Crossing the Rubicon

John D. Caputo, *series editor*

PERSPECTIVES IN
CONTINENTAL
PHILOSOPHY

EMMANUEL FALQUE

Crossing the Rubicon
The Borderlands of Philosophy and Theology

TRANSLATED BY REUBEN SHANK

FORDHAM UNIVERSITY PRESS
New York ■ 2016

This book was originally published in French as Emmanuel Falque, *Passer le Rubicon: Philosophie et théologie; Essai sur les frontières*, Copyright © 2013 Editions Lessius, Brussels, all rights reserved.

Cet ouvrage, publié dans le cadre du programme d'aide à la publication, bénéficie du soutien du Ministère des Affaires Etrangères et du Service Culturel de l'Ambassade de France représenté aux États-Unis.

This work received support from the French Ministry of Foreign Affairs and the Cultural Services of the French Embassy in the United States through their publishing assistance program.

Ouvrage publié avec le concours du Ministère français chargé de la Culture–Centre National du Livre.

This work has been published with the assistance of the French Ministry of Culture–National Center for the Book.

Printed and bound in Great Britain by
Marston Book Services Ltd, Oxfordshire

18 17 16   5 4 3 2 1

First edition

(Copyright page continued on page 193.)

In honor of Blandine Larnaud (1938–2012)

Contents

Philosophy is the servant of theology—Mary is indeed the servant of the Lord (Lk 1:38). But may the servant not pick a fight with the mistress and may the mistress not reject the servant, for a stranger would soon come who would quickly bring them to agreement.

—Charles Péguy, "Note conjointe sur M. Descartes,"
in *Oeuvres en Prose Complètes* (Paris: Gallimard
et Pléiade, 1992), 1458 [English—Trans.]

Crossing the Rubicon

Introduction

MATTHEW FARLEY

In June of 2013, I went to Paris to study *Passer le Rubicon* with Emmanuel Falque (there was at that time no English translation—a want that Reuben Shank here patiently redresses). Gladly, we held many of our conferences in the environs of Jardin du Luxembourg at the *Café Doucet*, cornerwise from the L'institut catholique de Paris, where Falque was, at the time, Dean of Philosophy. In one of those meetings over a Kronenbourg, Falque impressed upon me his respect for the integrity of the unbeliever. After all, the unbeliever these days, Falque explained, is no longer Dante's contemptuous Farinata, whose denial of the immortality of the soul is now considered a biblical precept;[1] nor is the unbeliever Bernard of Clairvaux's Wend "infidel," who merely believed differently; nor even is today's unbeliever Henri de Lubac's atheist humanist, who passionately sought to refill the depleted "sea of faith" with various quasi-messianic projects, whether Feuerbach's humanist Eucharist, Marx's classless society, or Comte's altruistic positivism.[2] The unbeliever today, Falque concluded, is our colleague at the water cooler: she gives gifts at Christmas; she regards Richard Dawkins as quizzically as Ken Ham; she regrets all theological contretemps. Falque agrees with Nietzsche, then, that atheism today takes the form not of a virulent war but of an "overrunning and leaving behind of God."[3] But where Zarathustra would condemn the deicides for their amnesia, Falque regards the average atheist today as nescient rather than forgetful.

1

In taking this current state of guiltless unbelief as a given, Falque departs significantly from the apologetic tenor that characterized the previous generation of religiously inclined French phenomenologists who sought to overcome Heidegger's critique of ontotheology. The thought of God as a *prima causa* of beings, Heidegger argued, eclipses the question of being as such. If God is the infinite anchor for the chain of finite beings, how could God be anything other than a being, and what is "being" anyway? The God of ontotheology inevitably serves as a philosophical *deus ex machina* introduced to rescue metaphysics from incoherence. Better to let metaphysics die the death, many theologians concluded, but does this mean that God dies, too?

While biblical theologians such as Karl Barth sought to establish revelation as an Archimedean point prior to reason and neo-Thomists such as Karl Rahner sought to elucidate God's mysterious immanence within transcendental experience, French phenomenologists such as Emmanuel Levinas, Jean-Luc Marion, and Jean-Yves Lacoste wondered whether Husserl was right that the Absolute had to fall under the knife of the phenomenological reduction. Thus Levinas contended that the Absolute continues to impinge upon us in the ethical demand of the other; Marion locates the Absolute in givenness (*Gegebenheit*); Lacoste finds the Absolute in liturgical experience *coram deo*. Such efforts prompted Dominique Janicaud to bemoan "the theological turn in French phenomenology."[4]

In marked contrast to his predecessors in phenomenology, Falque does not martial arguments for God's place within our aptitude for experience. On the contrary, Falque takes Bonhoeffer's challenge to heart: "we have to live in the world *etsi deus non daretur*" (as if God were not a given).[5] Accepting that God is no-place (*u-topos*), Falque thinks that the onus is firmly on the believer to present her beliefs simply as believable, above all, to herself, not necessarily to-be-believed by others.[6] Believers ought to liberate themselves from the idolatrous thought, which insinuates itself into so much apologetics, that theism is somehow necessary for good behavior. Recognizing with Jürgen Moltmann that theology "is no longer necessary for the practice of beneficence . . . but can finally be cultivated for God, and the infinite joy that he inspires,"[7] theologians can now adopt a more ludic tone. "I would only believe in a God who could dance,"[8] Zarathustra exclaims. Falque wagers that the perichoretic Trinity, no less than the dithyrambic Dionysius, may satisfy Zarathustra's conditions for belief.

Moreover, Falque cautiously descries a disciplinary boon to the ignorance that characterizes current atheism. Distanced from the Marxist materialism that dominated the French academy in the 1960s and 1970s, phenomenologists in France today are tackling what used to be considered expressly theological themes. Unbelievers such as Alain Badiou and Jean-Luc Nancy, for example, are returning to Christian texts in order to discuss love, revelation, and authority with remarkably little prejudice. Thus Christina Gschwandtner plausibly makes the case that phenomenology has effectively replaced natural theology as the shared idiom of church and world.[9]

Still, Falque thinks that if the theological turn in phenomenology were more candidly embraced, then theology and philosophy would have to coexist in joint practice and mutual enrichment. As it stands, phenomenologists such as Michel Henry, untrained in theology, freely take up eccentric theological projects such as *I Am the Truth*, while literate theologians such as Jean-Luc Marion remain ticklish about cross-courting their disciplines. Orbiting without overlapping, "both disciplines—philosophy and theology—are dirempted of the specific components they have to offer one another."[10] What Falque thinks philosophy offers theology is the intelligibility of its own claims. What theology offers philosophy, conversely, are disruptions or solecisms (de Lubac) that purposively break language in order to describe phenomena that hitherto escaped it.

Moreover, as a medieval philosopher by training—he wrote his dissertation on Bonaventure at Paris-IV Sorbonne—Falque sees beyond Pascal's influential separation of the god of the philosophers from Abrahamic fire to an earlier time when Christian thinkers such as Clement of Alexandria thought of themselves as philosophers rather than theologians. The Christian literary deposit itself just does not support the fast distinction between philosophy and theology that Pascal supposed. To remove proto-phenomenological moments in Christian sources in the manner of Jean-Louis Chrétien, for example, perpetuates the mistaken view that philosophy is a separable product from Christian culture. Let us take human finitude, for example. Falque contends that, in the West at least, the finitude of Dasein's horizon that many Continental philosophers now take for granted originated as a *theological* claim. It was the heft of the *creatio ex nihilo* that first led theologians such as Athanasius to deny the co-divinity of *nous* and the One. In other words, Christian theologians stood in contrast to pagan philosophers in their denial of an anthropological basis for the *capax infini*.

Falque notes that even Augustine, who first formulated the trenchant opposition of *fides* and *ratio*, could only do so with categories borrowed from ancient philosophy. Falque, for his part, cannot be mapped onto any model of relationship between *fides* and *ratio*—neither a traditional relationship of complementarity (Aquinas), nor dialectic (Barth), nor mutual indifference (Kant). Falque, in fact, resists all attempts to model the relationship between theology and philosophy in advance by disciplinary fiat: whatever the differences are between philosophy and theology, and Falque does not gainsay differences, they can only be clarified along the way by a joint practice.

Falque sees himself, therefore, as fulfilling Charles Péguy's prophecy that begins *Crossing the Rubicon*: "a stranger would soon come and quickly reconcile them [philosophy and theology]." Still too unknown in English-speaking countries, Falque *is* that stranger. In the image that controls the opening pages, Falque boldly presents himself as a Caesar crossing the Rubicon, sallying into the boundaries between philosophy and theology. Falque wants to pick a fight with whatever powers continue to treat philosophy and theology as if they were separated by some ancient Panthalassa, rather than by a mere rivulet in Emilia-Romagna.

And so Falque inevitably confronts his *Doktorvater* Jean-Luc Marion, who has always claimed to mind the difference between philosophy and theology. Falque's ongoing battle with Marion—which began in print in his "Phénoménologie de l'extraordinaire"[11] (2003) and continues in his most recent *Le combat amoureux*[12] (2014)—may strike us as just another example of academic patricide were it not for the fact that Falque has defended this (so far unidirectional) *disputatio* at great theoretical length. Quoting Heidegger, Falque claims that his "amorous combat" with Marion stems from an "adverse intimacy" and "intimate adversity" that surpass mere argument.[13] What is at stake for Falque is not this or that thesis of Marion, as we shall see, but a "type of humanity."[14] Whosoever side the reader finally takes, she will appreciate Falque's efforts to get outside his own wheelhouse in sustained polemics with an *immortel* of the Académie française.

Since English readers are likely to know the basic contours of Marion's work but next to nothing about Falque's (unless they should have chanced upon George Hughes's English translation of *Métamorphose de la finitude*,[15] Falque's contribution to Kevin Hart's *Counter-Experiences*,[16] or Chris Hackett's new translation of *Dieu, la chair, et l'autre*[17]),there can be little better way to introduce Falque than to sketch his profound disagreement with the "type of humanity" presented by Marion. Marion, we know, alighted in the American scene in his 1997 debate with Jacques Derrida at Villanova University. Though most attendees of that debate grant the laurel to Derrida, Marion proved himself capable of integrating negative theology and phenomenology in a way that made revelation thinkable. After his first English publication, *God without Being*, in 1995, Marion "finally elects to stay on a track that remains philosophical,"[18] becoming more and more widely read in the Anglophone world at each step.

In his clarion call for greater frankness about the intrinsic confusion of philosophy and theology, Falque thinks that Marion's various efforts to defend himself from Janicaud's charge of covert theologizing indicate that Marion doth protest too much. In clever latinate wordplay, Falque alleges that Marion has not so much "gone forth masked" like Descartes (*larvatus prodeo*) but has rather masked his controlling theological convictions, "masked before God" (*larvatus pro Deo*). "[Marion's] theology, apparently disconnected from phenomenology," claims Falque, "nevertheless constitutes for man his ultimate reason for being."[19] Marion's philosophy, like Descartes's, is profoundly inflected by a theological idea of the Infinite in the form of second-degree saturation, and we will have much more to say about this later.

In the meantime, we should note that it is not that Marion's philosophy is marked by theology that troubles Falque; it is rather that Marion styles the finite human subject as an obstacle to the Infinite. Descartes's confession that "I have only ever discussed the Infinite to submit myself to it"[20] Falque imagines equally true of Marion. Marion is on record as calling Barth long-winded,[21] but the Barthian scheme of his philosophy of givenness cannot be denied. Marion shares Barth's theology of rupture that prioritizes the divine decision over and against the human response: "God not only demands a decision of man," Barth thundered, "God himself constitutes this decision."[22] That God is known first as a negation of the human is one matter on which Bultmann and Barth agreed: "Knowledge of God is first of all the knowledge a man has of his own limits, and God is considered as the power that shatters these limits."[23]

Marion, too, maintains that the Infinite confronts us not gently as it did for Elijah in the "still, small voice" (*qol d'mamah daqah*, 1 Kgs 19:12), but as sheer counter-intentionality—as the inundation of intention by intuition and as the effacement of the gifted one by the gift. "The theologization of givenness, against which Marion constantly puts himself on guard," Falque contends, "is Marion's essential power."[24] As evinced by this telling sentence from §24 of *Being Given*, Marion seems to hypostasize givenness and to lend it a predestinating agency that can only be called God-like: "It [givenness] gives in the measure it shows, *to whom* it renders capable of receiving it."[25] Humans in this syntax cease to be nominative hermeneuts and become instead dative recipients of divine donation. By decentering the subject in order to overcome ontotheology, Marion has only rendered the finite human subject objective to an infinite subject that assails it with givenness without sufficient reason as if it were merely a "filter or prism,"[26] as in Young's experiment. Falque would agree, therefore, with the conclusion of Joeri Schrijvers: "For Marion, humans are the object and the objective of the given. The active and autonomous subject is replaced by a passive instance."[27]

Falque ingeniously traces back Marion's estimation of the finite human subject to a broader tendency among phenomenologists to neglect the body. Christina Gschwandtner rightly recognizes Falque's revisiting of Edmund Husserl's productive distinction in *Ideas I* of flesh (*Leib*) as the immanent "mineness" of the body (*Körper*) as the cornerstone of Falque's entire thought, and so we would do well to dwell on it here.[28] For English speakers, the word "flesh" denotes "meat," the most concrete part of the animal, but this is exactly the opposite valence that Husserl's German assigns to *Leib*, "the sole object in my abstract layer of world on account of which I feel."[29] As Chrétien has noted, it was Aristotle whose "radical and patient investigation of touch" premeditated Husserl's distinction between flesh and body.[30] In what Walter Ong termed "double sensation," Aristotle first noticed the phenomenal oddity of touch: "in the perception of objects of touch," Aristotle says, "we are affected not *by* but *along with* the medium"[31]—that is, in touching a "not me," we are immediately aware of the "me" doing the touching. The flesh is, quite simply, the "me" that is co-indicated in bodily acts.

Husserl developed the flesh/body distinction to frame his disagreement with the Cartesian treatment of the body as an extended thing (*res extensa*) on par with other extended things and therefore incapable of furnishing indubitable self-knowledge. Husserl allowed "body" to stand for the Cartesian body as a thematized object that senses the world "over there," but used the word "flesh" to designate the Aristotelian reflexing of touch in a self-feeling "here." Husserl calls the flesh "the sole object in my abstract layer of world on account of which I feel."[32] The distinction permits Husserl to avoid treating consciousness as a static structure without surrendering it to an entirely ego-logical account. "The specifically spiritual Ego," Husserl writes, "finds itself dependent on an obscure underlying basis of traits of character."[33] Before the body is ever objectified qua body, therefore, it is experienced in a field of self-affectivity. To adapt an example from Michel Henry, we do not say "my ears hear the fading sound of cicadas at summer twilight," but "*I hear.* . . ." The reality of the flesh, as the immediate inner experience of *my* body, denies Cartesian hyperbolical doubt its opening gestures. We never can prescind from belief in the ego.

Jean-Luc Marion picks up on Husserl's discussion of the auto-affective dimension of flesh in *Ideas II* via Michel Henry, via Merleau-Ponty. In

Chapter 4 of *In Excess*, however, Marion defends Descartes from Husserl's criticism that the *cogito* entails a false start. In fact, Marion endorses Descartes's aim in the *cogito*—that is, to wonder about the conditions of the possibility for self-access that we take for granted in daily affairs. Husserl fails to do the same in the transcendental reduction. Moreover, whereas Husserl insisted that phenomenality is shared between the phenomenon and transcendental consciousness, Marion insists that phenomenality belongs by right to the phenomenon. Marion maintains that the ego is not a primary endowment but is rather given by the flesh: "I do not give myself my flesh, it is it that gives me to myself. In receiving my flesh, I receive myself—I am in this way gifted to it."[34]

In his insistence on the primordial givenness of the flesh, Marion challenges the perfect fit of noesis and noema in Husserlian intentionality. Usually there is a structure of adequation between appearance and what appears, but the flesh, as the condition of possibility for appearance, never itself appears, and so escapes all adequation. Marion calls this *paradox*. I cannot "take" my flesh "as" anything, since my flesh is thoroughly reflexive with the intending self. "Since in this sole case the perceived is one with the perceiver," Marion concludes, "the intentional aim is accomplished necessarily in an essential immanence, where what I could intend is blended with the possible fulfillment."[35] Marion calls the flesh *absolute*, since it saturates the intentional horizon, prevents other objects from appearing, and overthrows Kant's category of relation.

Far from considering the flesh a sort of *hapax* in the phenomenological lexicon, Marion considers flesh paradigmatic of three additional types of saturated phenomena: the historical event, the idol, and the icon. Marion thus types the expansion of saturated phenomena in increasingly theological terms. In §24 of *Being Given*, Marion goes so far as to affirm the logical *possibility* of second-degree saturation, the paradox of paradoxes, the *paradoxôtaton*: Revelation. All saturated phenomena, Marion notes, mark degrees of givenness, so there is nothing illicit in wondering about a maximum of givenness—the apparition of some burning bush that overawes the beholder. Kathryn Tanner thinks that this isomorphism between Marion's philosophy and theology along the terms of saturation is perhaps too tidy a fit and risks a form of the very "revelation physics" that Marion himself cautions against in Eucharistic piety.[36] The logical possibility of second-degree saturation may open up a path for God's return from Kantian noumenal hinterland—"God's right to inscribe himself in phenomenality"[37]—but, Tanner worries, perhaps at the expense of reinscribing givenness as yet another secondary idolatry. Falque would agree with Tanner with the proviso that Marion's thought is theomorphic rather than isomorphic, since his theology controls his philosophy in a way that his philosophy does not control his theology.

We do not get from Emmanuel Falque a deep philosophical critique of Marion's interpretation of Kant: for that we would need to turn to Shane Mackinlay.[38] In fact, Falque agrees with Marion's central doctrines about the flesh: in contradistinction to the attempts of Berent, Romano, and Mackinlay to blend autoaffection and heteroaffection, Falque affirms with Marion and Henry the radical immanence of the flesh; Falque also agrees with Marion's mature position in *The Erotic Phenomenon* that flesh is singularized in love of neighbor.[39] Falque's quarrel with Marion's method is that he overcorrects against the naturalistic positivism that so worried Husserl by forgetting the body: "What yesterday seemed like a gain (a recognition of the subjective body), reveals itself today by way of repercussion as a loss (a total absence of discourse on the objective body)."[40] Phenomenologists have focused on the relative clarity of perception and intentionality to the neglect of the abyss of the body that Jackson Pollock pictured in "The Deep." Falque correctly points out that Husserl himself in *Ideas I* only sets flesh over and against body to abandon a false conception of the body as the putative empirical half of the *psychosomatôn*. In *Ideas III* Husserl, in fact, proposes a proper science of "somatology" that integrates the physiological and experiential dimensions of the body.

Throughout the course of his decade triptych—*Le passeur de Gethsémani* (1999), *Métamorphose de la finitude* (2004), *Les noces de l'agneau* (2011)—and most recently in this present work, Falque has worried aloud that contemporary phenomenologists, not just Jean-Luc Marion, but also Michel Henry, Jean-Louis Chrétien, and Jean-Yves Lacoste, have turned Husserl's distinction into another Platonizing fissure of the human being: "The ancient dualism of the 'soul' and the 'body' is today over and done with, but a new combination has taken its place: the 'flesh' and the 'body.'"[41] To disembowel the flesh of its body parts, as it were, leads to an effective bracketing of what Falque calls our essential animality (*bestialité*, alas, a word that does not translate well into English).[42] Falque dares to follow Edgar Allen Poe's "descent into the maelstrom" of the human animal body[43] and to discover there the liability of its organs, the abyss of its appetites, the difference of its genders, and the "impassible passibility" of its corporality.

Falque's oeuvre is best characterized by a sustained attention to the body in Christian thought. Neo-Platonic dualism, we know, was rather soft compared to other ancient varieties: for Plotinus, the body is at least dimly illuminated by form and is not to be identified with the evil material substrate (*stérêsis*).[44] Still, Falque's early work on Irenaeus, Tertullian, and Bonaventure convinced him of the "solidity" and "visibility" of the Adamic body in Christian anthropology compared to the neo-Platonic, as well as its potential for dynamic conversion.[45] In *Les noces de l'agneau*, Falque develops a comprehensive theological narrative encompassing the phase changes of the human *qua* animal. Falque begins by conceding that animality, as subject to evolutionary time, is perhaps an unstable construct.[46] Falque then steers a middle course between Augustine, who sets us apart from animals by denying animals *vox*, and Rousseau and Schopenhauer, who reduce us to animals. Intermediary to beasts, bodies without consciousness, and angels, consciousness without bodies, humans are by design *conscious bodies*.[47] By rejecting their particular form of human animality, however, Adam and Eve devolve into beastly animals. This is where we find ourselves east of Eden—sharing an accidental commonality with the beasts.

Instead of extending phenomenality to revelation like Marion (saturation), Falque focuses on God's condescension into the finite body (limitation).[48] The figure of the Lamb represents Christ as a beast vulnerable to brutality. Christ exemplifies "the ordinary and indepassible experience of human finitude."[49] Heidegger was wrong when he opined that Christian belief in heaven prevents one from reckoning with death and from enjoying its authenticating "moment of vision" (*Augenblick*). In *Les noces de l'agneau*, Falque reads Jesus's cry of dereliction as an expression of radical existential angst unadulterated by beatific vision. The servant should not expect doctrines to sweeten the bitter cup that the master himself had to drink. Moreover, unbelievers do not necessarily grapple with death more authentically just because they lack religious doctrine. For example, the cosmologist who takes sham comfort in our inevitable return to stardust in some Wordsworthian rolling around of organic matter has perhaps not yet seriously reckoned with her mortality in the manner demanded by the Gospels.

In the Passion, Christ transfers the suffering he *has* as an animal in a body to the human flesh that he *is*, thus bringing meaning into the abyss of uncontrolled passivity. The Eucharist of the Lamb, in turn, "transubstantiates" our beastly chaos into the cosmic humanity of the trinitarian perichoresis.[50] "Grace does not destroy nature," Aquinas says almost as if an aside, "but perfects it."[51] Falque takes Aquinas's side here. In contrast to theologians of rupture, Falque advocates a theology of metamorphosis, whereby grace perfects our fleshy bodies.

Against Marion's suggestion that humans in order to know God need their intentional structures reversed and exploded, Falque asserts, "We must hold as impossible and contrary to human freedom all the bedazzlement that would give itself all at once without any transcendental conditions of receptivity."[52] Falque thinks that the Protestant emphasis on the kerygmatic rupture is false to the real symmetry between God's governance and human agency. Again, Aquinas solves the problem of human decision by distinguishing between primary and secondary causality: "God is the cause of the decision of all those who decide."[53] The finite human retains her integral structures and in this way contributes to the co-governing of the Creation. Falque agrees with Heidegger that to restrict finitude to talk of human imperfection is to leave intact a more inclusive Infinite guaranteed by some nonhuman perfection. Falque argues instead for the "positivity of finitude," a finitude that is independent of the Infinite (plenitude of God) *and* the Finite (the insufficiency of the human, which only leads to repositing the Infinite as the corrective to human defect). Falque finds a theological ally here in Eberhard Jüngel, who thinks that theologians, no less than other men and the Son of Man, must take seriously "the possibility of nonbeing without coming to talk of God."[54] Falque's methodological alliance with Jüngel prompted Emmanuel Thorpe to reproach Falque for adopting atheism as an *a priori existentiel*.[55]

Falque is more open to theological metaphysics than Marion, since, like Denys Turner, he does not regard all metaphysics as susceptible to ontotheological critique. Aquinas's doctrine of divine simplicity, for example, demonstrates that God precisely in God's infinitude is *other* than a same/other binary. Falque, for his part, embraces a Bonaventuran "monadology without preestablished harmony" in which God is "all in all" (*tô pan*): "That is to say, nothing remains outside the Word—neither ourselves nor the totality of creatures who are linked together in the depths of his being."[56] Sensitive to Nietzsche's critique that Christians invented a shadow world, Falque nevertheless points out that Nietzsche misreads Paul, for whom the difference between the earthly body and the resurrected body is not one of substance, suggesting another world, but one of quality, suggesting a different manner of inhabiting the same world. It is the Resurrection, in fact, that provides Falque license to endorse this non-Leibnizian monadology.

Falque's debate with Marion's inversion of Kantian categories comes to a head with Marion's problematic account of Resurrection in §24 of *Being Given*. There Marion claims that Christ is the "saturated phenomenon *par excellence*," since Christ manifests all four modes of saturation. Moreover, Marion considers the inability of the disciples to name, place, track, and see Christ as telltale notes of revelation's counter-intentionality: Christ is an "irregardable phenomenon," the "counter-gaze of the Other," and the "absolute phenomenon that annuls all relation."[57] In *"Larvatus pro Deo,"*

Falque levies a varied set of objections to Marion's Christology here: Marion renders the extraordinary miracle of Christ ordinary; Marion makes a phenomenology of resurrection impossible because we cannot *take* the resurrected Christ *as* anything; Marion focuses on the Resurrection as convicting the finite of its finitude rather than metamorphosing the finite.[58] Most drastically, Marion brackets the problem of the Resurrection as historical actuality in favor of reducing it to an object of consciousness such that "the miracle no longer bears on a physical event but only on my way of looking at things."[59] Marion betrays a rather unexpected affinity with Bultmann in denying Resurrection faith objective contents.

Let us now return our attention briefly to the work at hand, *Crossing the Rubicon*. Falque presents here a highly digested and gestural "discourse on method" à la Descartes—that is, an explication of the philosophical principles that have guided his work all along. One cannot help but think of David Tracy's *Blessed Rage for Order* as the nearest English analogue. Just as Tracy's work is catholic in the breadth of the humanist disciplines it envelops, Falque's work is catholic in its attempt to reconcile hermeneutics and phenomenology: Falque yokes the Protestant "sense of text" (Ricoeur) with the Jewish "body of the letter" (Levinas) under the broader rubric of a catholic "phenomenality of text." The written letter is just one mode of textual phenomenality: Falque argues for a thicker "hermeneutics of the body and the voice."[60] Just as Hegel faulted Kant for his "pusillanimous failure of nerve" in stopping short of reason's identity with the noumenal, Falque faults both Ricoeur and Levinas for gesturing to doors that they refuse to open.

Falque roughly patterns the argument of *Crossing the Rubicon* after the six steps of Bonaventure's *Itinerarium Mentis in Deum*. Like Jüngel and Jean Greisch, two theologians he expressly admires, Falque adopts in the first three steps a methodological atheism, beginning *in via* with the human condition rather than *in patria* with the *totaliter aliter* God. For, as Kant once remarked, to begin with the didactic assumption of God is to undercut the heuristic question of whether, and how, God is to be found in human experience. That "we have no other experience of God than the human" Falque takes to be a *pons assinorum* that surprisingly few theologians dare to cross.[61] While Falque is heavily influenced by von Balthasar in his thinking about the Trinity, he is nevertheless compelled to take Karl Rahner's side in analyzing the condition for the possibility of faith in God.

Falque does not go in for anonymous Christianity, but he does deny that there is such a thing as an unbeliever in the broadest sense. Falque points out in these opening steps that religious faith, in fact, is founded upon an originary faith (*Urglaube*) in the world: neither Cartesian doubt nor Husserlian *epoché* actually breaks up our perceptive trust in the "there it is" of the world. This insistence on the faith natural to our "common humanity" is likely to rankle both certain kinds of believers and unbelievers.[62] Against believers who "would like to catapult faith onto a pedestal above and beyond humanity,"[63] who think that faith begins in doxastic certainty in divinely revealed truths, Falque reminds them what Bonhoeffer said: "being a Christian does not mean being religious, in a certain sense, it means being a man."[64] Against unbelievers who think that faith is as retrograde as the spleen, Falque insists, "Nothing is harder to believe than the absence of belief."[65]

Granted that faith in the world is foundational, how does one acquire religious faith as such? Again, Falque's strategy is to indicate a common threshold space shared by believers and unbelievers to make religious experience and decision less strange. In step 4, Falque conspicuously avoids the language of mystical negation that runs from Philo of Alexandria to Jean-Luc Marion—for instance, God-without-attribute (*aplous*, Philo); God-without-being (Marion). For Falque, as for Heidegger, mysticism is not "an escape into the ineffability of mystery but rather a lived experience . . . the lived experience [*Erlebnis*] overflows the mystical."[66] As for religious decision, Falque presents a Kierkegaardian notion of "onto-logical choice"[67]—not the superficial grocery-store kind of choice between alternatives, but the kind of choice that involves being chosen concomitantly. The response to the Christian kerygma, Falque argues, is not unlike the decision to get married or to take a job: all involve being chosen first. In step 5, Falque asserts that it is finally in the common experience of Christ's sufferings that philosophy and theology "overlap" (*tuilage* or "tiling"). The Resurrection, finally, is God's promise to transform philosophy into theology, physics into metaphysics, suffering into joy.

In step 6, "Finally Theology," Falque leaves the borderlands and crosses into the far *patria* of theology. While Falque readily concedes that not all theology need be confessional and that philosophers such as Blondel, Ricoeur, Levinas, Marion, and Lacoste are in their rights to remain at the threshold of confession while seeking theological spoils, Falque points out that minding the gap inevitably reinforces what de Lubac diagnosed as the Tridentine *duplex ordo* compromise: the separation of nature and supernature, philosophy and faith, world and church, depths and heights. The refusal to confess, in short, is not innocent of its own theological commitment. For his part, Falque thinks that our experiences of grace and glory are just as likely to be obscure as to bedazzle, to underwhelm as to overwhelm. The "type of humanity" that Falque stands for is the unrecognized Christ en route to Emmaus—his body hidden in Eucharist.

Falque anticipates that many will not be convinced by his thought experiment in *Crossing the Rubicon*. To return to his plucky Caesar analogy, Falque admits that he may not win the decisive battle at Pharsalus. In the meantime, if all Falque accomplishes is to confuse the reader about pat distinctions between philosophy and theology, he can claim at the very least a pyrrhic victory.

In the end, Falque does not ask us to undergo a mental itinerary that he has not undertaken himself. A believing philosopher who happily works across from the Sorbonne at an ecclesial university, a confessional Catholic who nevertheless insists on our finite horizons, a philosopher and theologian who advocates a "unified difference" of disciplines,[68] a writer who quotes pontifical documents and Husserl in the same breath, Falque models in his own person the fecund integration that he advocates in these following pages.

Opening

The Great Crossing

We have said that the notion of an individual substance includes once and for all everything that can ever happen to it. . . . [Thus] there is a reason why [Julius Caesar] crossed the Rubicon rather than stopped at it, and why he won rather than lost at Pharsalus.[1]

Leibniz's term *monad*, found in his *Discourse on Metaphysics*, is sufficiently well-known that it should give us no reason to pause. It is far more important to compose a philosophical plea capable of justifying an enterprise begun years ago. To begin, I will meditate on the Rubicon, a river (*flumen*) or small coastal waterway of Emilie-Romagna in northern Italy that once knew a singular destiny. To risk the crossing of this boundary was to violate the Roman Senate's laws. Nevertheless, a now well-known general decided to cross fully armed. With all his legions, he passed the boundary that separated Italy from Cisalpine Gaul, marching upon Rome with the intent of overturning Pompey. He crossed the little watercourse on January 12th, 49 B.C.E. This crossing transformed the destiny of humanity. Julius Caesar certainly did not doubt what was at stake in his decision. Indeed, the future emperor famously proclaimed, *"alea jacta est"*—"the die has been cast!" Later, the historian Suetonius would recount in detail the events that came to pass. Yet the ambition of the general was not immediately recompensed; he lost a number of legionnaires who were unwisely sent into battle. Nonetheless, history was on the march. The battle of Pharsalus quickly completed that which the crossing of the Rubicon failed to accomplish.[2]

§1. A Breakthrough

To cross the Rubicon again today, as it were, in writing a treatise on the boundaries between defined disciplines is to run the risk of losing the battle, although the outcome of the war is not at stake. The relation between philosophy and theology in France has recently shifted. To deny this would be to act in bad faith or in such great blindness that we would seem to be guided by nothing but ignorance of that which has transpired. Beneath the staggering blows of hermeneutics and the scalpel of the phenomenological surgeon, locked doors have already given way. This book aims first to take account of this recent event. In other works I have set forth the relationship between medieval philosophy and phenomenology. Today we await a great *disputatio* among contemporary phenomenologists to clarify the precise relation between phenomenology and theology. Meanwhile, a task remains to be accomplished: to characterize the ancestral relation between philosophy and theology in a simple but incisive *Discourse on Method*.[3]

Attempting to cross the Rubicon thus calls for "a great crossing." The itinerary may be quite short, since the river itself is narrow. At the same time, it may be weighty with the consciousness of the high stakes—as Caesar himself hesitating still to cross at the ford or to recognize that, in reality, he had already crossed long ago. Certainly no cohort of foot soldiers will be brought along in this conquest. After all, it may well end in defeat. Whether or not the battle is won, the risk I take in writing is taken also on behalf of another only insofar as he himself accepts the task of reading—and thus also of giving himself over to the reading. Indeed, the confrontation between philosophy and theology is not primarily a matter of war. Rather, it is a matter of making a decision, of taking a position—leaving the sown word to die on its own or disseminate itself further ahead. John Chrysostom rightly reminds us that "God does not ask us to succeed but to labor, and our labor will be no less rewarded because no one has listened to us."[4] Such would be the modest, but nevertheless necessary, meaning of the breakthrough attempted here.[5]

This little book, or *libellum*, humbly draws on the model of St. Bonaventure's *Itinerarium*, wherein in 1259 he summarized in six steps the procedure he had long been following. It thus follows the ambition of the medieval *Breviloquium*: to offer a sort of brief treaty that will suffice for the journey, at least for those who are emboldened not only to carry it with them but also to follow it. The Franciscan Doctor explains its origin and intent thus:

> That is why my colleagues have asked me, from my own modest knowledge, to draw up *some concise summary* of the truth of theology [*and philosophy*]. Yielding to their requests, I have agreed to compose what might be called a brief discourse [*breviloquium*]. In it I will summarize not all the truths of our faith, but some things *that are more opportune* [for such students] to hold. At the same time, I have added, under each topic treated, some explanation so that they might understand it.[6]

As in the case of the seraphic Doctor, a few friends and well-intentioned philosophers have solicited me.[7] Writing is not seized; it is received—especially when it is needed—and perhaps, it is even invoked. Moreover, it matters little whether the crossing of the Rubicon is a turning point instead of a march forward or another avenue of escape rather than a pursuit. All that counts in the act of crossing *this* Rubicon is the clarification of the practice that perhaps I would not have dared to undertake on my own. The results should show that at least it had to be tried.

Certainly one might accuse me, no less than others who profess to philosophize, of failing to vulgarize sufficiently and submit adequately to the demands for clear communication. Yet that charge fails to see that, especially in philosophy but also in theology, a certain mode of conceptualization must answer to the eminence of the questions. To deplore difficulty is also sometimes to refuse to rise to the challenge, as if understanding may be achieved without effort. I do not fear complexity but rather the illusion of believing myself the first to have come to think. Moreover, I fear the wrongful suppression of citations, as if understanding were easier when vulgarization masked history. It is appropriate to distinguish the act of thinking—including creating, inventing, distinguishing, deciphering . . . which are assigned to those whose job it is to think—from the task of vulgarization, which belongs to others, or if to the very same thinkers, only insofar as they do not eliminate all novelty in seeking excessive schematization. The challenge is obviously not to vulgarize following the appeal of those who simply wish that we would simplify their task. It is to continue to think rigorously with a concern to communicate, and most of all, to take stock methodologically of each point being made.[8]

The treatise presented here in its simplicity, brief character, and decided tone will not renounce the requirements posed by the matters to be exposed. Yet the excess of technicality will have been deliberately reduced or bracketed, since my works published elsewhere are sufficient to show, I believe, the solid foundations of the approach that has been underway now for many years. In this brief account, I will follow step by step the roadmap set forth in the following paragraphs, according to the carefully ordered succession of chapters. One does not cross the Rubicon without running a risk, as I emphasized earlier. One patiently awaits the day of Pharsalus, that victory may replace the defeat along with the overconfidence of the emperor at the first crossing. Following Heidegger, I have often called attention to the fact that thinking is deciding. The time has come to make that thought *qua* decision explicit, according to a "confession" that is all the more *philosophical*, since it consists in the act of deciding—that is, in the act most characteristic of all thinking.

§2. A Crossing

I will trace the stages of the itinerary that defines another and a new relationship between philosophy *and* theology with careful attention to their conjunction—*and*—rather than to their disjunction—*or*—as is most often practiced today. This brief "Discourse on Method" will indicate the significance and implications, first of the act of deciphering, second of choosing, and finally of crossing. The work will thus address (a) interpreting, (b) deciding, (c) crossing—that is, questions of hermeneutics, of the import of kerygma, and of boundaries between disciplines. This crossing will address these questions as much in dispute with those who went before as by discovering oneself transformed upon reaching the other side.

(a) First, I will enter into a debate with Ricoeur—not to take him to task but to discern fairly the value of his work. I will begin by asking, in Chapter 1, "Is Hermeneutics Fundamental?" I reply that understanding remains the horizon of saying as of every question. But it all hangs on what one *means by* understanding (describing or interpreting), as also on *what* one understands (text or life), and *how* one comprehends it (the short way or the long way). Catholic theology unanimously rushed into the breach created by textual hermeneutics, which indeed opened a space for an unusual fecundity that must be acknowledged. Nevertheless, I will question whether turning once again to this dominant approach remains adequate and fruitful for our thought today. If phenomenology finds itself engaged in the theological corpus, perhaps it is because, little by little, description is taking over from the unique act of interpreting, and life is taking its revenge on the text, which has become, today, nearly the only mode of the incarnate.

In this sense, the hypothesis of a "Catholic hermeneutic of the body and the voice," introduced in Chapter 2, will not contest all that Protestant inspiration generated, in particular the return to textuality, which renewed its way of thinking via biblical theology. Catholicism, however, properly affirms in its confession, as in its vocation, that the heart of its practice is found in the Eucharistic body and that the source of its conceptuality resides in the professed voice. In light of the absolute mode of carnal presence—from the Incarnation to the Resurrection through the *hoc est corpus meum* of the Passion—"Catholic" practice has this specific characteristic: it never leaves the thickness of the sensible. In this way, it rejoins the legitimate condemnations of Gnosticism by the early church fathers (particularly by Irenaeus and Tertullian), Aquinas's teaching on the absolute unity of the body and the soul (hylomorphism revisited in the light of the Gospel), the doctrine of the spiritual senses as rediscovered by von Balthazar (subjective evidence),[9] and finally, even the return to sensation fomented by Merleau-Ponty (following upon Cézanne, for example). In short, far from denying (textual) hermeneutics' solid foundations, the present treatise seeks rather to renew them. This work does not renounce the task of seeking to *understand* and even less to accept that one must always *decipher*. I will ask, however, whether (specifically written) linguistic voices are the only ones through which the Word becomes incarnate.[10] In opposition to *sola scriptura*, of which textual hermeneutics remains the heir after all (often without admitting it), I will set forth a *corpus totum* of a "hermeneutics of the body and voice," which Catholicism has rediscovered today. Rereading some of the best theological treatises (especially de Lubac), we will learn from theology, against the backdrop of phenomenology and classical philosophy, "what the body is capable of," indeed, what "we do not yet know."[11]

(b) The introduction to a hermeneutic of body and voice is followed by a debate with Merleau-Ponty and Bultmann. The expression "Always Believing," the title of Chapter 3, certainly does not indicate that everyone believes or even must believe. More accurately, we believe all the more in a *confessional* mode as we believe first in a *human* mode. This chapter is directed at all those who wrongly would like to catapult faith onto a pedestal above and beyond humanity, for the sole reason that it should always remain unconditioned. The goal is to establish the aforementioned hermeneutics of the body and the voice against a common, always given background. *No one believes in God if he does not first believe in the world—in fact, even in others.* Against all the lures of hyperbolic doubt or the phenomenological reduction, "some thing" or the "there is" always remains—irreducible as well as impossible to condense. Less of the order of the given as simple factuality, this "there is" (*es gibt* in German) imposes an originary trust precisely where classical philosophy teaches distrust or doubt, and the birth of phenomenology teaches prudence—that is, reduction. We always believe in the world and in others, as it were, "in advance," although experience will have taught us to suspect them or, more accurately, to distrust them. Religious faith, the *credo*, can graft itself upon, and only upon, this originary belief or *Urglaube*. The pedestal common to humanity waits its philosophical foundation in order to be "metamorphosed" theologically. The believer despairs sometimes of being the only one who believes. But if he recognizes in the other, not an atheist or a nonbeliever but a person "believing otherwise," and if he abstains from secretly baptizing them as "anonymous Christians," he will see that a *common believing* grounds also the *specificity* of his own belief, which does not permit him to flee from that which is common to our humanity.[12] Far from regretting the amphibology of believing—believing in others or believing in God—the confessing person will have the opportunity to respect and even to let himself be changed by the one whose belief is not bound intimately to his personal identity.

Nevertheless, to discover oneself thus "always believing," whether in a confessional or nonconfessional mode, removes nothing from the rightful foundation of religious faith. This is particularly true when believing encompasses, in a single movement, both "Kerygma and Decision" as described in Chapter 4. It is a mistake to consider the old quarrel about demythologization passé or already surpassed, as if Ricoeur's introduction of the symbolical in hermeneutics and the debate about enculturation, carried out by Hans Küng and Alois Grimeiller, have sufficed to resolve the question. To return to the thesis of demythologization is not merely to reactivate the myth of a pure faith, from which phenomenology itself is not free, and thereby to require again the "leap" of revelation, by which the *logos* would share nothing with human and natural reason. More accurately, to question "the decision of transformation" is to accept the necessary transformation of the concept of decision. A striking example is the event of birth, which is received before having been chosen, as brilliantly adduced by Claude Romano. What is true of birth is all the more true of confessional faith. "There is no choice" about having the choice; in the choice of non-choice resides paradoxically the greatest force of our choice. Of course, God definitely does not impose belief in him upon his disciples, as if freedom consisted only in recognizing oneself to be determined, as with Spinoza. But such *choice* is present in full force only insofar as the confessing person is no longer alone in deciding: the choice is determined always among two or three. After all, in the terms of Ignatius of Loyola, the "trinitarian colloquy" cannot be absent from the kerygmatic proclamation of the resurrected God.

(c) The final chapters turn to a dialogue with contemporary phenomenology. We often speak of methodology and the distinction between the disciplines. Theologians make a point of reminding philosophers that they incessantly surpass the boundaries set by human reason. Far from simply considering a given revelation—whether of daily life or the God of sacramentality—albeit forbidden to their discipline, phenomenologists make revelation the preferred object of their thought, alleging that they give new life to that which theologians were unable to renew on their own. First, I will acknowledge, necessarily, the immense fecundity of phenomenology for theology. Consequently, I will join in an extended debate with those who have made this field their life work. Yet the *counterblow of theology on phenomenology* from our perspective has not only been unconsidered but has yet to be carried out. Everything takes place as if we could and should be content with a theological phenomenology—using the phenomenologist's tools to describe the theologian's objects—without simultaneously asking ourselves about the signification of *a phenomenological theology* that would question, in its very modes of description, the truisms of phenomenology. The point is not to be a theologian instead of a philosopher or to show that theological objects manifest more clearly or most paradigmatically that which phenomenology only glimpses from a distance. The radical nature of my approach resides in its quest to indicate how attending to theology as such (not its objects alone) sometimes brings to light, in a rare flash, the limits of phenomenology. For instance, the horizon of finitude and its assumption by Christ on Holy Friday, his birth and his renewal in a "birth from above" in the Resurrection, human *eros* and its transformation by the *agape* of the Eucharist, approaching the materiality of the body solely on the basis of the anti-Gnostic reality of Christ incarnate—each of these already provides grounds not to persist in the simple *use* of phenomenology, albeit in order to renew theology. In its content—Incarnation, Resurrection, Eucharist—and its methods—in particular the necessary accounting for historicity—theology has the means to "turn back" to phenomenology in a counterblow that may *also* be claimed by a philosopher who does not conceal, at least from himself, the necessity of a common, ecclesial practice of theology. In short, the essay on *Borderlands* attempted here does not define a priori the limits of philosophy and theology. Instead, it discovers them a posteriori in light of my previous works, whose method and foundations this treatise aims but to evaluate.[13]

The hypothesis of a "tiling and conversion" of philosophy by theology, proposed in Chapter 5, will clarify the precise contributions of reflections on crossing boundaries, after the model of a discourse on method.[14] The distinction between philosophy and theology, particularly in contemporary [French] phenomenology, is not or is no longer, a question of their respective objects. We have gladly seen prayer introduced by Chrétien, liturgy by Lacoste, the Eucharist by Marion, and even the Incarnation by Henry. Each object was welcomed as new and worthy arrivals to the field of phenomenology, according to a seldom-matched criterion of *descriptivity*. The difference between philosophy and theology consists less in *what is studied* (the object), than in their specific *points of departure* (from below or from above), their proper *ways of proceeding* (heuristically or didactically), and the *status* of the objects analyzed (according to the category of possibility or effectivity). Nevertheless, in philosophy as in theology, the horizon of finitude will always remain primary, at least as a function of that with which, as humans, we are *first* confronted. Duns Scotus paved the way for an "unsurpassable immanence," inherited by modernity, even if, as I repeat emphatically now in this work, the resurrected Christ alone has the means to open that immanence to a dimension of eternity.

Certainly and to everyone's enduring regret, the believer would like to posit transcendence directly and rid himself, right from the start, of his pure and simple humanity, even the humanity of his "brothers," as Bernanos attempts, or the court of the Gentiles (*gentes*) who ceaselessly mill around *that* transcendence. Such an act, however, confuses the point of departure with the destination. It fails to see that to begin with finitude is not to imprison oneself immediately in it. Catholicism suffers at times from a naïve irenicism that calls into question its very credibility, as if the wonder of the newborn were a given and the newborn must not also, always undergo the *pathos* of existence right from the very beginning. If the supernatural, indeed, remains "necessary and inaccessible"—whether in philosophical terms, as with Blondel, or in theological terms, as for de Lubac—it is gained only by an action *of God himself*, who in his Resurrection decides to open the doors that until then had remained closed. If Christ had not "delivered us from death" (2 Cor 1:10), he would have accomplished nothing, neither releasing the chains of sin nor overcoming death's obstruction.

The Resurrection changes everything: it is the place of philosophy's conversion by theology—that is, the place of the passage of the aforementioned finitude to the resurrected Christ. The servant philosopher builds on the "tiling" as the meeting point of the human and the divine according to a structure of "overlaying" and deliberately refuses the leap that is quite common in contemporary phenomenology. He will accept the honor of the welcome or "the call from the heights" (Prv 9:3) of the theologian's dwelling. What the history of philosophy until now has denounced as slavery or serfdom he will come to consider *diakonia* or service. The conversion of philosophy by theology thus builds on the initial horizon of finitude, asserted by Duns Scotus, and on the structure of overlaying discovered in the resurrected Christ incarnate, following Aquinas. It is accomplished in the "trinitarian monadology," which integrates all human acts (in fact all that we are!) in the trinitarian God, the crucible in which everything undergoes metamorphosis, following Bonaventure. In the words of von Balthasar, commenting on Bonaventure, "Nothing is produced in a human being that is not first produced in God, apart from sin."[15] This dictum is not only a dogmatic confession, but also the high point of a discourse on method, carried out at once philosophically *and* theologically. Indeed, to stop on the threshold of one discipline—immanence in the case of philosophy, or transcendence for theology—prevents us from seeing and understanding how profoundly these thresholds and disciplines are bound in the God-man capable of unifying and incorporating them into the mystery of the Trinity.

Ultimately, we come to Chapter 6: "Finally Theology." Admittedly this phrase may resonate as the cry of a philosopher who ends up leaving his prerogatives behind. Having abandoned the human to plunge into the divine, he frees himself from an obscure past in favor of a highly desired transcendence, such that he believes himself to be immaculate. Nevertheless, the *lectior facilior* of the passage from philosophy to theology will not occur. "Finally theology" also amounts to the philosopher's acceptance of theology's invitation with a sigh of relief, since the injudiciously erected barriers will no longer need to be raised and manned. More importantly, to proclaim "finally theology" means to catch sight of theology "at the end" ("*en-fin la théologie*") of the crossing of the Rubicon. Reaching the end of the crossing does not result in forgetting everything, but rather in weighing all that took place in the crossing, according to a truly transformed humanity—yet without amnesia as to its ineliminable burdens. The human strides across the world as a "limited phenomenon," according to the Thomistic maxim of the principle of proportionality, whereby "nothing can be received over and beyond one's measure."[16] This finitude cannot be surpassed; its undergoing is the philosopher's task. The theologian is loved, desired, and carried by God himself all the way to the Trinity, in order to convert or "metamorphose" his finitude. But at the same time, the theologian's vocation is to offer his finitude there, giving it up to the care of revelation itself. No one is "more fully a philosopher" because he stays on the threshold of the disciplines or carefully separates the one from the other in his own corpus—quite to the contrary. Questioning disciplinary boundaries requires also that we accept all subject matters. Crossing the Rubicon is actually to carry out the crossing; inspecting the banks of the river is helpful but serves only to distinguish them better. Far from standing strictly by the discipline's requirements (to remain a philosopher rather than a theologian, a phenomenologist rather than a metaphysician), the philosopher and theologian should recognize that *existentiell* or better yet, experiential questions are ultimately at stake in the upcoming philosophy and theology. Thus, in the end, *existentials* are described by phenomenology and at the same time put to work by theology, until they are entirely transformed and "metamorphosed," as it were, from a counter-blow of the Trinity.

§3. An Experience

As with St. Bonaventure, the six stages of our *itinerarium* end upon a sort of *apex affectus* or intimate union of humanity with God—now understood as the total incorporation and transformation of the human in the divine. Ignatius of Loyola and Hadot have taught us that at least at their origins, and perhaps also ever since, theology and philosophy were and have always been "spiritual exercises."[17] Utterly forgetful of this fact, we wrongly separated metaphysics from phenomenology and dogmatic theology from biblical theology, or even from mystical theology. We could continue debating the necessary foundations to surpass metaphysics, which I would argue is already mostly surpassed today, or continue marking ever and again the borders of an ontotheology, which in my eyes are impossible to determine. Rather, we should be expecting from philosophy a description of *the great traverse* of *experience* as a putting oneself in danger (*Erfahrung*) and not simply as auto-affected experience (*Erlebnis*). The great crossing or the "self-apprenticeship through suffering," drawing upon Aeschylus's *pathei mathos*, will teach us perhaps how we ourselves have moved: it may disclose nothing but the blow that we experienced, albeit nearly "against our will." Indeed, sometimes we have been given the concepts as well as the method and path by which we have advanced. At the same time, we most often believe mistakenly that we are capable of deciding everything. We must recognize that usually we have no other choice than to assume our choices, letting ourselves thus be "girded by another" for a journey we did not think we would make (Jn 21:18). Such is the boldness of the philosopher *but also* of the theologian, or yet of the believer *and* of the human as such, as soon as *together* and in the *unity* of a same being, that they perform an act of thinking as an act of exposing themselves.[18]

"The more we theologize, the better we philosophize."[19] This is the saying that I have repeated carefully, time and again, and will not cease proclaiming—though I am first and foremost a philosopher. To rediscover the conjunction of the disciplines, beyond the disjunction or the leap carried out so frequently today, entails knowing how to situate oneself—moreover, to do so all the more precisely when the crossing of the Rubicon has been completed, after having ventured to stand on each bank. Rather than staring at each other stonily, insensitive to the other's proximity, or concealed beneath the mask of Janus, philosophy and theology will return or, better yet, will travel to meet each other in the end, and the philosopher live all the better at home in his native land:

> Happy are those who, like Ulysses, have enjoyed a beautiful journey, or like that other one who won the golden fleece, and then returned, full of good practices and reason, to live amidst his parents the rest of his days![20]

PART $\boxed{\text{I}}$

Interpreting

Is Hermeneutics Fundamental?

In this crossing of the Rubicon, the trumpets first sound in homage to Ricoeur. Yet I will conclude with an accepted and even affirmed gap between his hermeneutics and the approach advanced here. Any tribute to a master must reflect his greatness as well as his limitations, at least in the context of a legacy to be both received and transformed. Of course, one could proceed with pure and simple repetition. Ricoeur's concept of distanciation, however, may be productive at this juncture, prompting the declaration that the times have changed and that one must orient oneself anew. After all, the "long way" of linguistics, philology, or semiotics is no longer so significant today. I will inquire whether a *Catholic*-inspired hermeneutic may continue to refer theologically and philosophically to *textuality* alone, or whether it must not also address *the body and the voice* as the source of its renewal (see Chapter 2). Further, even if they are irreducible, confessional ties—Protestant Christianity for Ricoeur or Judaism for Levinas—create conceptual distances. A *critical* approach, in the sense of judgment or of bringing under scrutiny (*krinein*), is thus essential. It must be equal to the task of discerning what remains to be preserved at the heart of the tradition, yet cannot be repeated. To honor the thought of an author, however famous and prolific, is not to reiterate it, but to extend it or even reconsider it from another vantage point. A hermeneutic is *fundamental* only insofar as it is grounded in a mode of existence adequate to its object. In this way, it would have the merit of teaching us at the very least to better differentiate ourselves—but most importantly, to identify ourselves more precisely.

This chapter will question the validity of the grounds of textual hermeneutics for our thinking today as well as its contemporary retrieval, nearly word for word, in theology and even in philosophy. I will respond to the breakthrough of a hermeneutics that might be called *fundamental*. This latter predicate as well as the chapter title is obviously inherited from Levinas's contributions in his confrontation with Heidegger.[1] Chapter 1, "Is Hermeneutics Fundamental?" will first probe Ricoeur's Protestant hermeneutic, centered on the *meaning of the text*. Second, it will investigate Levinas's Jewish hermeneutic, shaped by *the body of the text*. This initial study will thus create a space in Chapter 2, "For a Hermeneutic of the Body and the Voice," for the possibility of a Catholic hermeneutic, anchored this time in *corporeality* as the center and heart of the activity of interpretation. This argument is patently not a matter of a quarrel between confessions, even less between religions. In reality, what matters is the kind of relation that grounds the interpretation of the message—mediation of the text or exposition of the body. This initial, fundamental orientation is usually not interrogated, or at least tends to be accepted without question.

Gregory the Great's phrase at the beginning of his *Homilies on Ezekiel* is widely known: "Scripture grows with its readings" (*Scriptura cum legentibus crescit*).[2] This claim may offer hermeneutes and even contemporary phenomenologists a way to breathe new life into biblical interpretation as it struggles to renew itself. The profound purport of the phrase calls neither for the proliferation of readers nor for their transformation in order to bring the text's fecundity to fruition. *Readers* do not grow in reading scripture. The opposite is true: *scripture* grows as it is read. In other words, the biblical text frames a unique and exemplary relation between reader and text. Whether understood as an ego or appropriation that ultimately always maintains its primacy, *I* am not the one transformed by reading the text. Rather *the text itself* grows by virtue of my reading; *it lives from my life*, rather than exclusively my living from it. Certainly, to make of the text a "Living [Being]," even a body capable of growing and experiencing with us a sort of intercorporeality, is astonishing. Paul Claudel, however, does not hesitate to affirm, "[the Bible] is a living being that grows and develops before our eyes."[3] Henri de Lubac also, reflecting on Origen, asserts:

In this way, Scripture seems like a first incorporation of the Logos. He who is by nature invisible can be seen and touched in it, as if in the flesh that he was then to assume; and reciprocally, this flesh is a letter that makes him readable to us.[4]

It could not be clearer. Writing [*l'écriture*], at least when it is biblical (but perhaps not exclusively so), is a life that addresses itself to a life. It is a Living Being that turns toward a living being or, in my perspective, *a body that speaks to a body*. If there is a hermeneutic in a Catholic mode (I will explain later what I mean by "Catholic"), it will be not only of the text but also of the body, and not of speech alone but also of the voice.

I will thus investigate the possibility of arriving at the body without remaining attached to textuality and of finding our life in the Bible rather than making the Bible live in us. This inquiry is most urgent today. Having rightfully deployed its conceptual treasures, textual hermeneutics seems to be gasping for air—not for lack of fresh elaborations, but because it waits for its release from the stranglehold of the text. Phenomenological description has, at least *de jure*, the capacity to set it free. As I already noted, one of the premises of the present treatise is that:

> The excessive attention to the *support* or *mediation* sometimes kills that which it supports or conveys: the often-unsayable meaning of experience, which it still seeks to describe.[5]

Let us be on our guard, however. This is not the opening to a trial of intentions; quite to the contrary. Philosophical hermeneutics—Ricoeur's certainly, but also Gadamer's—rendered and still renders service to theology in ways that we cannot not deny or even denounce. Indeed, the syntagm of hermeneutical theology has become the vestibule through which one must necessarily pass. Historical reasons suffice to justify the close collaboration between hermeneutics and philosophy as well as theology, corroborating its function of "transversality."[6] Furthermore, the hermeneutical relief in theology as in philosophy had perfectly legitimate motives, at least in its day.[7]

§4. The Hermeneutical *Relief*

The Hermeneutical Relief in Theology

The hermeneutical relief follows the pattern of the "four senses of scripture." Hermeneutics returns afresh to an examination of the plurality of interpretations. Moreover, it too consists in a historical reappropriation of various models of philosophy by theology.

The letter teaches "that which took place" (*littera gesta docet*), allegory "that which you are to believe" (*quid credas allegoria*), the moral sense (tropological) "that which you are to do" (*moralis quid agas*), the anagogical sense "that towards which you must tend [or extend?]" (*quod tendas anagogia*).[8]

The Dominican Augustine of Dacia, a contemporary of Aquinas, wrote this celebrated summary of the four senses of scripture around 1260. His statement can serve as a guide to trace the context and signification of the hermeneutical renewal when it arose and was in full swing at the beginning of the 1970s in France, now over forty years ago.

In 1975, when Ricoeur published his famous text "Philosophical Hermeneutics and Biblical Hermeneutics" (later included in *From Text to Action* under the heading "For a Hermeneutical Phenomenology"), textual exegesis in its theological articulation appeared in some ways to have run out of steam.[9] It had already exhausted all the resources of the historical-critical method, which after all had been entirely justified on its own grounds. Attention to the referents and to the sources introduced an increasingly diverse set of traditions (Yahwist, Elohist, priestly) and of events (Exodus, Exile, David's Court) to the reading of the scriptures. Consequently, what takes place in a given situation is what primarily counts—that is, *the gesture* at the level of *the letter* (*littera gesta*) or the literal sense. Paradoxically, the historical-critical method did not aim to reproduce what took place *as* it took place or *as* it is written. Rather, it sought to indicate what took place in terms of *the means* or other *circumstances* of the act of writing, which suffice to explain how and why it was written in this way and not otherwise. Still, a considerable step had been taken. Genesis could be understood finally as a "myth" precisely because it did not take place as it was written but because other accounts or places explain that it was written in such and such a way and not in another (for example, in comparison to the Babylonian myths). No explanation, however, was given for the function of the myth itself. With the historical-critical method, the attachment to the referent remained always essential, in fact self-evident, even if the referent itself had changed. The reader is no longer immediately facing the letter of the text in its location in the text, but the place and the context where the text was written and from which it can be explained. It is noteworthy that pastoral ministry has also carried out this exegetical approach, remarkably so in France, convinced that any faithful person who has undergone Christian and theological formation is wise enough to distinguish between the various sources, to bring to light the distinct contexts, and to rearrange the texts.

The textual hermeneutic that Ricoeur brought to life offered the relief that exegesis and theology in the late 1960s did not anticipate or no longer expected. The text itself—and the text by itself—is a world. This is the claim underlined by "The Hermeneutical Function of Distanciation" (also first published in 1975) where writing or more specifically literature "may abolish all reference to a given reality."[10] Distanciation consists in a triple reduction or *epoché*: emancipation from the one who wrote the text (the author), emancipation of the one who receives the text (the reader), and emancipation of that to which the text refers (the referent). All that remains then is what Ricoeur calls "the autonomy of the text":

> [D]istanciation is not the product of methodology and hence something superfluous and parasitical: rather it is constitutive of the phenomenon of the text as writing. At the same time, it is the condition of interpretation.[11]

This is another huge step forward. The great virtue of theological hermeneutics is to have drawn out its implications. The notion of *the world of the text* bestows autonomy upon the text and thus produces its semantic unity: in this way, the text is self-sufficient in its referential function.

> My thesis here is that the abolition of a first-order reference, an abolition effected by fiction and poetry, is the condition of possibility for the freeing of a second-order reference, which reaches the world not only at the level of manipulable objects but at the level that Husserl indicated by the expression *Lebenswelt* [life-world] and Heidegger by *being-in-the-world*. . . . For what must be interpreted in a text is a proposed world.[12]

The world of the text means that in effect the text is world-forming; as such, one could say that it "worldifies." I have maintained that the concept of "life-world" is Husserl's great legacy to Ricoeur's hermeneutics. Yet I will show that this gain comes with a loss particular to a so-called "Protestant" hermeneutics. It results in the detachment and absolute autonomization of writing relative to speech and also to the body and the voice, which support all writing.

To this concept of world and as a consequence of distanciation, Ricoeur then adds, not as an appendix but as a defining moment, "the appearance of the subjectivity of the reader" and "the appropriation (*Aneignung*) of the text, its application (*Anwendung*) to the present situation of the reader": in short, he propounds the capacity "*to understand oneself in front of the text*" and of "exposing ourselves to the text and receiving from it an enlarged self."[13] The text takes me for an object or, more accurately, for its principal subject. *I* am its addressee, although I will never reduce it to my singular personality as its recipient. Indeed, as a reader, "I find myself only by losing myself."[14] But the purpose of the loss is first and foremost that I find myself or that I am found by the text, such that in the end, I remain still the addressee, even the object, of this writing addressed to me. "The text is the medium through which we understand ourselves. [The] appearance of the subjectivity of the reader . . . extends the fundamental characteristic of all discourse, that of being addressed to someone."[15] In appropriating the text, I am appropriated, albeit first by disappropriating myself of myself. In order always and minimally to constitute "me as myself," the other of the text constitutes me as "another myself."[16]

We see, or at least should sense it now. Textual hermeneutics frees us from the methodological fetters of historical-critical exegesis. It finally becomes possible to read or to reread the text for itself, independently of its sources. The text necessarily says something to *me* by *its saying* the very same thing or perhaps even saying something else—only as long as its correct understanding gives rise to my appropriation. In this instance, pastoral practice also confirms the developments of hermeneutical theology, and vice-versa. The Word [*Parole*], or rather the text, is no longer studied in the objectivity of a given history. Consciousnesses in their intersubjectivity, struggling to tell each other their stories, share the text—to risk the presently, altogether overused verb "share." The text's world-forming effect for me can also be a world-forming effect for others. As a result, we face the numerous deviations known to arise in the incessant projections of oneself into the text, against which Ricoeur constantly struggled.

Returning to the four senses of scripture, textual hermeneutics no longer aims at grasping a literal meaning relative to what the letter teaches (*littera gesta docet*), as did the historical-critical method. Its aim is the moral or tropological meaning—that is, what one has to do (*quid agis*): it seeks primarily what the text has to say to me, rather than what it says in itself. The doing here is not only poiesis—even if Ricoeur's movement *from text to action* unfolds logically—but praxis: the world of the text "forms and transforms the reader's being-a-self in accordance with his or her intention."[17] A tropological approach turns the text into the place of my own transformation: my own world will inhabit the text's world only insofar as I become capable of finding myself there in the end.

As scripture becomes autonomous in its separation from speech and from the body, the text is understood to transform me as it modifies my egoity, but it never truly makes me destitute. Two shifts are needed: a hermeneutics of the body must succeed to a hermeneutics of the text, and an incorporation of the self in scripture must substitute itself for a transformation of the self through scripture. These two newly highlighted traits belong to a hermeneutic inherited more from a so-called "Catholic" ritual of the body—namely, the Eucharist—and of the world—that is, the Gospel of All Creatures—than from the "Protestant" ritual of the text, or *sola scriptura*, and of grace, or *sola gratia*. Indeed, the historical-critical method's focus on the literal sense and the textual hermeneutics' quest for the tropological sense have dominated, at first and rightly so, our reading in the modern era.

Nevertheless, today the time has come to deploy an *allegorical* sense—that is, what you are to believe—and even an *anagogical* sense, or that for which you must aim. Moreover, in this endeavor one must truly accept, in a quasi-monastic way, to be a *displaced-self* as well as to be *displaced from oneself and totally incorporated in the body of another* who is not oneself and never will be. "The beginning is the pure, and, so to speak, still mute, experience that now has to be brought to pure expression in its proper sense," to restate the famous phrase from Husserl's *Cartesian Meditations*.[18] But this road toward meaning will not, or will no longer, be made by virtue of hermeneutics—a graft that has taken too well and has in some way detached itself from its trunk, that is, from phenomenology. Instead, it will come to fruition rising from the same bedrock or under the impulsion of the same seedling, by virtue of which any first word or utterance remains silent or of the order of the *infans*, even if subsequently it were to say something or express itself. As Romano asserts, "Indeed, there exists an autonomy of the prelinguistic order, of pre-predicative experience with regard to superior forms of thought and language."[19] He continues:

> Authentic hermeneutics is phenomenology and phenomenology is accomplished only as hermeneutics . . . which would render superfluous the "graft" of the one on the other, to pick back up Ricoeur's famous image. Hermeneutics and phenomenology would be the flowering of a same "essence," of a same bud.[20]

The Hermeneutical Relief in Philosophy

The hermeneutical relief in theology, by way of biblical hermeneutics, depends on its relief in philosophy, as it took place in the relation between phenomenology and hermeneutics. For Ricoeur, hermeneutical phenomenology depends on "the graft of the hermeneutic problem onto the phenomenological method."[21] The historical situation of philosophy, along with the exhaustion of the historical-critical method in theology, could not but give textual hermeneutics every right and privilege of position; and at least at that time, it was fully justified to do so.

During the resurgence of the human sciences in the 1970s, sociology, linguistics, and psychoanalysis were the most powerful forces of renewal. In that context, there was no question nor was it even conceivable to deploy a hermeneutic and even a philosophy that did not proceed by way of those mediations. Indeed, it is surprising that today they have totally disappeared, or nearly so, in many arenas of contemporary philosophy, in particular in phenomenology. Four decades ago, the choice one faced was straightforward, and the alternative was clear-cut. In "Existence and Hermeneutics," the opening essay to *The Conflict of Interpretations*, Ricoeur indicates emphatically that "There are two ways to ground hermeneutics in phenomenology. There is the short route, which I will consider first, and the long route, the one I propose to travel."[22] I will later nuance this opposition in light of its presupposition (see Chapter 3, §11). The well-known gap between these two ways requires no lengthy explanation at this point. In sum, the short way is the ontology of comprehension, inherited from Husserl with his notion of *Lebenswelt* and from Heidegger with *Dasein*. The long way consists in analyses of language, inserting and imposing the mediation of history, as in Gadamer's work, or the mediation of the text, as in Ricoeur's. Whether via history or textuality, the long way becomes the indispensable detour to ground the act of interpretation. All that truly counts is the deliberate, contextually responsive decision "[to substitute] for the short route of the Analytic of Dasein, the long route that begins by analyses of language."[23] In Ricoeur's eyes, this choice has an unavoidable result that is perpetually recovered and subsequently reiterated.

The "short" intersubjective relation is intertwined, in the interior of the historical connection, with various "long" intersubjective relations, mediated by diverse social institutions, by social roles, by collectivities (groups, classes, nations, cultural traditions, etc.).[24]

[We] understand ourselves only by the long detour of the signs of humanity deposited in cultural works.[25]

While feigning to adopt the short way in "The Hermeneutical Task," Ricoeur asks himself, "Why not stop here and simply proclaim ourselves Heideggerian?" The hermeneutist responds, "a philosophy that breaks the dialogue with the sciences is no longer addressed to anything but itself."[26] In other words, only a return to the sciences justifies the strategy of the detour by the long way and condemns the direct access of the short way in an autarky of thought that the philosopher is unable to justify, at least historically.

The movement from the short way to the long way is actually more than a simple choice: it is a turning point for phenomenology, perhaps even for philosophy itself. Phenomenology, especially with Husserl and Heidegger, was forced to bracket the human sciences—even the positive sciences—by classifying them as "ontic" in contradistinction to "ontological." Precisely here, the Ricoeur of the hermeneutics (rather than of *The Fallible Man* or *The Wounded Cogito*) turns his back on all that was exclusively existenti*ell*, or better existenti*al*, in Husserl and Heidegger. The hermeneutical philosopher rededicated understanding (*Verstehen*) as necessarily bound to the explanation of the text and not only to the explication of the self. He mediates all experience through language and culture, which do not obstruct experience but actually make it fully accessible as well as give it meaning: "It cannot, therefore, be said that the passage by way of explanation destroys intersubjective understanding. This mediation is required by discourse itself."[27]

A twofold context is now evident: a theological context, shaped by the exhaustion of the historical-critical method, and a philosophical one, where thought reengages the human sciences. These two factors led to the insistence, on the one hand, on the tropological meaning of the text, which first of all and exclusively addresses me, its reader, and on the other hand, on the acknowledgment that only the passage through mediations or via the long way could justify the detour required to return to the sciences. Theology benefited from its consideration of mediations, institutions, historicity, textuality. Philosophy did so in its engagements with linguistics, semiology, sociology, and even psychoanalysis. One question, however, remained unresolved in the eyes of the hermeneute who was reading Heidegger and perhaps even devoting his entire life to seeking its resolution: "*how can a question of critique in general be accounted for within the framework of a fundamental hermeneutics?*"[28]

A Fundamental Hermeneutics?

Levinas raised the decisive question, "Is Ontology Fundamental?"[29] I now ask, "Is Hermeneutics Fundamental?" The terms of the debate are the same, but the intentions are different—even opposed. I will first consider Levinas's thought and then turn to Ricoeur's. For Levinas, the fundamental character of ontology is picked up or rather deflected by the yet-more fundamental character of ethics or of the figure of the other. Any relation to a being is indeed nothing but its comprehension as being in light of our being. Following Heidegger, he asserts that we can "let it be as being," but adds emphatically—"except for the other." The other in his ethical relation does not let me be, and I do not let him be within the basic ontological horizon of comprehension, even in terms of some simple mode of being of Dasein. In Levinas's words:

> Is our relation with the other a *letting be*? . . . Not at all. The other is not first an object of understanding and then an interlocutor. The two relations merge. In other words, *addressing* the other is insepa-rable from *understanding* the other.[30]

In Ricoeur's work, what is fundamental takes a detour, or more pre-cisely turns back explicitly to the general or the regional. Ricoeur fully assumes Gadamer's gesture. Gadamer initiated the "movement of *return from ontology toward epistemological problems*" over against Heidegger.[31] This is a movement, on the one hand, toward a general hermeneutics, addressing epistemic problems of method, and, on the other, toward regional hermeneutics, which accounts for specific objects of the historical sciences, including semiology and sociology.

For Levinas, then, ontology is not fundamental *enough*, since the "other" furnishes another and new foundation. For Ricoeur, hermeneutics is *too* fundamental, since it excludes all modes of explanation other than the understanding—that is, from the exclusive mode of Dasein. The fields of ontology and hermeneutics diverge. But the crucial question arises pre-cisely at this divergence: is it appropriate to radicalize the foundational or the existential as Levinas does or to externalize it and even to regionalize and mediate it along with Ricoeur? In essence, it is not a matter of "truth or method" (*aletheia* or *epistemê*) but truth *and* method—ontological unveiling *and* ontic sciences. Such is the indissoluble tie that Ricoeur defends, to the point of accusing Gadamer sometimes to fall back into the disjunctive on account of his proximity to Heidegger.[32]

A "but . . . !" of opposition, or a "save for . . . !" marking the exception is at the heart of Levinas's "Is Ontology Fundamental?" as he responds to Heidegger with the protest "except for the other." In the same way, my question "Is Hermeneutics Fundamental?" bears a *but* or an *except for*, at least in the context of the interpretation of Ricoeur's hermeneutics. Despite the putatively straightforward fact that hermeneutics, theology, and even phenomenology are intimately interwoven, it is necessary first to assess phenomenology's capacity to resist its marriage or simply its flirtation with hermeneutics. Today French philosophy, or philosophy in general, comprises so many turning points that we no longer know where we are or where we are going. We have encountered Ricoeur's "hermeneutical turn of phenomenology," Janicaud's much debated "theological turn in French phenomenology," Gadamer's "phenomenological turn of hermeneutics" as articulated by Jean Grondin, or now the "phenomenological turn in theology," as seen in certain contemporary attempts at phenomenological Christologies, for example.[33] Of greater significance than these turning points, certain ruptures have been experienced—without being expressed. Naming them entails at least displaying them, if not also analyzing them.

The weak echoes of hermeneutical phenomenology among the French phenomenologists (Henry, Chrétien, Derrida, Marion, Lacoste) are surprising—all the more so in light of their resounding impact among theologians, particularly in centers of Catholic training but even more so outside France. Contextual factors alone insufficiently account for this unexpected result; conceptual articulations probably illuminate it better. Janicaud asserts in Chapter 4, "Articulations/Disarticulations," of a noteworthy work entitled *Phenomenology "Wide-Open"*:

> Phenomenology and hermeneutics remain, as much in their origin as in their relatively recent autonomisation, more disjointed than jointed, without being foreign to one another. . . . Ultimately, what differentiates and reciprocally situates phenomenology and hermeneutics (without articulating them properly speaking) is the delimitation of the former within a horizon of elucidation or a horizon of upgradation (*mise à jour*) (a stabilization of a horizon of realization of presence/absence) and the illimitation of the latter in the twists and turns of the reading and of the interpretation of reference texts (for which the link to the sacred is perhaps never totally inexistent).[34]

The standpoint advanced here should now be clear. Without attacking the distinction or relation between phenomenology and hermeneutics, the exact character of their relation can be made explicit such that one may even decide between the two. In its apophatic function as a *clarifying* or *bringing to light*, the phenomenality of the *logos* is not and never was "understanding," even less so "explanation" in the sense of textual interpretation as mediation.[35] Heidegger's thought is centered on the simple ontological mode of being of Dasein. Ricoeur's work revolves around its relation to the ontic realm of the sciences of interpretation. In the first case, the heart of the matter is the simple art of living without apprenticeship. In the second, it is the art of reading with its discipline and its methodological requirements.

We will therefore turn to the following two questions: (1) Is not the detour through the text, in fact exclusively through *the mediation of the written text*, what finally makes Ricoeur's graft of hermeneutics onto phenomenology autonomous? (2) Should not the hermeneutical *relief*, as understood in its Catholicity, move in the direction of *corporeality* rather than *textuality*? All the while, we would leave the nobility of Ricoeur's Protestantism untouched, which Catholicism may indeed have expropriated by fully assimilating the basic return to textuality; and we would preserve the greatness of Levinas's Judaism, which Christianity, even Catholicism, may also have recuperated in misappropriated interpretations, for instance, of the figure of the other—by confusing the trace of the face and the sacrament of the brother. These are the questions that, particularly in the context of Catholicity, contemporary philosophy is entitled to raise not in order to accuse others—far from that—but to learn from the *differences*, including the confessional ones, about the present state of its proper *identity*.

§5. Confessional Hermeneutics

The Protestant Hermeneutic or the Meaning of the Text

It appears at least incongruous, if not also inappropriate, to speak of a *Protestant* hermeneutic, or a *Jewish* hermeneutic, or yet a *Catholic* hermeneutic, since the question of interpretation is not first of all a matter of religion or of confession, but of philosophy and its mode of conceptualization. Ricoeur always made this claim; Levinas did so all the more fervently. Each of their philosophical projects can and should be understood independently of any belief or faith conviction. Their arguments should be accessible to all, and possibly shared unanimously, and not be fossilized in some idiocy to which only those who share the confession would be capable of acceding. Yet, of course, something of the domain of conviction remains. We never think outside of a "primordial ground" (*Urgrund*) in Husserl's terms. Our departure points followed by thought's first germinations depend on this ground, even if our subsequent clarifications do not. If there is a Protestant hermeneutic in Ricoeur's work, it is not because his hermeneutic emerged, developed, and was then further elaborated in a Protestant context (in fact, it seems paradoxically to have had a greater impact in Catholicism). Rather, it deploys one of the basic principles of Protestantism, perhaps even its principal axiom: the so-called notion of *sola scriptura* or the return to scripture as *text*. As a result, neither the body—as really present in the bread in the Eucharist—nor the tradition and the magisterium handing on and interpreting the biblical message, the very pillars of Catholicism, can rival scripture or detach themselves from the *text*. But *Fides et Ratio* insists that "For the church, the holy Scripture is not the only reference point."[36] Moreover, Benedict XVI, in his apostolic exhortation *Verbum Domini*, asserts emphatically, "the Magisterium of the Church, which is not above the Word of God, has the responsibility 'to authentically interpret the Word of God, whether written or handed down.'"[37] A hermeneutic of the body and the voice that one may call Catholic stands in sharp contradistinction to a hermeneutic of the text and scripture that one may call Protestant. This Catholic hermeneutic cannot accept the double detachment of the text from the word [*parole*] and the body, and of the word from the Eucharist as incorporation in the church as a body. At this point it becomes clear that Ricoeur's *philosophical* choice guides his *theological* decision.

Ricoeur's Philosophical Choice

In "Phenomenology and Hermeneutics," Ricoeur argues that "the Husserlian demand for the return to intuition is countered by the necessity for all understanding to be mediated by an interpretation," such that "mediation by the text, that is, by expressions fixed in writing but also by all the documents and monuments that have a fundamental feature in common with writing," account for the elucidation of the chains of "transmission of historical tradition."[38] More precisely, because it is text and not speech, as clarified by "the hermeneutical function of distanciation," "writing renders the text autonomous with respect to the intention of the author."[39] Indeed the text, insofar as it is written and not spoken, takes absence from its author as well as from its referent, and even from its recipient, at least with respect to the particularity of a single reader. The *medium* of the text is not, or no longer, strictly the *means* of interpretation but also its proper, exemplary, and nearly exclusive—or at least paradigmatic—*place*.

Ricoeur's Theological Decision

As indicated, the consummation of the "world of the text" in "[understanding] oneself before the work"—namely, the function of distanciation—could lead and, in fact, did lead hermeneutics to tropology or a notion of appropriation as the process that "forms and transforms the reader's being-a-self"—but at the cost of the lived experience of the text itself.[40] In addition, the systematic reduction of the spoken word to scripture, as suggested in "Philosophical Hermeneutics and Biblical Hermeneutics," is not self-evident. As a hermeneut and as a confessing Protestant, Ricoeur emphasizes that a Catholic approach must understand that

> biblical hermeneutics receives an important warning from philo-
> sophical hermeneutics: it must not be too quick to construct a the-
> ology of the Word [*Parole*] that does not include, from the outset
> and as its very principle, *the passage from speech* [*parole*] *to writing*
> [*écriture*].[41]

This warning is highly relevant, since theology so frequently elevates the Word [*Parole*] over scripture.

Nevertheless, these two imperatives—the choice of the medium of the "text" or of language in philosophy and, in theology, the surplus of scrip-ture over the Word or over the world—are neither philosophically nor theologically self-evident.

The Philosophical Imperative

In conversation with recent philosophical discourses, I first pick up the thread of Romano's questions in *Au coeur de la raison*, where he cites Ricoeur and Gadamer and also denounces the inversion of the relation of language to the world:

> It is then no longer (according to these authors) because we are in the
> world that we have language; it is because we have language that we
> are in the world. . . . On this point, Ricoeur expressly follows
> Gadamer. He even takes one step further toward *a linguistic ideal-
> ism*. By virtue of the primacy that he grants to writing and to the
> text in general in his definition of hermeneutics, he tends to substi-
> tute for language in its widest extension, a textual model that is
> meant to *mediate* all understanding of the self and the world. . . . In
> short, the text is here clothed with the power to transform a simple
> environment into a world.[42]

Yet, at the very least, these theses regarding the mediation of the text—for instance, the scriptures for Ricoeur or a cluster of traditions capable of constituting a history for Gadamer—are not beyond dispute. From a philosophical perspective, we certainly cannot ignore the prelinguistic experience of the body, nor, for that matter, can we ignore affectivity and sensibility, from which language receives—much more than determines—signs. Descartes reminds us, in the second part of the *Discourse on Method*, "we were all children before becoming adults, and . . . it was necessary for us to be governed for a long time by our appetites and our teachers, which were often opposed to each other."[43] Such is the infancy of the human that we ought not to forget, at the risk of losing the *inf-ans* or all that which is speech-less (*in fari*)—all that constitutes our flesh.

The Theological Imperative

In addressing Ricoeur's theological claim, I argue in a Catholic mode that the text or the book of scripture (*liber scripturae*) does not necessarily over-shadow the book of the world (*liber mundi*)—rather, the opposite is the case. God did not first give Adam some scripture (tablets of law or a parchment) and only later, in the Garden of Eden, give himself to Adam in speech and in nature. In fact, humanity's loss of its ability to read or interpret nature (on account of sin) is exactly why humans needed scripture as the relay for the book of the world (in order to find the world within it). The Seraphic Doctor teaches in a famous text of the *Hexameron*:

> When humans fell and lost their knowledge, there no longer was anyone to lead them back to God, . . . this book [*iste liber*], that is, the world [*scilicet mundus*], was then as it were dead and defaced. Therefore another book [*alius liber*] was necessary, by which humans would be illumined in order to be able to interpret the metaphors of things. That book is Scripture [*autem liber est scripturae*].[44]

Indeed, for Bonaventure, who faithfully builds on Brother Francis's *Canticle of the Creatures*, and also for a so-called Catholic hermeneutic, the "book of the world" precedes and founds the book of scripture. In its use of metaphors, scripture serves only as substitute for the book of nature in its post-lapsarian state. No scripture was needed in Eden; nature spoke fluently of itself.[45]

The deliberate choice of the long way in Ricoeur's hermeneutic of the text over the short way of Heidegger's hermeneutic of being-in-the-world or facticity has been contested, in one way or another, ever since the medieval period (fully recognizing the obvious anachronism of this claim). Far from being the model of writing, reading has certainly been an aid to deciphering—not primarily to the deciphering of texts that very few monks knew or were able to read but to deciphering the presence of God directly in oneself and in the world. This latter knowledge and ability were more uniformly shared. Hugh of Saint-Victor wrote the following superb lines, which were reiterated in their entirety by St. Bonaventure:

This sensible world [*mundus iste sensibilis*] is as a book written by the finger of God [*quasi quid am liber est scriptus digito Dei*]: each creature considered in itself is as a figure [*quasi figurae*] that has not been discovered according to the good pleasure of the human, but instituted according to divine judgment to manifest the wisdom of that of God which is invisible [*ad manifestandam invisibilium Dei sapientam*].[46]

In following and critiquing Ricoeur, I have thus set forth both philosophical reasons—dumb and silent experience—and theological reasons—the primacy of the book of the world over the book of scripture. Both reasons taken together forbid, on the one hand, the choice of the medium of the text as the paradigm of all reading, and on the other hand, the anteriority, or at the very least the primacy, of scripture over the spoken word or even over the body. Ricoeur's tenth study, "Toward Which ontology?" in *Oneself as Another* sought to remind us of this very problem, inflecting this time his discourse toward corporeality. It falls to me to carry out this task. I will do so now, in a first step by offering a cross-section of what (I have called) a Jewish hermeneutic. Understanding what it could teach us will provide an opening toward a form of catholicity with a distinctive hermeneutic.

The Jewish Hermeneutic or the Body of the Letter

As we discussed Ricoeur's Protestantism, so we will both respect and interrogate Levinas's thought in relation to his Judaism. My stance is the same here as above: not defiance but rather full acknowledgment—attentive nevertheless to difference. Hermeneutics, or more precisely, the *relation* to the text is at issue for Levinas as it was for Ricoeur. In Levinas's work, it is transformed or rather oriented "otherwise." Where the text was a medium for Ricoeur, it becomes a trace for Levinas. Where it was scripture or writing for Ricoeur, it becomes spoken word for Levinas. When asked about his proximity to Derrida and Blanchot, Levinas's quasi-posthumous avowal remains on this point as clear as possible and even decisive: "But *it isn't in terms of writing* that problems come to me"— however one understands in this instance the act of writing or reading scripture.[47]

On what basis then does Levinas begin to think or, better yet, "does God come to his mind"?[48] Not on the basis of the text alone, as in a Protestant hermeneutic, or beginning with the world or the body, as in a Catholic hermeneutic, but beginning with Talmudic glosses on the text, precisely because they give body to the text in what might be called a "Jewish" hermeneutic. Interpretation is a communal process in Judaism, or it is not interpretation. More specifically, it deploys the infinite saying of a spoken Word, which first is proffered, said, and heard *orally* in the said, although subsequently it will let itself be inserted in a written work. Levinas's thought no longer moves from the text to the spoken word but inversely from the spoken word to the text, such that writing marks the moment of inscription of a trace rather than the transformation of a medium. An interpreter of Levinas rightfully highlights that

> Revelation is the inscription of the spoken Word of God in the book where his saying lets itself be captured by the said, but at the same time, where he is also invited to share in the infinite amidst the multiple voices of those who constitute the interpretive community. . . . The God who inscribes himself, whose body is written (in scripture), makes the writing not into the sign of his transcendence but the trace of his retreat.[49]

Levinas's hermeneutics teaches, and therefore helps us to learn, two distinct movements with respect to Ricoeur's hermeneutics. On the one hand, we learn to superimpose a plurality of significations to the point of expecting a reading from the *community alone* and not from the individual. On the other hand, we learn to seize in the letter of the text *nothing but the trace* of an absence rather than the mode of a presence—otherwise, we run the risk of seeking, conversely, to enclose the world of the text, now eternally disappropriated, within the appropriating self.

Yet God enters the scope of the very text and inscribes himself in the text itself. Although in contrast to Christianity Judaism may have no concept of God's incarnation in a body, there is at play nevertheless a sort of incorporation of God in the letter: "a contraction of the infinite in scripture" or "a precarious dwelling place in the letters."[50] Levinas insists, "the idea of the divine incarnation is foreign to Jewish spirituality" (in fact, this was a sufficient reason for the respect he received in his Judaism); further on, he continues:

> But the fact that kenosis or the humility of God who is willing to come down to the level of the servile conditions of the human . . . is demonstrated in the first instance by the biblical texts themselves. The terms evoking divine Majesty or Loftiness are often followed or preceded by those describing a God bending down to look at human misery or inhabiting that misery.[51]

In other words, if God does not come in a body as in Christianity, in Judaism he inscribes himself as a body, consecrating the letter of the Torah, exceptionally, not as text but as life, as a kind of incorporation of the *logos* (to return to de Lubac), or as a mode of dwelling for a God who would nonetheless not let himself be confined to it.

> For Levinas, God does not become incarnate. He inscribes himself. He descends into the letter: he inscribes himself and deposits himself in the letter. In other words, his body is a written body, or yet a body that writes itself. The letter then ensures the connection between body and writing. If God inhabits the misery of humans, he can only inhabit it miserably, that is, by making letters his dwelling.[52]

As a Protestant, Ricoeur was fleeing in a sense, and justly so within his hermeneutical perspective, from the literal sense in favor of the tropological sense. At that exact point, Levinas as a Jew rediscovers not the literality of the text (as in the historical-critical method), but the literality of the letter itself as the place God may dwell, extending even to "the ultimate materiality of the ink and the form of the book."[53] One more step has been taken toward what I am calling, somewhat abruptly, a "Catholic hermeneutic." By "Catholic" I am not indicating first off this hermeneutic's dogmatic character or force, rather simply its identity and specificity as determined by the movement I have traced thus far: on the one hand, from the *written text* to the *living* and *incarnate body* and, on the other, from the *professed word* to the *exemplified voice*.

The Catholic Hermeneutic, or the Text of the Body

From here onward, I will speak cautiously of "Catholicity" strictly as the name for a mode or manner of interpreting, wanting neither to impose it nor to universalize it. Today a form of ecumenism exists in theology and even in philosophy, which we would do well to claim, while at the same time the encounter with alterity should never exempt us from acknowledging our own identity. To illustrate, or actually to sing, with Claudel in his *Second Ode*—indeed the so-called Catholicity of this hermeneutic must be understood as praise for the created rather than a deciphering of textuality, and also of the thickness of corporeality rather than the appropriation of conscience seeking self-transformation:

> Welcome then, o world made new in my eyes,
> o world now one and whole!

O entire Credo of things visible and
invisible, I accept you with a *Catholic heart*!
Wherever I turn my head
I look upon the immense *octave of Creation*![54]

Such a relation to the world and certainly to my own being in the world
leads directly to assertions that are necessarily programmatic. First, the
philosophical eventuality of the short way over the long way comes to the
fore once again. Second, beyond mere theological possibility, an allegorical sense (*quid credos*—that which you must believe) and even an anagogical sense (*quo tendas*—that toward which you must extend) of hermeneutics
as well as scripture become theologically necessary.

First, the contemporary philosophical choice of, or return to, Heidegger's short way via the understanding of Dasein on this side of or over
against Ricoeur's long way though analyses of language should be understood here neither as the simple indulgence of a phenomenology that has
everything to win in breaking with hermeneutics nor as an absurd defer-
ence to the philosopher of Freiburg who could only be analyzed in our
exposition to him. In reality, the question is the meaning of hermeneutics
as well as of the phenomenology united and nearly identified with it. As
noted, it is no longer a matter of thinking hermeneutics *and* phenomenology but that hermeneutics *is* phenomenology. Moreover, this predicative
relation is reciprocal in the sense of an axiom for which all possibility of
"graft" is definitely eradicated or at least suspended: they are each dependent on the same "sap," as it were, although in different modalities, such
as "dumb experience" or "the world of life"—*describing* or phenomenology for the one and *interpreting* or hermeneutics for the other.

Although unjustified from the point of view of its root, Heidegger's
explicit and definitive renunciation of the term hermeneutics in his 1953
"A Dialogue on Language between a Japanese and an Inquirer" still has
something to teach us today:

> It can hardly have escaped you that in my later writings I no longer
> employ the term "hermeneutics." . . . I have left an earlier stand-
> point, not in order to exchange it for another one, but because even
> the former standpoint was merely a way station along a way.[55]

We know the philosopher's position and its origins because they were
frequently restated in his writings. In this dialogue, they are succinctly
described: "The term 'hermeneutics' was familiar to me from my theological studies. . . . Without this theological background, I should never

have come upon the path of thinking. But origin always comes to meet us from the future."[56] The heart of the matter, however, is not the origin as such—the theology at which we ordinarily stop—but its dependence on the hermeneutic to which it is explicitly, this time, united. The root term "hermeneutic" is suspect, even more than theology, which conceivably could have distorted everything. I am arguing that the turning point consists here in hermeneutics' capacity, in Heidegger's eyes, to obstruct "the journey toward the spoken word" if textuality becomes precisely a type of beingness or a regional ontology simply to be deciphered. For the rejected hermeneutics, the later Heidegger substitutes the notion of *speaking* to indicate a hospitality that, in Chrétien's terms, takes place in the "ark of speech," not in an episteme that hermeneutics could still inform. The first pages of Chrétien's *The Ark of Speech* describe this vividly:

> The animals have been gathered for human speech and brought together in this speech, which names them long before they are brought together, according to this same story, in Noah's ark to be saved from the flood and the destruction it brings.[57]

Second, the theological necessity of the allegorical sense—what is to be believed—and the anagogical sense—that toward which one must extend—arises from the reality that the aim of Catholic belief instills also a philosophical hermeneutic. In this case, however, it is a hermeneutic of the body rather than the text, as faced with Ricoeur, or of what I might call the Ark of *flesh* rather than speech as encountered with Levinas or Chrétien.[58] "The incarnation changes everything," emphasizes Merleau-Ponty in *Sense and Non-Sense*, shortly after describing Catholicism.[59] This formula is valid for phenomenology in terms of one's own incarnation as well as for theology or for the incarnation of Christ. I come not only to the *world* but also to the *text* with my flesh and body. Moreover, the text only becomes incorporated in me when I also become capable of incorporating myself in it, in the same way as we become incorporated in Christ or in the church. Further, Marcel Jousse's expressions are worth rediscovering today in the context of a Catholic hermeneutic of corporeality. When my "mouth" at once "eats and recites," such that "by my mouthful" of bread and spoken word, I eat the body at the same time as the book, I advance toward the two tables and become incorporated in the Word [*la parole*] by my incorporation into the Eucharist.[60] "Son of man, eat what is offered you," as uttered by the speaker in Ezekiel 3:1, which was taken up again in Revelation: "Go, take the scroll which is open in the hand of the angel who is standing on the sea and on the land." So I went to the angel and told him to give me the little scroll; and he said to me, "Take it and eat; it will be bitter to your stomach, but sweet as honey in your mouth" (Rv 10:8b–10a).

In a Catholic mode, we will thus no longer content ourselves with the ark of speech, which runs the risk of losing sight of the distinction of Christianity's "Word become flesh in the Son" amid Judaism's "speech become body in the text." I will suggest that "the ark of the flesh" may be understood both as "a body of speech to be recited"—that is, mouthfuls of scriptural verses—and a "Eucharistic body" to be assimilated—that is, partaking of a meal or even as contemplation or adoration. Indeed, Pope Benedict XVI underscores that "the spoken word of God becomes sacramental flesh in the Eucharistic event."[61] Therefore, insofar as there is an allegorical sense in a so-called Catholic hermeneutic, it consists in the fact that "what is to be believed" is first of all "a real presence" in transubstantiated bread in which the act of speech itself is also incorporated.[62]

A simple exegesis of the pericope of the disciples' experience on the road to Emmaus (Lk 24:13–35) is sufficient to confirm that an *other* Catholic hermeneutic of the body and the voice (see Chap. 2) must provide the relay for Ricoeur's Protestant hermeneutic focused on the meaning of the text and Levinas's Jewish hermeneutic oriented to the body of the letter. Christ is described as the exemplary first interpreter or hermeneute of the sacred texts: "Did not our hearts burn within us while he talked to us on the road, while he opened to us the scriptures? (διήνοιγεν ἡμῖν τὰς γραφάς)"(Lk 24:32). Significantly, his paradigmatic character appears only after, and not before, his manifestation and nearly simultaneous disappearance: "When he was at table with them, he took the bread and blessed, and broke it, and gave it to them. And their eyes were opened and they recognized him; and he vanished out of their sight" (Lk 24:30–31). According to the Second Vatican Council, in the Catholic liturgy the "table of Scripture" or the hermeneutic of the text does not precede ontologically but only chronologically the "Eucharistic table" or the hermeneutic of the body. Indeed, the hermeneutic of the text follows, and discovers its very foundation in, the hermeneutic of the body. The body of the text takes root in the body of the church—not the opposite. If the word of God is unique, it is heard *qua* text at the same time as it is eaten *qua* body; better, it only resonates on the eardrum, or is heard, because it is first tasted by the palate, or is manducated. Indeed, "the faithful are nourished in the Word of God at the double table of the Sacred Scripture and the Eucharist."[63]

In Origen's famous tripartite division of "three bodies," not only the (historical) "body of flesh" and the (textual) "body of Scripture" are essential, but also and most importantly the (Eucharistic) "sacramental body" by which all three are bound to one another in an intimate knot. St. Jerome later underscores this point, "when we are listening to the word of God, . . . God's Word and Christ's flesh and blood are being *poured into our ears*," such that "the Holy Spirit fashions *the sacramental body of Christ*, as it fashions in Mary his *body of flesh* and the *body of Scripture*," as Origen had already suggested.[64]

§6. Toward a Phenomenality of the Text

Intentional Lived Experiences

The phenomenality of the text overtakes a hermeneutics of the text. The "lived experiences" (*Erlebnis*) of the reader, but also those of the author and perhaps even of what takes place *in* the text itself, will no longer be considered "dead material." Rather, drawing further on the terms of Husserl's transcendental phenomenology, they are "intentional" lived experiences—that is, "a consciousness of."[65] If for Ricoeur a triple reduction of the author, the reader, and the referent makes the world of the text appear clearly as such, what takes place *in* the text—and almost independently of the text—between the characters at play *within* the text proceeds indeed on a yet to be discovered and never to be reduced life-world (*Lebenswelt*). It is reasonable to maintain that the text will always provide support for the events and characters *in* the text: we should never detach ourselves from the text in the act of reading that consecrates the crossing. Nevertheless, we do not always require the medium of the text to "mediate" us. The finger that points to the moon will never mistake the finger for the target, at the risk inversely of confusing the target and the means to reach it. The demonstration of the phenomenality of the text will depend certainly, but in part only, on the context, which is itself borrowed from an unforgettable lived experience—whether via a historical or referential hermeneutic. But in addition, precisely in the "life" that it seeks to exhibit and, as it were, is inherent and even incarnate in it (as in a hermeneutic of the "facticial life"), a true "lived experience of a consciousness-of"—or a mode of intersubjectivity—is now seen at work among the very actors in the text, albeit without always keeping strictly to the textual language that provides access to it.[66]

Intersubjectivity

The following example, drawn from the Gospels—"good news" (*eu-vangelia*) understood precisely as a lived experience and not exclusively as a text—may be helpful. A phenomenological meditation on the anguish of Christ before death consists first in seeing him, Christ-*himself*, experience the intersubjective sphere in which he is engaged with Peter, Jacob, and John. Second, it describes him in relation to his fear of dying in the account of "the cup." Third and finally, it is to contemplate him passing all the way through the narrow path of anguish when he will accept to surrender himself—in Christ's well-known utterance: "nevertheless not my will, but thine, be done" (Lk 22: 42b). In this case, we are first and foremost facing neither *text*, although the text may set us in motion, nor *ourselves* from whom we must first learn to turn away in order to see him truly as he is showing himself. This lived experience is first his own before I share it: it is in letting it be as itself—the allegorical sense—that I will then be able to be challenged or even troubled—the tropological sense.[67]

What is "to be read" and indeed "to be lived" in the proclaimed Gospel surely occurs in all literature—as with Flaubert's Madame Bovary or yet Stendhal's Julien Sorel, for example. There also intersubjectivity is at work and the play between the characters themselves matters at least as much as, if not more than, their effect of challenging me. In fact, their only intent is to displace and incorporate me into their own world. Moreover, with the "word of God" and especially with the account of the incarnate *Logos*—that is, the good news—the particular case modifies the rule (which typically in literature is determinative). The account of Christ at Gethsemane—but also and perhaps more than anywhere else, the prologue of the Gospel of John—produces the unique and exemplary observation that "the one of whom we speak"—namely, Christ—is at the same time "the one who speaks"—that is, the Word [*Verbe*]. This identification of the locution (the God of whom I speak) and the locutor (the God who speaks to me precisely when I speak of him) is original as well as extraordinary. It is precisely in this identification that one finds the specificity of the sacred text and in fact the fullness of its unicity. In complete agreement with Ricoeur:

> Theological hermeneutics present features that are *so original* that the relation is *gradually inverted*, and theological hermeneutics finally *subordinates* philosophical hermeneutics to itself as its own *organon*.[68]

In other words, without overgeneralization, it is appropriate to recognize that the theological itself may modify the philosophical to the point of transforming its structure and even making it secondary (as in Ricoeur's hermeneutics), even if it remains but a *hapax legoumenon* that he never brings to its term or, at least, never erects as a rule.

My hypothesis—and the Catholic hermeneutic unfolding in this text—entail the following key point. Although the text cannot serve as a unique basis for interpretation, we should, however, recognize its exemplary structural modification of theology understood as the identification of its "object" (discourse about God [theo-*logy*]) and its subject (discourse of God [*theo*-logy]), provided that we pay more attention to the *epiphany internal* to the text or to its *own phenomenality* than to its sole mediation by language. The biblical *logos* articulates, par excellence, the apophantic mode of being (*apophaneisthai*) of Christic language: "showing Him showing himself"—more than we seeking to show him; "claiming Himself addressing himself to us"—though we seek to communicate him by evoking him. Indeed, we must recall Heidegger's claim, the pioneer of a hermeneutic of facticity grappling with textuality: "*Logos*, as speech really means *deloun*, to make manifest 'what is being talked about' in speech. Aristotle explicates this function of speech more precisely as *apophainesthai*."[69]

Intercorporeality

We should thus seek, and we will perhaps then find, intentional lived experiences (that is, consciousness-*of*) in a hermeneutic of facticity rather than textuality. Such a hermeneutic of facticity attends to what arises from the *intercorporeality* of lived experiences *of what*—and *of the One* who—is spoken of and speaks in the text (what I call the allegorical sense in relation to Christ), rather than focus on the trial of *the one* who reads the text and in that way exposes himself at the same time as he appropriates the text (what I call the tropological sense in relation to the reader). The Philippians hymn proclaims, "Let the same mind be in you *that was in Christ Jesus*" (Phil 2:5)—not the reverse. *I* am thus not first, and don't first understand *myself* "in front of the text" (to pick back up an expression dear to Ricoeur).[70] On the contrary, the text is there *in front of me* as if I were saying "*let me be read* with authority by the Holy Scriptures."[71] To cite Chrétien's new proposition that is yet to be deployed philosophically, "When faced with the Bible, *every appropriation must at the same time be a disappropriation*" such that "it is necessary for the intelligence to make itself a prayer in order for it to become exegete, that is to say, *to read as it allows itself to be read*."[72] I do not first encounter God in God's "letter"—

whether as the historical-critical reference or the trace of the Torah or in *my* lived experience of consciousness—that is, in the tropological aim of the textual hermeneutics. Rather, it invites me to incorporate myself into its fleshly lived experience—the allegorical aim, even anagogic, of the hermeneutics of the body.

The approach via the phenomenality of the text thus reverses the perspective of a textual hermeneutic. Where hermeneutics suggests that the text takes me as its aim, phenomenality maintains, at the fore, the character of the text as event in its pure and simple alterity, albeit to incorporate me into it and thus not let me become a total stranger to it. The transcendental aim of a text that, in the same way as nature in Kant's understanding, would respond only to "the questions we ask it" is utterly and consciously eliminated. The alterity of disappropriation replaces the egoity of appropriation. Claudel strikingly insists, "But to say that we question the Scriptures is incorrect. It is better to admit that the Scriptures question us and find for each of us, throughout every age and generation, the right question."[73] Moreover, the inauthenticity of the *happily* lost reader—all the more "himself" as he has accepted not to find himself—follows upon the authenticity of a being-there who is capable of managing everything. Indeed, Claudel, as already noted, claims that "[the Bible] is a drama, I would say, not enacted by us so much as through Him, just as the actors of the Old Testament lived through Him."[74] *My* lived experience—the moral or tropological sense of textual hermeneutics—does not therefore matter, or very little, in light of the displacement and disorientation of my egoity and in view of its own alterity—that is, the allegorical, even anagogical sense rising from the text's phenomenality. In reality, I will truly rejoin the text as a "never appropriated" lived experience and the place of a paradoxical "intercorporeality" only in turning away from the text as mediation.

The epoché of a true hermeneutics of the factical life (see Chapter 4, §13) suspends not only the author in his genesis, the referent in its historicity, and the reader in his singularity, but, also and most significantly, the very textual "base" in its role as the incessantly imposed "medium." The aim of this last bracketing is to come to all that is ineffable and silent in intercorporeal relations or in the *infans* (not as "the struggle to speak" but) as the engendering of a body, which is ceaselessly being knit together. The body of scripture always waits for the bodily combative embrace with its reader, and in this "dumb experience" alone is said, or rather is heard and lived, what the text does not say. The text opens on the "white" of *A Roll of the Dice* (to draw on Mallarmé), itself waiting to be undergone (*ex-periri*) rather than simply expressed. Joseph Conrad professes with regard to literature, which I adopt in all its detail, and all the more so, for a hermeneutics of scripture:

My task which I am trying to achieve is, by the power of the written word, to make you hear, to make you feel—it is, before all, to make you *see*. That—and no more, and it is everything. If I succeed, you shall find there according to your deserts: encouragement, consolation, fear, charm—all you demand—and, perhaps, also that glimpse of truth for which you have forgotten to ask.[75]

Neither text nor writing as with Ricoeur, neither letter nor trace as with Levinas, the phenomenality exhibited in the act of reading is thus, in a Christian or rather a Catholic mode, that of the *body* or, better yet, of the bodily, "hand-to-hand combative" embrace of the reader always in a struggle with "what is spoken," letting himself be displaced, even forgotten, in an incorporation where the Eucharist, of course, constitutes the key event. Moving from the *meaning of the text* in the Protestant hermeneutic to the *body of the letter* in the Jewish hermeneutic and finally to *the text of the body* in the so-called Catholic hermeneutic, the focus shifts to the voice rather than writing and to incarnate flesh rather than embodied speech. Indeed, held at all times in a body, the quasi-carnal voice of the incarnate Word [*Verbe*]—thus not only his spoken word and even less so his text—resonates still today in scripture such that, "in the Word" precisely, we might "live bodily" in the whole fullness of divinity (Col 2:9). In listening "almost with the ears of our flesh," in St. Francis's phrase, and according to a "conversion of the senses" as Bonaventure taught, we will hear his voice more than we will read his text and we will find his iconic presence rather than his quasi-amnesic trace. Thus, I can conclude with Hugh of Saint-Victor's admirable text that will serve as the guiding thread for the next chapter:

The word of God closed in human flesh appeared visibly a single time and now, each day [*Quotidie*], this same word comes himself to us under the cover of a human voice [*humana voce conditum*]. Certainly its manner by which it makes itself known to humans is different according to whether it's by his flesh [*per carnem*] or by the human voice [*per vocem humana*]. And yet, in a certain manner [*quodammodo*], the voice of the word must be understood at present as the flesh was then [*hic intelligenda set vox verbi quod ibi caro dei*].[76]

2

For a Hermeneutic of the Body and the Voice

Hic intelligenda est vox Verbi quod ibi caro Dei—"the voice of the Word must be understood at present as the flesh of God was understood then."[1] This single formula from Hugh of Saint-Victor is sufficient to illuminate the Catholic hermeneutic of the body and the voice as introduced so far. The reminder is certainly appropriate. A "Catholic" hermeneutic should not be opposed to a "Jewish" hermeneutic or to a "Protestant" hermeneutic in a confessional struggle, which fortunately today is by and large left behind. Catholic theology lives in an ecumenism of good taste; it regularly recognizes its debt to Jewish or Protestant contributions to theology— contributions it should safeguard. These contemporary approaches are not, and never have been, modes of condemnation. The inflection orienting their thought is solely significant (see Chapter 1, §5). Ricoeur's Protestant hermeneutic, with its focus on the meaning of the text, insisted on the book of scripture rather than the book of the world as its anchor. Levinas's Jewish hermeneutic centered on the body of the letter sought to show how the sacred text itself becomes the trace of the materiality of an inscription, which incessantly returns to the text without our ever being able to be freed from it. As observed in Chapter 1, we face the medium of the text on the one hand, and on the other a quasi-carnal inscription. Thus, the written text is primary in Protestantism and Judaism according to a truly necessary "liturgy of the Word," but in a Catholic structure it designates only one of the "two tables"—the other being the Eucharistic table—where we consecrate as well as celebrate.

Instead of assimilating or alternately rejecting everything Ricoeur and Levinas offer, I expect the most from each author: that each remain "such as he is"—first anchored in his own tradition. I will not reproach the former his privileging of the meaning of the text anymore than the latter his making himself the champion of the "body of the letter"—quite to the contrary. Nevertheless, we should ask ourselves: has not the resumption of Ricoeur's textual hermeneutic in the context of Catholic theology some-how concealed the significance of bodily reality and therefore of the Eucharistic "this is *my body*"? In addition, has the recuperation of Levi-nas's notion of the trace in a number of philosophical discourses not lost sight of the thickness of alterity—for example, in the gap between "the face" and "the sacrament of the neighbor"? In short, by over-privileging the influence of non-Catholic thinkers (whose own grounds are neverthe-less clearly solid), has Catholic thought not in some way retreated from its own identity, forgetting to take root in its specific ground: *hoc est corpus meum*, "this is my body"? Significant theological questions are thus at stake and call for new approaches. An*other* and a *new* way remains to be traced—not to be in opposition to those who have preceded us but to find in them nourishment and fresh orientation.

In light of these questions, my work has followed a distinct Catholic approach, not primarily in order to wave some Catholic banner but to focus specifically on Christ incarnate. Indeed, we cannot be satisfied to relate everything only to "the lived experience of the flesh" (the phenom-enological *Leib*) without rooting it in the very "organicity of the body" (*Leib* in Nietzsche's sense of the term). The "counterblow of theology on phenomenology," to which we will return (Chapter 6, §20), demands the revision of the commonplaces of phenomenology itself. Nothing entails or in fact guarantees that it is sufficient to speak of the "flesh" to account for the "body" of Christ incarnate—even of his Eucharistic body. What is true eventually for the Resurrection as a "lived experience of the flesh" (*Leib*) cannot be said in the same way for the Eucharist as "the organicity of the body" (*Körper*). In this way, my book *Metamorpho-sis of Finitude*, which addressed birth and resurrection, had been waiting for its counterpart in the work entitled *Les noces de l'agneau*, dealing with questions of the body and the Eucharist. The specific goal of the chapter on "L'embardée de la chair" was showing that the entirety of the body could not be articulated in phenomenology alone and that in particular its organicity required new and otherwise-deployed thinking. "La philoso-phie à la limite" then takes aim at our bodily life, which is made of pas-sions and pulsations, falls under the scope of what we can no longer say, and reaches that chaos or "*tohu wa-bohu*," which Christ alone in his

Eucharistic gift or his "this is my body" is capable of rejoining as well as indwelling. If such is the character of the wedding to be celebrated, Christ's gifts will join up with our "portion of animality" in the effigy of the sacrificed Lamb, assumed and transformed in the figure of the resurrected Christ.[2]

The other side must also be addressed, although it may be more difficult, since it was insufficiently developed in my previous works. What is "speaking," especially when it must be once again and persistently rooted in corporeality? In other words, if "the Word became flesh in order that flesh become word," in Mark the Ascetic's frequently cited and beautiful phrase, how do we understand the "flesh of the word" rather than simply the "word of the flesh" and the "body of speech" and not only the "speech of the body?" By dint of insisting on the primacy of corporeality in philosophy, ethics, and theology, does not speech risk losing its frequently and justly declaimed preeminence? If Catholicity cannot abide exclusively by the Protestant hermeneutic of the meaning of the text or the Jewish hermeneutic of the body of the letter, is it not waiting to find its own status in an *incarnate Logos*?

I claimed, or at least tried to show, in *Les noces de l'agneau*, that "this is my body" is brought forth as much by the performativity of speech (in §33, "Oeuvre en prose") as by the impossibility for the body alone to signify (§24, "Les failles de la chair"). Yet God speaks *and* speaks to us today as yesterday, even if in another mode or in an ethos to be rediscovered at this time. No longer able to build anew on the foundation of the specific medium of the text or the exclusive corporeality of the letter, the Catholic problem remains: to recount the status of a *logos* or a speech ever incarnate. The "Voice" or the *phonê* is no longer a simple instrument of communication but the most intimate of phenomena, chosen by God to identify himself today. Indeed, Jesus responds at the tribunal before Pilate: "whoever is of the truth listens to my voice" (*akouei mou tês phonês*; Jn 18:37) or, earlier in the same Gospel, the "good Shepherd" is the one who opens the door to the lambs, who "listen to his voice" (*tês phonês autou akouei*) because they "recognize his voice" (*oti oidasin tên phonên autou*; Jn 10:3–4).

§7. Aphonal Thought

In the fourth century, the grammarian Servius wrote, *De vocis nemo magis quam philosophi tractant*—that is, nobody discusses the "voice" more than philosophers.[3] This formula should be, or perhaps should have been, taken literally in philosophy as also in theology. Philosophy without *the voice* would remain nothing but a voiceless philosophy, such that the "forgetfulness of the voice" (which is probably more fundamental) would take over from "the forgetfulness of being." More acutely, a true Christian ethic of the body requires *an ethos of the voice*, at the risk of leaving the spoken word, which continues to be given to us today, forever disincarnated. When the body and the spoken word are unified, such that there is no voice without body or spoken word without voice, the exercise of the voice requires then neither the absence of the locutor (as with the text) nor his complete presence in a face-to-face (the speaker may remain hidden but not absent, by letting his voice be heard). The spoken word takes bodily form in the voice, at the same time as the voice gives a bodily reality to the spoken word. This "forgetfulness of voice" must be brought to light, without which the recurrent and inappropriate arguments based on the dualism of speech and silence would never come to an end. Chrétien underscores the point while restricting it, however, to the realm of the call:

> There are innumerable reflections on language. There are many reflections on speech. But there are *very few on the voice itself.* The voice is paradoxically silenced by most deliberations on language, albeit not as the material means of its realization.[4]

Hence the question before us: by dint of insisting that the *logos* is language per Ricoeur or speech per Levinas as inscribed in a text, have philosophical and theological hermeneutics not been bereft of their basis in corporeality—*in the voice itself*? Moreover, have not the recent advances in phenomenology truly reintegrated the voice as the very mode of thought as it repeatedly withdraws into a silence on whose basis, sometimes, there is no longer anything to formulate? Furthermore, has the insistence on the voice in the Bible—*qol* in Hebrew, *phonê* in Greek, and *vox* in Latin—not been sufficiently weighty to the point of becoming a veritable *topos* for theology? Certainly, the Gospel did not omit speaking of the voice: from the voice of John the Baptist crying in the desert (Jn 1:23), to the voice of the Father at the baptism of Christ in the Jordan (Lk 3:22), to the loud voice of the angels and the living on the day of the apocalypse (Rv 5:12). In short, has not philosophical and theological thought become aphonal—not that it does not speak but that it neither gives voice to anything nor is voci-ferant?

Phenomenology without Voice

We could be led to believe that the voice has recently been reintegrated into phenomenology in the time between Derrida's *La voix et le phénomène*

(1967) and Chrétien's *La voix nue* (1990).[5] The breakthrough achieved by these two works is unique and valuable in that they open to another and new "voice/way" in phenomenology. Nevertheless, it deserves to be radicalized or, at the very least, brought to its term in order to give voice to the voice. As a matter of fact, for Derrida the voice is never "proclaimed": it only designates the internal phenomenon of "hearing oneself speak to oneself in oneself" or "being heard in the other." As a result, the voice consists only in my own resonance to myself or in the echo between the other and myself. As a precursor to Henry, Derrida writes:

> The operation of "hearing-oneself-speak" is an auto-affection of an absolutely unique type. . . . To speak to someone is undoubtedly to hear oneself speak, to be heard by oneself, but also and by the same token, if one is heard by the other, it is to make the other *repeat immediately* in himself the hearing-oneself-speak in the very form in which I have produced it.[6]

Trapped in the nets of Husserlian commentary and the question of signification, in a sense, the Derridean voice does not speak. It resonates inside oneself or in the very interiority of the other, without truly vociferating or being addressed. Certainly one must recognize the phenomenologist's virtue in having defined the voice as the locus of "one's proximity to oneself" in interiority, in "hearing oneself" more than in "seeing oneself" or "touching oneself." For Derrida, when I speak, I speak first of myself and in myself, in a sense right there beneath my skull. In this resonance, an auto-affection from which I can never detach myself plays itself out—in contradistinction to "seeing myself" or "touching myself" from which I can always separate myself (turning my gaze away from the object, or ceasing to touch "myself").[7] Yet in our eyes, the essential is still lacking: the voice is not articulated in relation to the body at this point. At the most, it is kept within the limits of a consciousness fenced in by subjectivity.

On my reading, this solipsism of the voice, which repeats at will the Cartesian solipsism of thought, follows from the philosopher's more fundamental grounds—that is, the primacy of the *gramma* over the *phonê* and the preference for grammatology over phonology. It all really depends on the interpretation given to Aristotle's well-known formula set forth at the opening of his *De interpretatione*: "spoken sounds are symbols of affections in the soul, and written marks symbols of spoken sounds."[8] *Of Grammatology* (1967) deplores the fact, on my account wrongly so, that the *gramma* or the written sign is defined by Aristotle only in terms of its dependence on the *phonê* or the voice. Caught in a deviation of a "phono-centrism" that has not been liberated from the metaphysics of presence (since one must *be there* in order to speak), the *"graph"* is thus called to enjoy its autonomy akin to Levinas's trace, and thereby may claim its non-dependence upon the spoken system. In *Of Grammatology*, Derrida asserts contra Rousseau's little voice of conscience that "the history of truth, of the truth of truth, has always been . . . the debasement of writing and its repression outside 'full' speech."[9] Thoth, the god of writing, then comes to power in "Plato's Pharmacy": the science of signs, or more precisely of written traces or *gramma*, gains preeminence over linguistic speech [*la parole de la langue*] or the *logos*.[10] In the eyes of the philosopher, the latter is always oriented toward the mode of presence and thus toward meta-physics. In short, as Agamben underscores rightfully in his masterful seminar notes on the forgotten phenomenon of "the Voice": "if [in Der-rida's work] metaphysics is that reflection that places the voice as origin, it is also true that *this voice is, from the beginning, conceived as removed*, as Voice."[11] In other words, the voice must no longer simply inscribe itself in signs or the signs free themselves from the voice as with Derrida. Quite to the contrary, the voice must be heard to give voice or be concretely embodied. Thus, grammatology must receive itself from phonology as the mode of presence of alterity and no longer as only the panegyric of a forgotten trace.

The passage to Chrétien's *Voix nue*, a worthy relay to Derrida's *Voice and Phenomenon*, could then make us believe in an actual utterance of the voice. Yet the "naked voice" is *denuded of voice*, precisely. It is found within a Heideggerian notion of the call, according to a relay of the requisite and the response, which is widely circulated today, even overused (consider Heidegger, Derrida, Chrétien, Henry, Marion). The thickness of the voice disappears beneath the declinations of the call: "the discourse of conscience never comes to utterance," following Martin Heidegger, and thus "con-science only *calls* silently."[12] Indeed, the call only "*speaks* in the uncanny mode of silence."[13] Furthermore, the "voice of conscience somehow speaks of guilt," and yet "the call 'speaks' *nothing* which could be talked about': it only highlights that which must be understood [*Verstehen*]."[14] Paradoxically, the Heideggerian voice does not speak. More accurately, it neither cries out nor vibrates with its so-called tonalities (*Stimmungen*). It remains utterly "aphonal," entirely enclosed in the sphere of the intimacy of the conscience according to the oppositional prism of speaking and silencing, which in reality does not make space for the vociferation of the voice itself. Dasein, as also the whole of phenomenology, appears properly speaking "voiceless" (*a-phonê*). In Agamben's words, Being-the-*Da*, or "Being-the-*there*," is "possible only through . . . the experience of the taking place of language in the removal of the voice."[15] The "naked voice," to return to the introductory syntagm by Chrétien, certainly responds always "to an anterior voice that it only hears in responding to it—a voice that precedes and exceeds it." But this trajectory runs "from the crypt to the throat to the intimacy of the ear, breathes while traversing the air," and contains a secret, which sometimes goes so far as to "leave the voice breathless and suspended—silencing it without the word's being able to leave it."[16] Caught in the Heideggerian concepts of call and response, all contemporary phenomenologies of the voice appear to forget the most trivial thing from which we are unable, however, to detach ourselves: there is no voice without a body, no alterity without the present vibration of an incarnate being. The "ghost of a pure language," in Merleau-Ponty's terms, still haunts the banks of phenomenology—certainly not in the Husserlian purity of the algorithm, today long left behind, but in the ideal of a voice so stripped of flesh in its structure as a call that it forgets to root itself in corporeality and also to cry out:

> There is thus an opaqueness to language. . . . Our analyses of thought give us the impression that before it finds the words that express it, it is already a sort of ideal text that our sentences attempt to *translate*. But the author himself has no text to which he can compare his writing, and no language prior to language.[17]

From the Naked to the Raw Voice

To rediscover a true ethos of the voice—a voice that speaks authentically, that gives voice to . . . or "voci-ferates"—we will not keep it bound to Heidegger's call of conscience, anchored in writing with Derrida, or yet, as Chrétien would, let it run out of breath in order to expose itself in the silence of an exhausted saying. The "naked voice" waits for its other model or its counter-model: the "raw voice."[18] Indeed, if the voice proclaims itself, if it attaches itself to a body without ever turning itself off or running out of breath, it is because it must be heard first in its "crudity" or rawness, which has no part in a certain "cruelty." The raw [*crue*] voice, according to the French syntagm, is not raw because it is cruel [*cruelle*] but on account of its brute or unworked state ("raw" as in uncooked and not-yet-prepared food), that is, just as brutal in its singular expression as inalterable in its identity—for instance, the "harsh light" ["*lumière crue*"] when the sky begins to darken. The voice contrasts and marks the contrast as it attaches itself to the body and singularizes it, such that "one's own" is oneself and the "other" is other.

The other is recognized paradoxically by his voice as well as, or even better than, by his body or even his face. The other's voice brings him close (in the past, as "hidden," or today, in the mode of the "tele–phoned"). He manifests himself in its timbre, is heard in the fine grain of its vibration and the modulation of his breath, and deploys himself in the mode of his speaking more than in the spoken words themselves. Indeed, clearly one recognizes one's friend and one's neighbor most definitely by his voice, so that it is sufficient to hear him speak in order to say that *it really is him* who is actually playing the role of the addressee. The greatest certainty is not found exclusively in the visibility of the corporeal and even less so in the invisibility of thought, but in this *intermediary timbre* between the sensible and the intelligible, whereby he approaches and seeks to identify himself. At the end of the "line," today more than ever virtualized, resonates the voice of one whose given location, city, region, even country, I do not—or no longer—know. Beyond all geographical coordinates and sometimes even within the very mode of transportation wherein the passenger himself does not know how to locate himself, the only sound is the grain, or the barely articulated breath, of the other: "it's me." The call no longer resounds in order to be audible in the sense of something heard in its articulation. It is found *a minima* in the mode of a sound that is disdainful of any first name. The strict carnality of the "I" and the "you" through which we hear ourselves simply by vibrating substitutes itself, in the recognition of the voice, to the aptly named concept of the surname by which we seek to identify ourselves. Frequently, there is no need to name oneself when our voice is "dialed in" or predictable—consecrating the *far* of the *phonê* (*tele*-phoned) as one of the modes, in reality, of the greatest proximity. The identity of the body expresses itself also sometimes there where it is hidden, even if *eros* fails to be content with that. Not truly absent from a text from which the speaker would have definitely withdrawn, the voice resonates as another modality of the presence by which precisely the other indicates itself as the beloved. Merleau-Ponty again perceives and grasps it clearly:

> A friend's speech over the telephone brings us the friend himself, as if he were wholly present in that manner of calling and saying goodbye to us, of beginning and ending his sentences, and of carrying on the conversation through things left unsaid. Because meaning is the total movement of speech, our thought crawls along in language.[19]

The love of the other as "the singularity of his voice" is thus the confession in which the beloved resounds. In fact, at times, even quite often, there is no need to speak with each other, other than to make resound "the loving timbre" of the one whose presence, however, remains hidden. The whispering of the beloved, even simply his breath, suffices to recognize the depths of his familiar presence, which nevertheless remains always foreign. His raw voice resonates without being naked and, even more clearly, without being retained in a trace from which all orality would have been removed. Indeed, nothing is missing more than the voice, especially as soon as the beloved is at a distance. Absence certainly does not prevent its renewed proximity, albeit in the technical mode of the always ready-at-hand "telephone call." Death, however, eliminates the voice with a pain that the call of desire cannot satisfy. I recognize my beloved by her raw voice. My call, then, becomes all the more desperate when I can no longer hear her voice. The supplication of the voice deepens the chasm of the oft-unsatisfied absence. Indeed, precisely by way of her absence, the other truly plays for me—even for my body—the role of the addressee. The lover in the Song of Songs begs his spouse in a vocal expression of conjugality, which everyone may experience: "let me hear your voice" (Sg 2:14), which can then be heard echoed in the Gospel of John, where this time, the friend of the bridegroom "is full of joy when he hears the bridegroom's voice" (Jn 3:29).

Perhaps at times a phenomenology without voice has detained thought in its aphonal mode as if to cut off the vibration of the one who addresses me. In omitting this intermediary body between thought and corporeality, philosophy has perhaps not sufficiently listened to the resonance of the voice—at least in its rawness. The scriptural texts, however, never fail to echo it and even to provoke it. The occurrences of *qol* and *phonê*, as we have emphasized, are so numerous that there is no need to insist on this fact. Yet theology itself, following the example of hermeneutics but also sometimes of phenomenology, has often missed the vociferation whose echo the sacred texts receive or to whose cry they give voice. Indeed, the "raw voice" is often lost amidst the effort to find the meaning that muffles its timbre. Finally, the dereliction in the Passion will also be smothered as soon as the call no longer lets the voice resonate or when "Holy Friday is always perceived in the light of Easter," or yet, as Péguy claimed, when one sees "the crucifixion in the fructification of the resurrection."[20]

Theology of the Voice

The voice is thus always "raw," or theologically speaking should be so construed. In one sense, as already introduced above, it is raw because it always gives itself in a brute state (in its "crudity"), by which the voice personalizes itself in its expression rather than exposes itself in the anonymity of a call—*voci-ferates* more than demands, cries out rather than convokes. Such is the paradigmatic case of the "great voice" (*megalê phonê*), a more accurate translation of the "great cry," of the day of dereliction: "at three in the afternoon, Jesus cried out in a loud voice: *Eloï, Eloï, lema sebactani?*" (Mk 15:34)—which means, "My God, my God, why have you forsaken me?" After philosophical or more precisely phenomenological thought's aphonia or "lack of voice," the aphonia of theological elaborations emerges now, following the same pattern. Most often interpreted in light of Psalm 22, the "great voice" of Jesus on the cross is only heard in terms of the resounding "Why?" In silencing the vociferation (the cry of the voice) amidst its signifying (the why), we lose what it signified originally—not only the interrogation of the meaning (why?!) but the tearing of the body.[21] As indicated by the following verses:

> With a loud cry, Jesus breathed his last. The curtain of the temple was torn in two from top to bottom. (Mk 15:37–8)

and

> by a new and living way opened for us through the curtain, at is, his body. (Hb 10:20)[22]

The voice is thus first and foremost "raw" in philosophy in light of its brute character or its crudity if it does not get lost in the entanglements of the call and the signified; in theology, if it does not tone down the "great voice" amidst the innumerable reasons of its "why."

The voice is "raw" ["crue"] in another sense as well: in its "belief" ["croyance"] in addition to its crudity or its carnal density. To believe in God theologically speaking is also today *to believe in his voice*, perhaps even more than in his body. Assuredly, the Word became flesh for his disciples; this was the meaning of his Incarnation. But *for us* after his Resurrection appearances and the Ascension, also insofar as we are situated on the other side of the closure of the Canon, the Word is no longer present in the flesh but *in the voice*. To obscure the vociferation of the voice in a theology no less "aphone" than philosophy is to forget not only the question of the expressivity of words but also the thickness of the body itself. Since there is no opposition of the body to the voice—after all there will never be a voice without a body—the voice occupies the topos of the flesh for us today. There where yesterday the disciples saw and touched the Word on the basis of his flesh (*ab ejus carne*), we encounter him today on the basis of his voice (*ab ejus voce*). I already noted, without yet making it explicit, the basis of a hermeneutic of the voice that may be called Catholic, found in Hugh of Saint-Victor's foundational text:

> The Word of God clothed in human flesh appeared *visibly but once.* *Now, each day*, this same Word comes to us under the cover of a *human voice.* To be sure, he makes himself known in different ways, whether it is according to the flesh or the human voice. Yet in a certain way, the voice of the Word must be understood at present as the flesh was so understood then.[23]

This "Word of life" that the disciples' ears "have heard," that their eyes "have seen," and that their hands "have touched" (1 Jn 1:1), indeed can no longer be heard, seen, and touched in the same way today. But *his voice* remains, as Hugh of Saint-Victor indicates. Moreover, it remains audible insofar as the being of his now-hidden body, albeit hidden under the species of the Eucharist, does not cease speaking to us.[24] No longer seeing his body, we hear his voice: we recognize it by its manner more than its matter, by its tonality more than its visibility. Then—his *flesh* singularized him as made known in his face and the kinesthetic movements of his body, when he was seen and heard by his own. Now—his *voice* personalizes him for us in its tone, style, and timbre, when we read and listen to his spoken word, when we eat and praise him—the one who has entered, however, into the order of the unseen. In no way retrenched in the invisibility of a *quidam* that would not or no longer want to manifest itself, on the contrary, God makes the choice, not to avoid being seen, but to let himself be seen *otherwise*: that is, heard. In Claudel's language, when "the eye listens," the ear also "makes visible." The voice of the good Shepherd, whose voice the lambs know (*oïdasin tên phonên autou*), is opposed to the voice of the strangers (*allotriôn tên phonên*), whom they do not know (*ouk oïdasin*) (Jn 10:3–5). In this known voice, the Shepherd does not so much say something as he makes himself known. He speaks less than he resonates in his spoken word. He makes himself not only "word in flesh" but also "word in voice." The "incarnate God," in the strict sense of the term, becomes for us the "vocalized God" but not without a body, not having lost his body. This God is here, today, enfleshed in language that could never abstract itself from the body that uttered it, although it would remain hidden to us to this day.

§8. The Voice Is the Phenomenon

To rediscover the meaning of the voice or to finally let the voice "give voice" entails no longer enclosing the voice in language or words in their significance. The voice is found between silence and the spoken word. In this forgotten third, the reality of the incarnate Word is set forth—the human word certainly, but also that of God, since he uttered it first in his flesh. "And the Word was God' (Jn 1:1)"—Hilary of Poitiers comments on this phrase in his *De trinitate*: "the word is a sound of voice [*sonus vocis*], a naming of things [*enuntiato negotiorum*], a verbalization of thoughts [*elocutio cogitationum*]."[25] The fact that the "voice [that] cries in the desert" (Jn 1:23) is John the Baptist's rather than the incarnate Christ's does not dispense the second once he becomes the first, namely the Messiah or the anointed of God, from the duty of also using it—quite the contrary. To the Baptist's voice that cries out to the ends of the horizon of the inhabited world without concern for its reception is opposed the voice that speaks at the very end with a "great voice" or the *megalê phonê* of the Son who addresses himself to his Father, to the one who appears, however, to have abandoned Christ on the cross. To say "I am the voice" (*egô phônê*) does not exempt Christ from being it all the more so by offering himself precisely at this time fully in and through his eternally given body, since "Eucharistic" before resurrected. The Messiah himself, following the example of John the Baptist, otherwise "gives voice" to and from within his flesh, recapitulating in himself that which the first Adam had already localized in the act of creation to which his father also had called him. "For just as at that time God spoke to Adam in the evening, and seeking him out," as St. Irenaeus underscored in an allegory of the two testaments, "so in the last times, by means of the same voice [*per eadem vocem*], seeking out his posterity, he visited them."[26] As Word of the Father, the Son is also its *voice*, or at least he receives it in his being there for us today incarnate, in light of a vocality to be rediscovered today. Philosophically speaking, we would thus no longer be able to separate the voice and the phenomenon. Certainly, Derrida correctly emphasizes that "the voice *is* consciousness."[27] But in this complete identification of consciousness with the voice, the voice does not speak or no longer speaks, as I have already shown. It remains, on the contrary, all the more "aphone" in that it inhabits the reflexive threshold or rather the interiority as "resonance beneath the cranium" as the very place of the revealed. As a phenomenon giving itself to consciousness, the voice is exhibited in the work, but is not properly speaking vociferated.

The Language of the Voice

The attempt to deliver the voice, or to no longer treat it as a voice possessed by the message it bears (conscience, call, debt, being), entails disengaging it from language (*logos*)—more specifically, from writing (*gramma*)—for which it appears, however incorrectly, always destined. A reversal must take place, which has certainly been suggested but properly speaking never thought through. Agamben confided to his friend Giorgio Caproni, "Long ago—we are told—our voice was inscribed in language. The search for this voice in language is thought."[28] To this "long ago" is opposed a *now* and even a *tomorrow*, which finally let the voice be heard, or at least express itself. In Agamben's striking formula, "thought is the suffering of the voice and language."[29] The reversal is complete and concludes by showing that the voice not only has the goal to signify but also and most of all to articulate or better yet to make vibrate what in fact would no longer be able to give itself according to the mode of consciousness or the call. It is no longer a question of the voice in language but *the language of the voice*; no longer vocalization to signify, but *the signification of vocalization*; no longer thought for speaking, but *speaking to think*. Finally, the voice begins to vibrate. Better yet, it exhibits itself in that it no longer leads only to thought but preserves also, in itself, the question of corporeality at the very heart of its singularity.

To rediscover the suffering of the voice, and thus its pathos as such, requires a return to its Aristotelian definition; simply cited for now, "the sound emitted by the voice are the symbols of states of the soul, in the written words are the symbols of the words emitted by the voice."[30] The book on the voice that Agamben regrets not having written, as indicated in the preface of the French edition of *Infancy and History*, would have shown, suggests the author, that "there is no articulation between phone and logos" or that "the voice has never inscribed itself in language"—Derrida's *gramma* being nothing but "the very form of the presupposing of self and and potency."[31] This untested trail must be followed today. Caught in language and, at the same time, in its inscription's target in a trace, the voice loses that *for which* it is made. Properly speaking, this *for which* is neither solely whining nor crying out by means of corporeality nor uniquely producing significations in the service of a well-articulated consciousness, but *for saying the pathemata* or the "symbols of the states of the soul" and even the life (*psuchê*) by which it manifests itself. The Greek expression of "the state of the soul in the voice" (*pathemata en tê phone*) in Aristotle's *De interpretatione* has in view less the "sounds emitted by the voice," as if the voice made itself the instrument of a pathos simply to be communicated, than the "place" or the "this" where these affects come to dwell and express themselves most profoundly. A literal translation would read as follows: "That which is in the voice (*ta en tê phonê*) contains the symbols of mental experience [the *pathemata* of the soul], and written words are the symbols of that which is in the voice."[32] First of all, the voice contains thus the pathos, only to afterward and eventually affix it in a written text as its possible, but only secondary, target. In opposition to Derrida, for whom the second term of the proposition—the writing of the voice or the *gramma*—is central, today it is appropriate to point out the primacy of the first: the *pathemata* "in the voice" as symbols of the states of the soul according to a finding that is certainly close to Henry's "phenomenology of life" but will not content itself to repeat an auto-affection where nothing is expressed externally, and all the less, voci-ferated.

The Pathos of the Voice

The detour through or rather the return to the definition of the human as *zôôn logikon* at the opening of Aristotle's *Politics* provides sufficient evidence for an expressivity proper to the voice. The voice expresses the "states of the soul" more than its nonsignified, and in opposition to the absolutely conscious: "man is the only animal who has the gift of speech [*logos*]. And whereas mere voice [*phonê*] is but an indication of pleasure or pain, and is therefore found in other animals."[33] A counter-reading of the famous definition of the human as a rational animal reveals the meaning of vocality. Indeed, if—since "it is characteristic of man that he alone has any sense of good and evil"—the *logos* declares the useful and the harmful followed by the just and the unjust, then there will always be *a hither side of the logos* within the *phonê*. In other words, if the absolutely conscious is on the far side of the *logos*, the distinctiveness of vocality is found on this side of the *logos* in an ethos of the voice that enlivens and grounds all ethics of values (yet without disqualifying it).[34] I have already explained this claim elsewhere in passages treating the question of animality where the meaning of the proffered voice also had to be rediscovered:

> the [*requête*] of the declined logos as discourse does not prohibit the *phonê* defined this time as voice; indeed the logos superimposes itself to the *phonê* or the discourse to the voice, such that the more originally (the voice or the faculty of producing sounds) sounds again its derived product (speech/the spoken word or the capacity to articulate according to thought).[35]

The voice is, in a certain sense, vague and undetermined in the spoken word; the latter finds its origin in the former—not the inverse. Writing affixes the voice, rather than the opposite. It is thus a mistake, as Agamben suggests in passing, that Derrida was able to see the intentionality of speaking in the *gramma* as the fourth term alongside the voice, the *pathemata*, and things themselves.[36] Aristotle does not speak for the purpose of writing, any more than he thinks for the purpose of speaking. An originary and shared speaking discloses the human voice as the premise and role of animality within humanity. To rediscover the *pathemata* of the soul cultivated in the *phonê*, or the joy and pain originally borne by the voice, is certainly not to return to our animal state but rather to recognize a common pathos from which everything is derived—within which all *logos* or discourse on values must be inserted, without which it would remain forever disincarnate: *"language is our voice, our language. As you now speak, that is ethics."*[37]

The Phenomenon of the Voice

Thus we will no longer or not only say, "the voice *and* the phenomenon" but "the voice *is* the phenomenon." In liberating the voice from its restriction to the functions of supporting the signification of language and its inscription in the letter, I will attend less to the link of the voice to the phenomenon of consciousness than to the dedication of the voice per se as the phenomenon. Specifically, the phenomenon to be seen or more accurately heard is the "great voice" (rather than the great cry) by which the Son declares himself in the *pathemata* of his "absolute pain," as overwhelmed by the feeling of abandonment and thus ready to be radically transformed.[38] *The voice of the phenomenon*, derived directly from the Heideggerian lineage of the call (conscience, being, gift, debt, listening) must now be transformed into *the phenomenon of the voice*, after the manner of a certain Kafka and Deleuze. In the metamorphosis of a human into a giant bug, Kafka describes how "Gregor had a shock as he heard his own voice answering hers, unmistakably his own voice, it was true, but with a persistent horrible twittering squeak behind it like an undertone."[39] A stranger to his own voice, Gregor Samsa gives voice to his pain and, at the same time, gives up his voice. Blurring the boundaries of the *logos*, Kafka requires that his hero complete his transformation (*Verwandlung*) to the point of returning to inhabit the greatest depths of his pathos, where precisely, and now in the words of Deleuze's commentary, "a language of sense is traversed by a line of escape—in order to liberate a living and expressive material that speaks for itself and has no need of being put into a form."[40] Pressed to give language to the voice—no longer only give voice to language—to the point of undoing the articulation of the signifiers themselves, it is necessary, to achieve now the complete reversal, to confer a body to the voice—no longer exclusively a voice to the body—such that the recognized community of an incorporated voice is substituted for the specific individuality of the proffered voice.

§9. The Voice That Embodies[41]

The Voice of the Body or the "Signifying" of the Voice

A hermeneutic of the voice has created a space for a new mode of the act of interpreting: interpretation is bound more to the body than to the significations of language (or of the text), which are the usual foci in the most frequent forms of deciphering. In effect, the body of the voice is not exclusively speech or the voice's body without which it would cease to signify. It could signify in the flesh and otherwise than in articulated language. Voci-ferating certainly can be a moaning or whining as in the example of a Gregor discovering himself addressed (supra)—*but only* insofar as he conveys a suffering, or rather a *pathema*, struggling to express itself. The voice articulates or articulates itself, although it cannot be reduced to articulated language and remains, for that reason, the boundary point between speech and corporeality. Aristotle states it clearly in a key passage of *De anima*:

> Not every sound, as we said, made by an animal is voice (even with the tongue we may merely make a sound which is not a voice, or without the tongue as in coughing); what produces the impact must have a soul in it and must be accompanied by an act of imagination, for voice is a sound with a meaning [*sematikos dê tis psophos*], and is not the result of any impact of the breath as in coughing.[42]

The matter is thus clear as it now stands and should now be underlined: a voice is not simply the emission of a sound (a cough is not a voice), and there is no voice without signification—without an expression of some pathos. The Cartesian idea according to which "the human alone speaks" is certainly false, if the claim's sole basis is the human's endowment with reason.[43] But the signifying activity of the voice is embodied in the human as soon as speech occurs. Indeed, this is the meaning of the articulated *gramma*, if peradventure, it comes to bear the trace of the *phonê*: "*vox quae scribi potest*, the voice that can be written—in short, always preexisting as written."[44] Writing does not set down the voice in order to silence it and imprison it. On the contrary, it makes itself the flux, as it were, the vehicle of the mode of "proffering." The *stylus* at the end of the feather—the style as exemplified in all writing as well as in all true literature—follows the movement of the voice in its timbre or vocal cords. In both cases as in all cases, the voice becomes flesh (*leiben*) as it incorporates a body: it signifies by indicating a mode of speaking, which seeks as best it can to articulate itself.[45]

As the transcendental condition of the body as well as of meaning, the voice seeks a body for itself rather than coming from the body. It irrigates the body with meaning more than it encloses itself in meaning. As with Spinoza's conatus, which can be read as a model of the power of the Eucharistic incorporation as well as of the Resurrection, the *force* or the *Holy* Spirit—thus also the voice or the breath (*ruach/pneuma*)—*desires the body* more than it takes its origin in a body and produces the *instituting signification* more than it has its provenance in the instituted meaning.[46] Merleau-Ponty underscores it in this way, justly under the title *Prose of the World*:

> the expressive operation, and speech in particular considered in its nascent state, establish a common situation which is no longer only a community of being but a community of doing. It is this conquering speech which interests us, for it makes possible institutionalized speech, or language [langue] possible. . . . It is not enough for speech to convey a meaning already through and through; it is necessary that it make it be.[47]

The Eucharist or the Body of the Voice

Returning to theology, the voice of the body of the incarnate Christ in the eyes of the disciples seeks a "body of the voice" specifically *for us* in which he comes to manifest himself. To emphasize again by quoting the already twice-cited passage from Hugh of Saint-Victor, "the voice of the verb is to be understood at present as the flesh was understood then." This same Son who according to St. Augustine "gave a voice to his body (*ex persona corporis [oravit]*)" is waiting now, I claim, to give a body to his voice.[48] The instituted words of the Eucharist—"take, eat, this is my body given for you"—first feeds itself from the instituting or conquering speech of the voice that conveys it. Jesus replies to Nicodemus, "the wind (or the Holy Spirit) blows where it will, and you hear the voice [*tên phônen autou akoueis*], but you do not know from where it comes nor where it goes. This is how

it is of anyone who is born of the Spirit [*geggenêmenos ek you pneumatos*]"
(Jn 3:8). As with the "listeners" [*ekousantes*] rather than the "observers," to
whom the cry of the "great voice" in the *megalê phonê* of the Son on the
cross (Mk 15:35) is addressed, the Eucharistic epiclesis of the voice invoked
by the priest provides the relay in the liturgy for the flesh incarnate, which
had been previously touched by the disciples. In the words of the liturgy,
"Make holy, therefore, these gifts, we pray, by sending down your Spirit
upon them"—your Spirit or your Voice or your Breath [*Spiritus tui rore*]—
"so that they may become for us [*nobis*] the Body and the Blood of our
Lord Jesus Christ, our Lord [*Corpus et Sanguis Domini nostri Iesu Christi*]."[49]
By virtue of *the voice of the Spirit* (*Pneuma* or *Spiritus*), Christ becomes
flesh or takes body in the Eucharistic bread even as the bread is incorporated into the body of the church. The catechism of the Catholic Church
adds this succinct commentary:

> In the epiclesis, the church asks the Father to send his "Holy Spirit"
> upon the bread and the wine, in order that they become, through his
> power [*operante virtute*], the Body and Blood of Jesus Christ, and
> that those who partake in the Eucharist become one body and one
> spirit.[50]

The Word in Voice

It should thus have been understood that a Catholic hermeneutic of *the
body and the voice* is necessarily rooted in the Eucharistic liturgy—in particular, in its epiclesis. The power of God transforms the bread all the
more into a body as the Word gives itself now to us *in the Voice* through
the Holy Spirit, as he gave himself beforehand *in the body* to his disciples
in his Incarnation. Thus, the Christ specifies at the hour of the announcement of his glorification: "it is not for me [*ou di eme*] that this voice [*phonê*]
has made itself heard, but for you [*alla di umas*]" (Jn 12:30). The *pro nobis*
of the voice provides in our present time the relay of the *in se* of his body
in its historicity. At that time, in the Incarnation, there was no body without a voice; today, in the Eucharist, there is no voice without a body.
Offering his body, God also imparts his voice through which and through
whom we recognize him. Proffering his (inspired) voice, he transforms it
into a body by the power of his benediction. The "way/voice of truth"
[voie/voix] is not only that which maintains a certain number of claims
(according to a wordplay that, in French, abounds in significance). It is
also, but not exclusively, that by which we belong to the "breath" of this
ecclesial space, ever newly generated in the Eucharist. It is necessary to

again remind us, "whoever is of the truth" [*o ôn ek tês aletheias*], listens to my voice [*akouei mou tês phonês*]" (Jn 18:37).

Neither a simple hermeneutic of the *meaning of the text* as in Ricoeur's Protestant mode nor a pure hermeneutic of *the body of the letter* as seen in Levinas's Jewish approach, the hermeneutic of *the text of the body* in its Catholic and Eucharistic deployment finds the raison d'être of its "speaking" as well as the meaning of its "embodying" *in the voice*. St. Augustine's famous formula in the *Enarrationes in Psalmos* on Psalm 85 is once again helpful: to hear "*our voice in him and his voice in us* [*in illo voces nostras et voces eius in nobis*]" is the goal of "seeing" and thus of adoration, and also of "eating," thus of manducation, in the Eucharistic transubstantiation.[51] Grounding the act of *interpreting* in the body (Part I) certainly does not suffice for the act of *deciding* with respect to a horizon of belief that could be shared by everyone (Part II). After all, still today a Voice makes itself heard—a Voice whose prophecy will be all the more listened to, insofar as "other voices" will come and join with it to constitute the *voiced Body*.

Strange duo where *I speak with two voices* and receive my spoken words:

> "This is my body," and *His voice is mine*,
> "Delivered for you," and *I am the one who says so*
>
> —Not echo but prophecy *in our allied voices*
> *and our two voiced bodies.*[52]

Deciding

3

Always Believing

It was necessary to interpret (Part I). It is now time to decide (Part II). The hermeneutic *of the body and the voice*, which I have named Catholic, opens unto "a phenomenology of believing" that grounds it. Where hermeneutics drew out *meaning*, albeit anchored in the body rather than in the text, phenomenology describes a *mode* of being-there rooted in believing. The experience of being-there and believing sends us back first to a human community. As we just underlined, ecclesiality opens a space for the Eucharistically incorporated voice, which gives a concrete body to the body—the church—empowered by the force that engenders it—the Holy Spirit. Yet we are incapable of considering, straightforwardly or unanimously, every human to be caught in the nets of such "catholicity." Universality (*catholica*) does not consist in subjugating everything, or worse, consuming everything, in a bodily confrontation, which some could certainly refuse. In philosophy and in theology, nothing is more to be feared than a position of predominance, as if confessing belief could decide everything in a single blow and turn into a "privilege" an election simply given at the beginning. Grace may truly be received and confer an exemplary character to a person, in particular to the saints. But the Christian will not be satisfied with extracting himself from the sphere of common humanity. The confessing belief in God draws first and always upon an "ordinary" belief in others or in the world. Forgetting this, we would run the risk of failing to see the human per se in whom we take a stand before all else. Each person can best be said in this sense to be paradoxically "always believing" in humanity and the world (advanced here in Chapter 3) before deciding on a specific belief, whether for or against God (set forth in Chapter 4). First, then, I must decipher and describe the common pedestal that provides the basis for the Christian's remembering—not forgetting!—the first meaning of his own incarnate being.

"Yes; but you must wager. It is not optional. You are committed."[1] Pascal's well-known sentence leaves us no choice. Or rather, we have no choice about having the choice. This is the meaning of this famous, yet so often misunderstood, argument of the bet. While able to choose this or that, the gambler cannot choose himself choosing. He is always in advance engaged in the act of choosing. Paradoxically, all choice thus rests on a non-choice: the non-choice of being able to choose, certainly, but also the one of having already chosen without having the choice. The human, as in the example of the gambler, is embarked on an existential game where it is necessary to make a good wager. The player guarding his turf does not only use his tierce as a pastime but dedicates it in lieu of his existence. Indeed, he is caught in the choice of not having the choice—at least the non-choice of gambling, although he could well lose as a result of his wager. If there is a decision, particularly in the *choice of believing* in this or that, it is founded nevertheless on *an absolute non-decision* that we must at least recognize, since we lack the capacity to determine it. Not only the theologian but also the philosopher, even "the human per se," is always concerned, surprised, touched, and even found by the object he considers as soon as he begins to think. Every philosopher as well as every artist or poet is, in some way, inserted in the tableau or "ushered up from the audience to the stage," in the words of the theologian Karl Barth, even if he were required to appear in person by the one whom he encounters—namely, God himself.[2] Even before any kerygmatic decision, the conviction of religious faith (as will be shown in Chapter 4, "Kerygma and Decision") is founded upon an originary philosophical belief or an initial faith (as first shown here in Chapter 3, "Always Believing"), in which it takes root, in that we *are-in-the-world* to see ourselves also as *being-for-God*.

Indeed, the choice is not, and probably never was, between "believing" and "not believing," at least with respect to our philosophical being-there in the world. It is only a question of asking ourselves *who* and *how* to believe, since, in any case, we always believe. The philosophical belief in the world precedes the theological belief in God and supports it through and through. Instead of baptizing so-called "anonymous" Christians à la Rahner and without falling back on the motif of identity as von Balthasar, we should accept, at least as philosophers, that the non-thematic may always be a remainder from the non-thematized or even the nonthematizable. More precisely, an originary belief or an *Urdoxa* in Husserl's term is always the basis of any belief: "an actual world always precedes cognitive activity as its universal ground, and this means first of all a ground of universal passive belief"—the very ground that justifies the creation of the neologism "primal-belief" (*Urglaube*) or "protodoxa" (*Urdoxa*).[3] In short, there is no "decided dis-trust" without an "originary trust." The implication is not that we can and must trust everything but that we always trust something and, in particular, our irreducible belief of being-there in the world. Only in this way are we able to distrust something, perhaps even the world itself. This "philosophical faith" that Merleau-Ponty later will call "perceptive" is the precise reason we cannot believe that it is possible not to believe, independently of whatever we may or may not decide to believe in. In a posthumous work, Merleau-Ponty suggests that:

> we have to situate that relation back within a more muted relationship with the world, within an initiation into the world upon which it rests and which is always already accomplished when the reflective return intervenes.[4]

The central question can now be drawn out from this observation of a *common faith*, at least insofar as the word "faith" is taken in its widest scope. In the framework of a prereflexive philosophy, if the word "faith" is not understood in the sense of a decision but as "what is before any position, animal faith,"[5] what then is the relationship of this originary faith with "*the* faith"—that is, with the act of faith or with religious belief? In other words, if it is necessary to find and propose a "perceptive faith" at the foundation of "religious faith," does the former exclude the latter, or rather, is it not its condition of possibility as its transcendental structure? There would be no decided faith in God—for example, in the kerygma— without an always-presupposed faith in the world, since we are always there beforehand, or are even always "the world." In excluding perceptive faith, as indefectible belief that we are in the world, from religious faith as an act of confessional faith, the very believers have sometimes excluded themselves from the "always believing" human community. In the same way, in denouncing confessing religious faith in the name of a presumably independent perceptive faith, atheists or nonbelievers do not or no longer imagine the ties that bind the profane world to the sacred world as if religious belief must necessarily detach itself from humanity. A continuum, beginning with a philosophical perceptive faith and carrying on to an anthropological religious faith, and then to a theological confessing faith, always remains to be posited, even though the act of confessing faith (addressed in Chapter 4, §14) demarcates a rupture relative to perceptive faith's common belief of always being "already there in the world" and even to religious faith's belief of being bound to some transcendence. In this way, I will claim that "philosophical belief" or "perceptive faith" is the place of the greatest human community—where both God himself and our act of confessing faith must become incarnate.[6]

Nothing is harder to believe than the absence of belief. Of course, this is true with respect to the believer, but also to the nonbeliever. Common to both is being and remaining "always believing." The evidence resides as much in our originary belief in the world (per Merleau-Ponty) as in auto-affection (following Henry). The first cannot but make us "believe that we believe," while the second cannot but make us "feel that we feel." In both cases, we encounter the same redoubling in a quest for the irreducible as also the unsayable. *There is* world as *there is* feeling, and in this *there is* arises the unavowed community of a shared being-there. We are thus "always believing" not first in God or even in humanity but in this choice of not having the choice: we are always engaged in placing a wager from which none would be able to divest himself a priori. If theology as the deployment of the revealed demands our adherence or non-adherence to what was provided in the act of faith, philosophy as the description of the given keeps us in a community of belief from which we cannot detach ourselves in any way in light of the originary or perceptive faith. The kerygma, or "the confessing decision to believe," always takes root in a perceptive faith as a philosophical engagement in believing. The distinctiveness of faith "in God" can only take root upon the common pedestal of faith through an irreducible passion of "believing in general." In forgetting that "we all are embarked," in Pascal's terms, certain believers risk too quickly leaving the riverbank of humanity to find themselves suddenly alone.

§10. A Belief at the Origin

The Irreducible Belief in the World

As Péguy taught us, "In the history of thought, Descartes will always be the French horseman who took off at such a good pace."[7] Indeed, I have no intent to reject the foundation of our modernity. Consciousness marks the greatness of a philosophy that we would be wrong in accusing of having rejected everything. Yet the contemporary "reduction," in the framework of Husserlian phenomenology, is drawn from the Cartesian doubt of modern philosophy. Where the latter nullified the world, the former suspended it or placed it between parentheses. As Husserl explains, *"we put out of action the general positing which belongs to the essence of the natural attitude."*[8] He differs in this way from Descartes insofar as Descartes inspects the world and its possible existence—thus making an ontic judgment—whereas Husserl questions and interrogates the very one who scrutinizes the world—offering an ontological judgment. Nothing of the Cartesian "thing" or the *res* remains for Husserl—including the *res cogitans*, insofar as the latter still ends up reifying the subject rather than opening it to the fullness of its modes of possibilities. The father of phenomenology clarifies further:

> I am *not negating* this "world" as though I were a sophist; I am *not doubting its factual being* as though I were a skeptic; rather I am exercising the phenomenological ἐποχή which also *completely shuts me off from any judgment about spatiotemporal factual being.*[9]

Nevertheless, a question arises that will serve precisely as the guiding thread for the quest for an irreducible belief. If every judgment regarding the existence or the nonexistence of the world and thus the entire natural attitude is suspended, what is the status of the very act of "placing in parentheses"? In other words, is abstracting oneself from all judgments about the world (the epoché) in order to turn to the acts of consciousness (intentionality) to gloss over or even blatantly disregard any positive indexical relation to the world (that is, this originary and spontaneous belief)—that I was qualifying as irreducible—that the world exists rather than not existing? If we can doubt the existence of the world, along with Descartes, or yet "place in parentheses" any judgment about the world, following Husserl, are we truly capable also of freeing ourselves from "our belief in the world," as Husserl indicates or instead as Merleau-Ponty debates?

Indeed, there are two levels in the phenomenological reduction. The first, easily achieved, is placing judgments about the world in parentheses. The second, more difficult to attain, is questioning the remainder from what is suspended—precisely the "judgment about the world." In passing, as it were, while Husserl was studying the "general structures of pure consciousness," he specifies:

> that which is parenthesized is not erased from the phenomenological blackboard but only parenthesized, and thereby provided with an index. As having the latter [an index], it is, however, part of the major theme of inquiry.[10]

The road here is narrow but nevertheless negotiable. It is not a question of renouncing the epoché—far from it—but rather recognizing the existence of another type of epoché. Alfred Schütz, a much too frequently and unfortunately forgotten disciple of Husserl, will call it the "epoché of the natural attitude." In this case, the human, who is actually always held in the grip of an irreducible belief, "equally uses a specific epoché, *other than that of the phenomenologist* . . . which does not suspend the belief in the exterior world and its objects, but on the contrary *suspends all doubt of their existence.*"[11]

Therefore, everything is reversed. Or rather, everything takes place as if *Ideas I* (1913) already announced the principal theme of the *Krisis* (1936): the lived world is the irreducible horizon of the life-world or the *Lebenswelt*. When we thought that all belief was necessarily suspended in *Ideas I*, it appears now more and more clearly that a kind of "faith in the world" actually endures, forever irreducible, despite the Cartesian attempts to doubt the world or to suspend judgment as with the early Husserl. In *The Crisis*, Husserl asks:

> What has become of them if now, in the psychologist's epoché, the taking of a position on any such positing is to be excluded? We answer: The very epoché itself frees our gaze not only for the intentions running their course within the purely intentional life (i.e., the "intentional experiences" [*Erlebnisse*]) but also for that which these intentions in themselves, with their own "what"-content, posit as valid in each case as their object.[12]

Despite the complexity of the debate, there are simply *two lives* (rather than two separate ways), or better, *two methods of interpreting a same life*. On the one hand, the conscious or intentional life carries out the phenomenological reduction, and on the other hand, there is a nonconscious or rather preconscious life whose residue remains irreducible—that is, belief in the world itself. Although I could believe or fain to believe that the world does not exist, or yet I could suspend all judgment about the world, *I could never believe that I do not believe in the world.* A "universal ground of belief in the world" remains nonreducible, or yet in the terms of Husserl's late researches/investigations:

> Everything, which, as an existing object, is a goal of cognition is an existent on the ground of the world, which is taken as existing as a matter of course. . . . *Consciousness of the world is consciousness in the mode of certainty of belief.*[13]

Of Philosophical Faith

The idea of an original faith in the world, or rather trust in the belief that I have of the world, makes the world paradoxically the highest and the most certain of truths in an originary attitude of trust rather than mistrust. That this faith may be philosophical and not only religious is one of the great lessons of phenomenology, which theology today would gain from investigating, albeit to let itself be transformed in the process. *Religious faith*, often wrongly mistrusting the world and the ordinary belief of humans, should recognize first the trusting attitude that abides in each and every one's originary *philosophical faith*—whether a believer or not. The belief of all humans in others and the world, if it is simply sympathy, always leads to the belief that others *are* rather than they are not, and inclines humans to entrust themselves to the world rather than distrust it. This belief serves as the foundation or the *community of belief* (this chapter) upon which the proper belief of the confessing Christian will be erected— the kerygmatic belief (the upcoming chapter). That philosophical faith can designate something other than religious faith does not come to pass at the expense of religious faith, as we often mistakenly believe, but constitutes its precedent. In reality, religious faith can only rest upon philosophical faith, wherein it finds the *community of humanity* needed for it to take root.

Despite the primacy of existential anguish, Heidegger marks after Husserl one of the essential moments of this movement of "secularization of faith." He preserves in his philosophical discourse the very thing that was first and foremost under the authority of the religious or theological attitude. In Freiburg in 1918, Heidegger writes of "Faith" in these words:

> This title [Faith] ranges over a multiplicity of modalities, which are not equal in the sense of species of a genus; rather, among which one is distinguished from the rest: *primordial doxa*, toward which the others are referred back *in a certain way*.[14]

One might certainly be surprised to see the young Heidegger preferring philosophical faith (*Urdoxa*) to religious faith (kerygma), although his seminar is preoccupied with the comprehension of Pauline writings. In fact, everything depends on the method according to which he is already reading St. Paul. Paradoxically, for this philosopher, the most ontological formula of Paul's epistles serves as the underpinning for a phenomenological interpretation of faith: "anyone who comes to [God] must believe that he exists" (Hb 11:6). To prevent all misunderstanding of this formula and to follow the most ordinary exegesis of the New Testament, the *fides qua* or the act of faith takes precedence here as always for St. Paul over the *fides quod* or the content of faith. To believe that God exists (*oti*) implies first turning toward (*eis*) the One whose presence we seek. The Pauline writings are in line with the eventual credo of faith: "I believe *towards* God [*eis*]—and not in God—the Almighty Father, creator of heaven and earth."[15] A good exegesis of the formula concludes that we do not *first* believe that God exists in order to, *second*, approach him. As "anyone who comes towards him" (*ton proserkhomenon tô theô*), we too believe in his existence (*oti estin*). Divine *existing* certainly arises in and from himself in accordance with the objective proofs that philosophy has sought, much more than theology. But everything actually turns on the "ways" or "approaches" to which we will return (§12 below), understood precisely in the sense of Aquinas's description of the diverse paths toward God, rather than in terms of ontic positions of existence.

Religious faith, insofar as it is not only a conviction about existence (to believe *that*) but also adherence to a mode of being (to believe *in*), will serve thus in the history of philosophy, and in a telling extension of its meaning, as a model for any structure of faith understood phenomenologically. A philosophical faith encountered and discovered by theological faith (for example, Heidegger's studies of St. Paul or St. Augustine) frees itself from theological faith less to deny it than to universalize it. We adhere to the world in philosophy as we adhere to God in theology in an originary posture—always given in advance—such that the philosophical faith in the world heuristically precedes the theological faith in God. Belief in God no longer leaves behind the whole and/or the rest of humanity: the "little remnant (of Israel)" is never more greatly reduced than when it ignores the "great remnant (of humanity)." Indeed, in forgetting humanity, which the claims of "Catholicity" or etymologically of "universality" cannot set aside, both Israel and Christianity find themselves caught up in a simple demand for the recognition of their identity.

Reducing and Understanding

The real problem of reduction in philosophy, understood now within the framework of an originary belief (*Urdoxa*), is then less a matter of reduction than understanding. In a formula of *Being and Time*, understanding (*Verstehen*) consists in the fact that the human "being discloses in itself what its very being is about."[16] The human or Dasein does not explain the world: he explains himself in his relations to the world. Understanding is always included in explanation, since the relation that I maintain with "'something as something' [table, house] lies before a thematic statement about it" and determines it through and through.[17] In philosophy but also in theology (§12), a primary or an elementary understanding (*Verstehen*) precedes all explanation (*Auslegung*). Understanding is not first a thematization but a *fore-having* or already understood turn of phrase, a sort of *foresight* or preparation for interpretation, and even a *fore-conception* or anticipation according to a determined and adapted conceptuality.[18] For Heidegger as well as for everyone since him, there is no way out of the circle of understanding and explanation. We "understand ourselves in understanding the world," just as we "approach God in believing that he exists." The essential is not to state or to think "the world is" any more than "God exists." All that counts at first, albeit not exclusively, is the interaction of the believer with the object of his belief—world or God— such that he cannot doubt its existence, at least as bound and addressed to him. I am "always believing" because always joined to the other in me, making my believing into my unshakable conviction as also my most proper mode of existence. Against all criticism of solipsism, I am never able to believe that I am alone, whether due to the absence of the world, the other, or God. Always present prior to me, the "other in myself" turns my "I" in the nominative into a "me" in the accusative, or even a "to me" in the dative, such that the grammatical first case (the nominative) always becomes the last case, or the one by which at the very least it is no longer appropriate to begin.[19]

Such a Husserlian double delimitation of belief and Heideggerian one of understanding would all be for the best if a certain prejudice—a tracing back to an absolutely pure origin of the subject—would not still survive in the famous ideal of a possible "absence of prejudices." Once again, hermeneutics (Part I) teaches phenomenology (here in Part II) a lesson. Indeed, we are "always believers" not only because a ground of belief precedes the entirety of our judgments about the world or because "understanding oneself in relation to the world" anticipates and structures the mode of explanation. The prejudgments or the opinions presumed not to resist the reduction remain always as its irreducible constitution and their mode of belief, in reality, always incompressible. Gadamer claims:

> Heidegger entered into the problem of historical hermeneutics and critique only in order to explicate the fore-structure of understanding for the purposes of ontology. Our question, by contrast, is how hermeneutics, once freed from the ontological obstructions of the scientific concept of objectivity, can do justice to the historicity of understanding.[20]

On the one hand, Heidegger advances a notion of understanding without history; on the other, Gadamer sets forth the historicity of understanding. This is probably the greatest dividing line between phenomenology and hermeneutics: the short way, on the one side, with Husserl and Heidegger, and the long way, on the other, with Gadamer and Ricoeur—according to an opposition that now must be nuanced to cross and pass beyond this one line of demarcation, already observed in Chapter 1, §4.

§11. The Prejudice of the Absence of Prejudices

Impossible Neutrality

The previously stated choice of the primacy of the short way over the long way (§4) and thus of phenomenology over hermeneutics should not obliterate the very question of precomprehension. Any lived experience of consciousness—the focus of phenomenology—always gives itself in a story or a history—the concern of hermeneutics. To scorn the story would be to uproot the very act of understanding from its ineluctable temporal dimension. The false combat between phenomenology and hermeneutics will thus not cease until each one will have assessed its distinct contributions without falling into an inseparable mixture or collage. Following the example of "the preemptive right of the infinite over the finite," the "Cartesian prejudice of the absence of prejudice," in this sense and quite correctly as perceived by the hermeneute Gadamer, must be counted as among one of the "greatest prejudices"—and, in my eyes, indeed, a very prejudice of phenomenology itself.[21] It is "the recognition that all understanding *inevitably involves some prejudice* [that] gives the hermeneutical problem its real thrust."[22] The presumed neutrality of consciousness for Husserl or of Dasein for Heidegger belongs in fact to a mode of philosophical idealism, which today should definitely be eradicated. Prejudice or "prejudices" that accompany us even within the lineaments of culture fashion our language as well as our historicity. In the terms of Merleau-Ponty, we must posit a fundamental obscurity of the human as also an opacity of language, without which we risk contradicting ourselves. To seek to eliminate it would not only justify the lures of the presumed transparence of the conscience but would also make us forget that everything only comes forth and becomes among the incomplete. We will not always bring to light the nonrevealed, but we will preserve it in the depths of the hidden. As Merleau-Ponty tells us:

Culture thus never gives us absolutely transparent significations; the genesis of meaning is never completed. . . . There is an opaqueness to language. Nowhere does it stop and leave a place for a pure meaning; it is always limited only by more language, and meaning appears within it only set in a context of words.[23]

Sum credundus

Therefore first philosophically, we are *always believing*—no longer simply because we dwell upon the ground of the primordial belief in the world, per Husserl, or because we deploy ourselves in the unsurpassable horizon of comprehension that proceeds and founds all explanation, per Heidegger. We are also "always believing" because an "impossible neutrality," according to Gadamer, and a "fundamental obscurity," in Merleau-Ponty's words, are the foundations of our being-there and give it meaning. Prejudice has a positive meaning, which the Latin never ceased to underscore, and the French, ever since Descartes, has all too often forgotten. *"Praejudicium"* signifies the act of coming beforehand or of judging beforehand in the juridical sense of prevenient hearings and precedents that serve understanding and not as the haste of the one who judges, as in the Cartesian sense.[24] The critique of opinion should become today an opinion of critique. Prejudices are always "conditions of understanding" and not the understanding of the the conditions required to divest oneself of expired or even defeated prejudices at work amid the Heideggerian "they."[25] Repeatedly asserted ever since Plato, the now classical condemnation of *doxa* or opinion would benefit from being newly questioned. The human is "always believing" first of all on account of his opinions and therefore also his beliefs, which are paradoxically more certain than the greatest certainties most often proclaimed by philosophy. The *sum credendus*—"I am credible"—precedes in its certitude Descartes's *cogito ergo sum* and even Heidegger's *sum moribundus*—"I am dying." We must resolve to recognize with Wittgenstein according to his accurate hypothesis concerning a "believing certitude":

> I believe that I have forebears and that every human being has them. I believe that there are many cities and, quite generally, in the main facts of geography and history. I believe that the earth is a body on whose surface we move and that it no more suddenly disappears or the like than any other solid body: this table, this house, this tree, etc.

If I wanted to doubt the existence of the earth long before my birth, I should have to doubt all sorts of things that stand fast for me.[26]

Believing with Certitude

As stated above (§10) and now confirmed with the rehabilitation of opinion (§11): it is true that we naturally live in the mode of trust rather than distrust, whether it is a question of philosophical belief in the world or theological belief in God, a matter of a same "perceptive faith" or "believing certainty" such that we consider and rightly believe in being rather than nonbeing. The fact that we know that Santa Claus does not exist does not prevent us from believing in him—quite the contrary. If a belief is a mental state and this state means recognizing that a certain representation is true, we could certainly doubt the adequation of the representation to the thing ("I believe *that* the sky is blue"), but not the *belief in the representation* ("I believe *in* the blue sky")—in particular when we entrust ourselves to beings that are dear to us, albeit imaginary ("I believe in Santa Claus"). Holding to one's own opinion always precedes its destruction. Moreover, its destruction (or deconstruction?) never—or rarely—succeeds in annihilating the opinion in question. Again following Wittgenstein: "And that something stands fast for me is not founded on my stupidity or credulity. . . . Mustn't we say at every turn: 'I believe this with certainty'"?[27]

Leibniz's great question—"Why is there something rather than nothing?"—picked up and commented by Heidegger can certainly provide orientation to metaphysics until it is surpassed. Precisely, something always precedes nothing, at least in the mode of belief that is the backdrop of our existence. *There is* world in philosophy as *there is* creation in theology. To be examined or at least noticed, the immediate and irreducible given of the *there is* prohibits the complete rejection of opinion or *doxa* as carried out from Plato's condemnation of the *pistis* to Heidegger's own discrediting of the figure of the "they." Indeed, Husserl as the latter's forerunner already noted:

> *This life-world is* nothing other than *the world of the simple doxa,* which *tradition treats with such disdain*. In the non-scientific life, naturally, it is not underappreciated in this way since, on the contrary, it delineates a sphere of actual corroborations—the very ones that make possible and give meaning to the whole of human interests, whatever their goals may be.[28]

§12. Faith and Nonfaith

Philosophical Faith and Confessing Faith

It has thus been established that there is "faith." But this faith must first be understood in the sense of *philosophical faith* by which we believe in our own belief in the world. We are unable to destroy such faith (by doubting) or suspend it (in the reduction) without falling into the double illusion of transparence and absence of prejudice—that is, without denying what truly constitutes our ordinary life as a life-world—our quotidian lives.[29] An important question remains—perhaps even the essential one. As soon as philosophical faith has been posited, what are we to make of "religious faith"? It is no longer simply the question of our adhesion to the world but of our decision to trust ourselves to another (God?) who would have come into our world. In other words, if the ambivalence of the word "faith"— philosophical or religious—provides a common base for all belief, is there not now an incompressible and necessary gap between the originary faith of the "always believing" human (here in Chapter 3) and the voluntary faith of the confessing believer (Chapter 4, "Kerygma and Decision")? I have signaled it: no religious faith beyond philosophical faith—that is, no belief in God independently of belief in the world, even if that means continuing to abide in the inextricable and just "pre-judices" of human beings, which God himself would come to inhabit and not take them away from us, as if he were some kind of "evil genius." Grounding himself on this *Urdoxa* or originary belief, the confessing believer recognizes the solid foundations of this philosophical faith, which belongs to his humanity per se, and thus lets God dwell there somehow, such that nothing of our primitive chaos or even our *there is* (*il y a*) would remain foreign to him. Rather than considering philosophy and theology as radically opposed or simply complementary, we should now recognize the same force of conviction in the one as in the other, which definitely connects them and does not prevent them from belonging with regard to the necessity of adhesion, to a same filiation and even a common sphere of belonging. Merleau-Ponty expresses it succinctly according to a formula that deserves further meditation today:

> Philosophy's relationship to Christianity cannot be simply the relationship of the negative to the positive, of questioning to affirmation. Philosophical questioning involves its own vital options, and in a certain sense it maintains itself within a religious affirmation.[30]

Certainly, as indicated in §10, the *perceptive faith* of philosophy is not to be identified with the *religious faith* of anthropology and with the *confessing faith* of theology (§12). Perceptive faith points to "the conviction that there is something, that there is the world, the idea of truth, the true idea given,"[31] whereas religious faith indicates a possible relation to transcendence, whether or not it is named. Finally, confessing faith assumes a given act of faith, no longer beginning with the sole self but also with an "other" who lives in me: "I no longer live, but Christ lives in me" (Gal 2:20). Indeed, there is a long road from the originary belief of this third chapter to the decisive affirmation of a faith received from God exposed in the next chapter. Rather than always abstracting confessing faith from the properly human ground in which it takes root, we should acknowledge that the community of belief—albeit according to an amphibology of the term "faith" *qua* perception and confession—is of greater import and supports more than putative ruptures, which definitely undo the properly human, thus also philosophical work in the act of faith, by dint of separating the orders. Merleau-Ponty concludes with a rare acuity:

> Will there ever be a real exchange between the philosopher and the Christian (whether it is a matter of two men or of those two men each Christian senses within himself)? In our view, this would be possible only if the Christian (with the exception of the ultimate sources of his inspiration, which he alone can judge) were to accept without qualification the task of mediation which philosophy cannot abandon without eliminating itself.[32]

That this reasoning from nonfaith to faith or from philosophical faith to confessing faith is sound does not eliminate what is proper to the philosophical or yet the phenomenological—quite the contrary. In fact, St. Paul testifies to it. Moreover, Husserl and Heidegger adopt the same line in such an explicit manner that a reading of the apostle to the Gentiles will also have the right to be exposited in philosophy itself: "remember that in that time you were . . . without God in the world" (Eph 2:12). The one "without God" (*atheoi*) or the "atheist" is not the one "against God": the era of paganism precedes and is even the foundation of the Christian epoch. Independently of all judgment about the solidity of the foundations of the passage from paganism to Christianity, we must conclude with Lacoste:

> The disturbing hypothesis of a humanity satisfied with existing "without God in the world" [Eph 2:12] must therefore be taken seri-

ously. Atheism is neither simply nor in the first place a theoretical problem: it is first an a priori of existence.[33]

This is in fact the point of departure and the incontestable primacy of phenomenology itself before any more-or-less mistakenly taken or declared "turn." In Husserl's thought, "life is atheist," at least insofar as God's transcendence is rendered inoperative [*"mis hors circuit"*] in *Ideas I*, "Naturally we extend the phenomenological reduction to include this 'absolute' and 'transcendent' being."[34] In the Heideggerian conceptuality of the 1922 "Natorp-Report," a philosophy of the factical life is "fundamentally atheistic," where

> to be an atheist thus means in this case to be liberated from the need and the temptation to speak only in terms of religiosity. Is not the very idea of philosophy of religion, especially if it does not take into account human facticity, pure non-sense?[35]

To suppose, then, despite such declarations, that existential atheism can remain, in the eyes of Martin Heidegger himself, "absolutely incompatible with the elaboration of a philosophy of religion," risks vitiating the perspective of the philosopher *qua* philosopher.[36] At the very least, the distinction between "philosophy of religion" and "philosophy of religious experience" must be clearly drawn in order not to remain with a trivial alternative between the philosophical and the theological (see Chapter 4, §13). I can now agree wholeheartedly that:

> Even if Heidegger himself might have declared that his studies in theology were at the origin of his philosophical questioning, we could nevertheless not *draw the conclusion* that his philosophy *issued from theology*, and thus that he himself was a *"crypto-theologian."*[37]

All things considered, we cannot "save" philosophy of religion as we save phenomena. Husserl's flux of consciousness, Heidegger's factical life, and Merleau-Ponty's perceptive faith require neither anthropology's *religious* faith nor theology's *confessing* faith. Moreover, there is no need to reject all belief in order to posit, at least initially, a threshold of unbelief at the origin of all philosophy. Despite being a believing and confessing Jew, Levinas is a well-known example of a thinker who respected through and through the horizon of philosophy as such, without presupposing, at least in the beginning, anything other than pure and simple humanity, albeit wanted and desired by God himself (Yahweh?):

To be I, atheist, at home with oneself, separated, happy, created—these are synonyms.[38]

By atheism, we thus understand a position prior to both the negation as well as to the affirmation of the divine, the breaking with participation by which the I posits itself as the same and as I.[39]

"Always believing" is thus not equivalent to "identically believing"—on the contrary. Philosophy of religion, and all the more so philosophy of religious experience (§13), in a sense require but one thing: to graft themselves onto a philosophy, period—one that forfeits no characteristic of humanity when speaking of God. Indeed, there are philosophies of the *threshold* and the *leap*. Nevertheless, in a too thorough separation of the Orders (as with Pascal's Three Orders), we will forget what "order" is all about: precisely and truly the possibility of passing from the one to the other, since they are intertwined rather than simply superimposed (see Chapter 6, §19). "Preambles to faith" are thus still necessary today—not because we need to reestablish a propaedeutic for a self-sufficient, confessing faith but insofar as a certain continuum must, however, not cease to be posited running from philosophical faith to religious faith, and then from religious faith to confessing faith, at least in light of the identity and common use of the term "faith."

Preambles to Faith

So far I have only announced, without sufficiently indicating, how the "ways for God" in the so-called "five ways" (and not proofs!) of the existence of God in Aquinas's *Summa theologia* (Ia. q.2 a.3) are also and first of all "ways for the human." To ask "whether the existence of God is self-evident?" (q.2 a.1) or better, "whether it can be demonstrated" (q.2 a.2), certainly did not entail in the Middle Ages that it would be self-evident or demonstrable. On the contrary, it implied that evidence "in itself" (*in se*) may not be as such "for us" (*pro nobis*) or that the "demonstrated by itself" (*per se*) must also pass by the "demonstrated with respect to us" (*quoad nos*). The key to the ways is not in their end—"what everyone names God" (*hoc set dicunt Deum*)—but in their beginning:

Because we do not know the essence of God, this proposition is not self-evident to us [*non set nobis per se nota*], but needs to be demonstrated by things that are more known to us [*quoad nos*], though less known in their nature—namely by effects.[40]

The cosmological ways relay the ontological ways in the *Summa theologia*, not simply by default but out of respect for the limit and for our limits, such that our status *in via* is philosophically primary, at least for us here below, and primes over our refuge in the celestial city *in patria*.

The preambles of faith thus do not indicate any content already given in philosophy, which theology would simply have to take over and assume, as if the philosophical were nothing but the auxiliary and instrument of the theological. A philosopher can remain simply "always believing." Moreover, the passage from philosophy to theology must be thought in terms of "pathways to travel" rather than contents to be claimed (Chapter 5, §16). The way takes precedence over the term as does the method and style over the content alone. Reread phenomenologically in relation to the hypothesis of an always believing human being, the preambles of faith lead from philosophy's perceptive faith to anthropology's religious faith and then even to theology's confessing faith. Aquinas explains, "The existence of God and other like truths about God, which can be known by natural reason, are not articles of faith, but are preambles to the articles [*sed preamble fidei ad articulos*]."[41] Indeed, the path to what is to be demonstrated (*ad articulos*) imposes the preliminary truths of faith (*preambula fidei*), and not the other way around. The existence of God becomes demonstrable in Aquinas (*demonstrabile* [a.2]) not on the basis of a Dionysian burst of truth waiting to be proven (as with Anselm's ontological argument), but precisely in a surprisingly modern way, by virtue of our own capacities for demonstration grounded in the given world. Such is the character of Aquinas's cosmological ways. In the mode of a negative theology, the *sense of limit*, rather than *the virtue of excess*, undergirds everything for Aquinas. In this utterly original way, the *theological limit* also rejoins *phenomenological finitude*.[42]

Rahner, and not von Balthasar, notices this enigma: what the theologian calls "transcendental experience" as the experience of transcendence—"an unthematic and anonymous, as it were, knowledge of God"—arises in the same way for the phenomenologist when he proposes some nonthematic knowledge—for example, Husserl's belief in the world, Heidegger's understanding, or yet Merleau-Ponty's perceptive faith.[43] Reasoning from phenomenology to theology, in that precise order now, is thus also sound. Theology involves the originary and the already-there such that the prereflexive is not, or is no longer, the unique prerogative of philosophy, although it may bring to light and to our attention this dimension of anteriority. In *The Foundations of Christian Faith*, Rahner insists:

> if it is clear that this transcendental experience is not constituted by the fact that one speaks of it; if it is clear that one must speak of it

because it is always there, but for this reason it can also be constantly overlooked . . . , then one understands the difficulty of the task we are undertaking: we can also speak of the term of this transcendental experience indirectly.[44]

The proximity of the theologian Rahner to phenomenology will only surprise the one who has neither perceived nor understood that Heidegger's horizon of understanding structures the whole of his *Foundations of Christian Faith*. The theologian adds that "the presuppositions which are to be considered here refer to man's essential being" such that "theology itself implies a philosophical anthropology . . . which gives an account of it in a humanly responsible way."[45] Rahner could also have been able to claim that the human can and must be "always believing," whether philosophically or theologically, even if he were to have done so by securing the phenomenological advancement of "understanding" upon the foundations of the Kantian transcendental—a move that we can no longer make today, any more than proclaiming the "anonymity" of the non-Christian who thus came to be inappropriately baptized. It is not a matter of taking sides in the famous debate between Rahner and von Balthasar. Rather, it is important to recognize that what Rahner brings to an anthropological discourse, von Balthasar reserves exclusively for theology. The "conditions of the revealed" belong also to revelation. This is the meaning of Rahner's notion of "the transcendental experience of faith," and from my own perspective, the path that leads from phenomenological belief in the world to theological and confessing belief in God. Therefore, I can claim that a same world, always "pre-given," precedes and founds all belief, whether philosophical or theological. To recognize this strong claim is not only to ensure a continuum but to anchor every proposition in *an originary there is, an overflowing of self* by self, or a *brute nature* that must now be questioned, less to unveil it than to ever better take root in it.

"There Is": From Brute Nature to the World of Silence

One might seek "chaos" or the "open abyss" in the framework of phenomenology but give up on ever truly finding it.[46] Certain indices would, however, permit one to find and identify it in the *Es gibt*, the *il y a* or the *there is* "on this side of the signifier" in the context of phenomenology itself, albeit approached as a simple, undeveloped hypothesis. The impossibility of phenomenology per se to lay everything out in the open—in particular the abyss of chaos—on account of the primacy of the signifier within intentionality does not entail that, in fact, it did not in a certain way see everything or nearly so. It is not only a matter of perceived limits but of the possibility for the philosopher himself to stand firmly at the extreme limit and to open a field of view that is properly his own, at least in his manner of entering it as well as walking through it. Notably, Husserl recognizes in *Philosophie première* that "we cannot stop ourselves from recognizing that it is conceivable that a continuous succession of concordant phenomena may be broken and transformed, to speak in Kant's terms, into a pure chaos of phenomena."[47] Then in *Ideas I*, the phenomenologist adds that in the "ruins of the world, I would still be an intentional consciousness, but intending/aiming at the chaos."[48]

Nevertheless, from Husserl to Levinas, Merleau-Ponty or Maldiney, belief in the world (as in God?) is radicalized, ruining this time the intentionality of consciousness as such in its very aim at chaos or the *there is*. In the end, consciousness was, for Husserl, always but "the residue from the obliteration of the world."[49] This is precisely what is no longer accepted today, as it led to a "disaster" for Heidegger or a "disbeing" [*désêtre*] following Maldiney, which phenomenology itself could not have imagined. The *there is* of the world or myself in the experience of insomnia, for example, indicates a hypertrophy of the presence of myself to myself in the event of the vigil, which entails that we always remain bound to being rather than to nonbeing. Thus, we are stuck in the invasion of the self by the self in the material life of one's own body rather than "passed out" in anguish over death, which would still make it possible for me to forget myself in a still philosophical and disincarnate consciousness. Levinas powerfully describes this reality during his captivity:

> The impossibility of rending the invading, inevitable, and anonymous rustling of existence manifests itself particularly in certain times where sleep evades our appeal. One watches on when there is nothing to watch and despite the absence of any reason to remain watchful. The bare fact of presence is oppressive; one is held by being, held to be.[50]

One should now see it or at least sense it. Levinas's *there is* (as well as Merleau-Ponty's) definitely leaves the "riverbank" of donation to be expressed in the hypertrophy of chaos, of the nonsignifier, even of the inassimilable. The "*es gibt*" *no longer gives*, precisely because the "*geben*" in the German expression as in its French translation—*il y a*—expresses less donation, with or without a donor, than the hyperpresence of the nonsignifier—that is, the overflowing of being eliminating even the very possibility of nonbeing and its always accompanying forgetfulness. *There is* an existent as *there is* bad weather or *there is* bread on the table in an amissible as well as incompressible way. Something of the order of the open or a chaos of existence, even of the brute thing, remains to which I will always be foreign and will lack all means of access to it, at least in the mode of a giving as also signifying. As Levinas writes:

> From a space without horizons, things break away and are cast toward us like chunks that have weight in themselves, blocks, cubes, planes, triangles, without transitions between them. They are naked elements, simple and absolute, swellings or abscesses of being.[51]

> This impersonal, anonymous, yet inextinguishable "consummation" of being, which murmurs in the depths of nothingness itself, we shall designate by the term *there is*.[52]

Merleau-Ponty himself celebrates this same confession, seeking—this time in "birthing" rather than "existing"—the brute or wild being from which the human is always drawn forth, on this side of all intentionality, which could yet circumscribe him and give him the power to signify. "The brute or savage being that has not yet been converted into an object of vision or choice is what we want to rediscover."[53] Rather than wild or even disordered, it would be more accurate to recognize in the brute being a kind of primordial anonymity, most often baptized "flesh" or "flesh of the world," which, far from signifying uniquely a matter, a spirit, or yet a substance, indicates rather an "element" or an "ontology of the visible," indicating this time "the concrete emblem of a general manner of being."[54] Here this path merges, in a certain way, with Blanchot's notion of "the neuter"—this "speech that has no center but is essentially wandering, always outside."[55] The *there is* of the author of *The Phenomenology of Perception* reaches the heights, or rather the depths, of the *khora* of Plato's Timaeus: "To return to the things themselves is to return to this world prior to knowledge" in the "'there is' which underlies [scientific thinking]."[56]

Nevertheless, one more step must be taken. There is or there was the time of "pure experience and one might say, mute still, that must be brought to express its own meaning."[57] But now, it is time to let the dumb speak for himself in other ways than speech, or perhaps even in the unique mode of corporeality. More accurately, the prereflexive will no longer find its end or goal in the reflexive alone as if it were only preparing for it or establishing its foundation as in Husserl's phenomenology, any more than the unconscious will orient itself to consciousness, as in Freud's psychoanalysis. An exploded and nonoriented "unconsciousness of the body," such as Nietzsche advances, is always impossible to synthesize amidst the diversity of our experience. To recognize this impossibility is a way not to flee the chaos from which we are fashioned.[58]

Whether it is a question of the phenomenological life-world extending from Husserl to Merleau-Ponty or the matter of mystery in theology, from Denis the Aeropagite to von Balthasar or Rahner, a "world of silence" remains—not simply that which is not appropriate to say but that which cannot and must not be said. The *there is* or *brute nature* does not always come to expression in its proper meaning, as if the linguistic term or the signified is necessarily the norm for what is to be expressed. We are always believers not because our convictions about the world or God must be expressed, but because they interweave the fabric of our existence much more profoundly than we could ever imagine. In terms of corporeality— even the Eros where the "this is my body" reaches rarely equaled heights— never to reach "coincidence," albeit in the simple experience of the touching-touched of myself as another, "is not a failure." The phenomenologist of *The Visible and the Invisible* insightfully recognizes:

> For if these experiences never exactly overlap, if they slip away at the very moment they are about to rejoin, if there is always a "shift," a "spread," between them, this is precisely because my two hands are part of the same body, because it moves itself in the world, because I hear myself both from within and from without . . . : it is only as though the hinge between them, solid, unshakeable, remained irremediably hidden from me.[59]

The question finally arises: what is the relation between this prior *there is*, on this side of perceptive faith and understanding or belief in the world, and the religious faith of anthropology—and even the confessing faith of theology? The answer should be clear: no one, or at the very least none such that we would want to think this of them, in such a simply proposed continuum as the kerygma, would crown a process whose steps lack full justification. The light of the transcendental does not follow self-evidently from the obscurity of the primordial. Certainly in Judaism but also in a Christianity that is capable of questioning its certainty as well as its assumptions, the *tohu-bohu*, and even the absence of God, is a starting point for norms, without which one runs the risk of masking too quickly with presence or yet Providence the abyss so often covered over on account of the incapacity to gaze upon it with clear eyes. Following Levinas, far from the exclusive character of epiphany attributed at times and mistakenly to the face, we must confess that "The rustling of the *there is* . . . is horror. . . . Rather than to a God, the notion of the there is leads us to *the absence of God, the absence of any being.* Primitive men live *before* all Revelation, *before* the light comes."[60]

Paradoxically, then, the prephilosophical or at least the prereflexive is indicated and situated upstream from philosophy itself and thus also consequently from the anthropological and the theological. The irenic character of a thought that posits God directly belongs neither to phenomenology undertaken and understood as the quest for the starting point nor to theology that is truly anchored in a foundational anthropology. "We do not have any other experience of God than that of the human" (§16), such that it is only "in passing through the human" that we will also come to God, in the Son who, precisely, became human (Chapter 5, §18). The "theological incarnate"—that is, the Word made flesh—does not come simply to superimpose itself upon the phenomenological incarnate—that is, the flesh of the human; it decides to dwell in it and transform it. The God-man reveals also the human *in the human* and *in becoming human,* even if only to lead him to recognize himself in his status as son of man and thus also of God. "Always believing" is a mark of the "in common" of an initial faith in the world (*Urdoxa*) shared by all humans, placing the seal of trust on what most often is an index of indecision or distrust— leading to the completion in death of what, however, always manifests the excess of life. To conclude with Chrétien:

> We have never professed this [philosophical and religious] faith and we never came to adhere to it: it is immemorial, and it has always already seized and held us. *Fides, fiducia,* as in the Latin. As with all faith, this one has the character of trust.[61]

4

Kerygma and Decision

In Chapter 3, I claimed there is no confessing faith outside of an original philosophical faith. A common ground of *believing* always precedes the *decided act* of believing. To recognize oneself as "believing otherwise" is then not to disregard faith or to condemn the so-called unbeliever. This position is neither a kind of ostracism nor a kind of conformism, nor does it aim to relativize. On the contrary, it arises from a real resolution. Believing *theologically* in God rests on first believing *philosophically* in the world or in others—whether via a Cartesian act of negation, a Husserlian suspension of trust, or in terms of a belief that is truly impossible to deny or eradicate.

An important question remains: how does Christian belief—a confession of faith according to the kerygma "this man [that you] put to death by nailing him to the cross, . . . God raised him from the dead . . ." (Acts 2:23–24)—change belief per se in any way? In other words, does religious faith, or more precisely confessing faith, only extend or complete philosophical faith—or does it not rather transform it? Recalling the "metamorphosis of finitude" or the Resurrection, I cannot but repeat, "Confessing faith changes everything."[1] Certainly the Christian is not extracted from humanity per se—quite the contrary. The structure of the act of believing as of the Resurrection consists in transformation rather than superimposition, conversion more than conservation: "The decision in view of transformation is inseparable from the necessary transformation of the concept of decision."[2] What may be true of birth, and in fact of any event, is all the more true of the act of believing. In Christianity, God is specifically (a) the one *through whom* we believe and (b) the one *without whom* Christian belief in him is precluded.

(a) We believe *through him* insofar as the One of whom we speak, Christ, gives himself paradoxically as the One who speaks to us—that is, the Word. Ricoeur rightly indicates that "the relation between the two hermeneutics begins its inversion when one considers the other side of narration, namely, the profession of faith. . . . In this sense, the word 'God' does not function as a philosophical concept."[3] Indeed, in the act of faith, what I believe (*fides quod*) becomes at the same time that by which I believe (*fides qua*). As emphasized previously, this is the contribution of biblical hermeneutics to the phenomenality of the text. The object of the Good News transforms itself paradoxically into its ultimate subject. Thus, the distanciation of the text is recognized as the medium by which an "other" speaks: not only the author (the evangelist), not strictly the reader (the disciple), but also and especially its inspirer (the Christ).

(b) We cannot believe *without him*, since every reassuring affirmation of faith would ipso facto destroy its very name of faith. As Barth insists, "Certainly no one would believe if he maintained that he 'had' faith, so that nothing was lacking to him, and that he 'could' believe."[4] Better yet, and this probably justifies Catholic theology's insistence on ecclesiality: no *credo* outside of a *credimus* (no *I believe* apart from a *we believe*). The believing community serves as the "humus" in which any decision of faith takes root. The idea of a pure faith as also of a pure philosophy, whether a theology wrongly purified of all tradition or a phenomenology putatively purified of all metaphysics, is as foreign to the act of believing as of thinking. If the old problem of "demythization" must now be reactivated, it is not to return to a quarrel that we believed forgotten but to attend to certain unavowed efforts that are waiting for further testing. To the Catholic character of the hermeneutic of the body and the voice founded in the Eucharist (see Chapter 2) corresponds the Catholic character of the affirmation of the kerygma and the decision in a believing community (Chapter 4). It should again be made clear that, without excluding or proscribing, a *confessional* philosophical posture does not conceal the specificity of its determination—following the example of the Jewish roots of Levinas's thinking and Ricoeur's Protestant heritage.

§13. Philosophy of the Decision

Decision and Demythologization

How could there be also a Catholic problem of demythization if the idea of a pure phenomenology without metaphysics actually only carries on the primordial, even Adamic, myth of a pure faith? A response via a discussion of the concept of decision in dialogue with Bultmann makes it possible to question anew the contemporary relation between phenomenology and metaphysics (see Chapter 5, §18). We are familiar with the many debates for or against Bultmann's initial thesis of demythologization. The primary objections or diagnoses remain in force and should be repeated: demythologization may result in a loss of historicity or ecclesiality for the sole benefit of a return to textuality. As one Catholic thinker declared, "The problem of demythization, and even more generally, the problem of hermeneutics is *a Protestant problem*."[5] It is important to observe that indeed Bultmann insists on the point that the problem of demythization is a problem of hermeneutics. But these objections and diagnoses should be reinterpreted today. As underlined in Chapter 1, §5, it is a mistake to reduce the debate to a simple opposition between Protestant and Catholic confessions as if it were nothing but a struggle between religious traditions. In reality, it is a question of positions, references, and modes of insistence: references to the weight of history, of tradition, or even of the church and the magisterium in so-called Catholic thought, over against the return to *sola scriptura* by means of a hermeneutic of the text in a so-called Protestant approach. If at first the status of scripture was at stake in demythization and thus in textual hermeneutics (recall Chapter 1, "Is Hermeneutics Fundamental?"), it is time to pick back up the debates from another perspective and on another ground provided by a notion of "believing confession"—in its relationship to culture and in relation to its possibility or lack thereof to define itself in a presumably purified mode (developed here in Chapter 4, "Kerygma and Decision").

A central thesis inherited from Bultmann's *Jesus* cannot but put our dominant hermeneutical approaches in question, inasmuch as it insists on personality rather than textuality and on the decision to believe more than on deciphering the message. According to Ricoeur, for Bultmann, "The kerygma is not first all the interpretation of a *text*; it is the announcement of a *person*. In this sense, the word of God is, not the Bible, but Jesus Christ."[6] A hermeneutics of the kerygma therefore accompanies a hermeneutics of the text. The first serves as a foundation for the second according to an order that one should not forget. The decision takes precedence over the interpretation. The encounter with the one of whom the text speaks takes priority over the mediation of the text, the allegorical and anagogical sense of the text over its literal and topological sense. *The encounter with a person* has yet to have been understood as the true intention of demythologization, although none could deny the coefficient of interpretation that necessarily remains in every act of believing as in every decision. Bultmann firmly asserts, "Christian preaching is *kerygma*, that is, a proclamation addressed not to the theoretical reason, but the hearer as a self. . . . Demythologizing will make clear this function of preaching as a *personal message*."[7] Where Ricoeur in his textual hermeneutics emphasizes the necessary interpretive distance that constitutes any text, Bultmann with his kerygmatic principle directly draws attention to the existential decision that is implied by reading the text.

Crossing the Rubicon implies crossing the river and rejoining its banks in order to better sketch its boundaries. The philosopher cannot rest satisfied with interpretation alone under the pretext that the kerygma is a theological matter. In accepting also to walk, at least for a little while, in the "shoes of the theologian" (Chapter 6, §20), the philosopher passes from the "being in common as always believing" (Chapter 3) to the "kerygma and the decision" (Chapter 4). Thus, he would not hesitate precisely in the context of faith—in relation to what is at play in the proclamation of the kerygma—to ask this key question: when one decides to believe, who makes the decision, or believes in the decision, to believe: the human and/or God? In other words, if in Christianity specifically it is not a matter of deciding for oneself but also and especially of deciding *with* and *through* another or others, "I no longer live, but Christ lives in me" (Gal 2:20), is it not appropriate in light of the Christian structure of eschatology, as suggested above, to transform the concept of decision in making the decision to transform oneself? Better yet, precisely in the Christian confession of faith, can one restrict oneself to the *believing* structure of faith alone, albeit philosophical belief, even if the one in whom one believes theologically transforms the object of the very belief and even the access to it? Does not the original belief in the world and in others (*Urglaube*) also wait for the One who is at its origin (the triune God), that this One may rejoin philosophical belief by inhabiting the interior of the acts of confessing one's faith within one's culture? In this way, would not the One at the origin be able to transform such faith rather than superimposing the confession of faith upon a culture presumably untouchable, and at times wrongfully denounced?

Today's changing context entails a possible mutation in the way of stating the meaning of the act of the decision. In the process of demythologization and in the steps by which it unfolds, Bultmann is not satisfied to simply repeat the Heideggerian "resolution" (*Entschlossenheit*) by applying it to faith and its kerygmatic dimension. The decision of the authentic Dasein (*Entschluss*) in Heidegger's work is not simply reiterated in the act of faith; it is also transformed and even radically inverted in Bultmann's confessional perspective. He writes:

> [The judgment of faith] claims that wherever resolution realizes itself ontically in that an actual man, being shattered by death, lets himself be thrown back upon his being-there and resolves in the situation and thus for himself, it is really a resolution of despair. . . . If for faith, all of the ontic resolution, freedom, and historicity of the man of unfaith is illusory, and it all really exists only in faith and in love, then the question necessarily arises how the faithless man is at all able to see these characteristics of human existence in existential analysis.[8]

On the one hand, we find the unbelieving Dasein and, on the other, the believing Dasein; there is despair for the one, and for the other, faith and love; on the one side, auto-decision and on the other, dependence upon another. The oppositions appear too simplistic to be but reiterated. As we will show, the "ruptures" should be seen as mistaken insofar as they simplify out of an excessive desire to purify philosophy as well as theology. Indeed, all contemporary [French] phenomenology does not cease to duplicate this duality: always privileging an inverted intentionality or the quasi-dogma of pure passivity over against consciousness's aim or the authenticity of Dasein.[9]

Certainly, this trivial alternative between intentional egoity and counter-intentionality or between claimed authenticity and a newly asserted and then questioned inauthenticity is not the endpoint. The reversal of a framework never leads one altogether out of the framework (whether it is a reversal of Plato, Kant, Husserl, or Heidegger). Phenomenological oppositions—Levinas's counter-intentionality, Chrétien's welcome of speech, Marion's saturated phenomenon, Lacoste's liturgy, Romano's event—are not a way out of a now simply inverted schema, which will again reverse itself, sooner than later. To say that I no longer decide alone does not mean, however, that I no longer have anything to decide as if I were submitting to the opening of the event, which would, in many cases, deprive the subject of his freedom. By dint of deciding the undecidable or wanting only the possible of the impossible, we could well no longer decide any-thing, or even decide not to decide, and consecrate this unique resolution as the highest achievement, however tenuous, of every decision. The status of experience in phenomenology as well as in theology is now in question. The possibility of passing to another, but necessary, determination of "phi-losophy of religion" depends on the legitimacy of whether or not one accounts for the decided act of believing—that is, the kerygma, in theol-ogy certainly—but also in philosophy.

Philosophy of Religion and Philosophy of Religious Experience

We will once again cross the Rubicon. We will turn away from philosophy of religion and toward philosophy of the religious experience—changing the paradigm rather than evolving within a timeworn model. Henry Duméry drew this line of demarcation already in 1957. It is worth redis-covering, if not pursuing: "We cannot but recognize the benefit of *the personal practice of religious experience*; *without being eligible*, it is often *a great help* in the critique of the religious object."[10] The decision is embod-ied, and it is inseparable from the object of a philosophy of religion. Far from letting any claim to analyze its object dwell in a logical and linguistic positivism, the subjective experience of the believer is, in this case, fully and explicitly examined. This is not to baptize every philosopher of reli-gion as a theologian, nor is it to claim that such a decision is necessary for all edifying discourses. Forced baptisms always fail to achieve their puta-tive ends; Heidegger's work itself often pays the price of such an unfortu-nate deed. As a good scholar of Bonaventure, Duméry distinguishes religious philosophy and philosophy of religion, or rather, and to be more exact, philosophy of *the religious experience* and philosophy of *religion*, precisely in light of the criteria of decision or adhesion. He identifies two types of philosophies or at least of philosophers: those who, for reasons of method, "forbid themselves from taking any premature position in favor of some determinate religious belief" in order to remain squarely posi-tioned in an exclusively philosophical perspective ("philosophers of reli-gion" such as Hegel, Schilling, Fichte) and those who "from within their very faith, seek to elucidate philosophically the reasons that led them to their adherence," while not renouncing philosophy, conceive its very activ-ity quite otherwise ("philosophers of the religious experience," such as Augustine, Pascal, Kierkegaard, Blondel, and much closer to us, Edith Stein, Simone Weil).[11]

Remarkably, these philosophers of the religious experience do not cease to be or, indeed, to claim to be first of all philosophers, even if they take the Gospels or the parables themselves as foundations for *Edifying Discourses*, as in the case of Kierkegaard. The "decision" or "adhesion" does not impair philosophy—far from it. While it is, in fact, appropriate to maintain a rigorous methodological atheism (Chapter 3, §12), such atheism does not prohibit all decision but only imposes a distinction between philosophy of religion and philosophy of religious experience. Heidegger himself was its apostle in his *Phenomenology of Religious Life*. A "hermeneutic of factical life" only finds its meaning and definition inasmuch as life, particularly when it is a question of religion, must be rediscovered, as it is, situated at the heart of things—otherwise we run the risk of simply objectivizing it as a subject matter whose science no longer concerns us. Heidegger's choice was clear, and the imposed title for his university seminar conserves its trace: *phenomenology of the religious life* rather than phenomenology of *religion* or of *religious consciousness*. Assigned the task of teaching "philosophy of religion" at Freiburg in 1921, Heidegger denounced the discipline to the point of mocking its science (rather than those who would have the intention of practicing it): "even women produce philosophies of religion (!)."[12] Following the jest (contrary to appearances, without any misogyny), the philosopher will refuse to construct another "philosophy" of that kind, which already saturates the thought of his time.[13]

"To renounce a constructive philosophy of religion" and "not to get trapped in the purely historical" is the direction that his program takes from its very beginning (in the 1918–19 course on medieval mysticism), and at least negatively speaking, called "a phenomenology of the religious life" in contrast to a phenomenology of religion. Inversely and positively this time, a true phenomenology of the religious life, or in my terms a *philosophy of religious experience*, must undertake to lead us back to pure consciousness and attain the essence of the religious phenomena by means of the lived experiences of consciousness. Mysticism, whether medieval or other, is not and never was for Heidegger an escape into the ineffability of mystery but a lived experience, a theory of this experience, a theory of living itself, or yet, a way of life. It is a matter of intending incarnate living (*Erlebnis*) rather than the excess of the given (*musterion*). I claim that this is the definition of the task of a philosophy of religious experience in contrast to a philosophy of religion or even to an escape into a phenomenology tarnished by a theology that is all the more present the more it is concealed. The lived experience overflows the mystical in that the latter unfolds as a theological mode of the former. The philosopher does not have the goal to supplant a theological approach but to recognize and accept that he will find nourishment in it for his own reflection on the human per se. In the coming years, thought will not yield to the false accusations of presumably building a new metaphysical discourse or to the devious calls to renounce the experiential in favor of the conceptual alone. The true task of thinking will be to bring to light the philosophical foundations of medieval mysticism. Finding in the mystery itself a theory of life is not necessarily adhering to it, but at least recognizing that such was the case for those who spoke of it.[14]

The Facticial Experience of Life

Does this mean then that one has to be religious, or simply confessing, in order to attain the essence of the phenomenon of religious life as such? No, it is no more necessary according to Heidegger's writings than in my own. Once again, the professor from Freiburg will explain that "only a *religious man* can understand *religious life* because, if it were not so, he would not dispose of an authentic givenness." This sentence does not mean that one must, at least via philosophy, "awake to religious life"—although indeed such an awakening may (fortunately?) come to pass, without having necessarily been sought.[15] Far from any apologetic intention, the return to the religious person or the religious life means nothing but "hands-off for those who do not feel genuinely at home here."[16] The facticial experience of life, which is the foundation of what I am calling a philosophy of religious experience rather than a philosophy of religion, seeks simply and essentially to recognize the principle according to which "the experience of the self"—the author of whom one is speaking and the very religious matter of which he is speaking—constitutes the ground upon which the discourse is produced: "the fact that the experiencing self and what is experienced are not torn apart like [two] things."[17]

Bernard of Clairvaux's phrase upon inviting his friend Henri Murdach to join the Cistercian order is most pertinent here: *Experto crede*, or "believe me who have experience."[18] A philosophy exists, and not only a theology, for which the coefficient of experience as a putting oneself in danger (*Erfahrung*) and not solely an auto-affected lived experience (*Erlebnis*) becomes a foundation for thought, refusing to abstract what cannot be separated. A philosophy of religious experience will never be the exclusive preserve of some, and definitely not for those who may have the privilege of sharing in its specificity. Adherence to the Christ of the Gospel is not the condition sine qua non for reading a work by Pascal or Kierkegaard, for example, any more than contemplating a tableau by Rouault or Caravaggio. Of course, these same thinkers or artists never thought, wrote, or painted outside of such adherence to an object of [a common] believing, marking, *at least for them*, their first (but not unique) intention. By dint of secularizing culture according to a rightful separation of the realms, we no longer see how the religious motif was never simply occasional but was primarily experiential. Thus, the specific character of what is studied will be described on the basis of *their* experience, or of inserting oneself within it—nevertheless without necessarily adhering to it confessionally. The "crossing of the Rubicon"—from philosophy to theology and vice versa—is for myself, as for anyone, all the more justified insofar as we make explicit where we went and are able also to return after having been transformed (§20).

The better one theologizes, the more one philosophizes. That is the methodological imperative suggested from the very opening of this present work (see the Opening, §3). It is missing in philosophy today, including in phenomenology. Moreover, not knowing who theologizes and when we theologize, we do not know who philosophizes and when we philosophize. The muddying of the boundaries is not a consequence of the return to the philosophy of religious experience, whether for or against the philosophy of religion, but a result of the mask worn by a philosophy that does not admit to also being theological, albeit in the passage of time and in the unity of the same person or researcher. The "decision of transformation is a transformation of the concept of decision" insofar as the kerygma, or the act of faith on account of the Resurrection, imposes a real change of paradigm instead of its constant evolution (or reversal) with respect to an ancient model. The movement from a philosophy of religion to a philosophy of religious experience imposes, therefore, a choice: either to take into account, or not, the choice of choice—that is, this time and explicitly so, the dimension of the kerygma in the very act of the believing or confessing decision.

§14. Theology of the Decision

The Choice of Choice

The problematic of the decision in philosophy, and even in theology, proceeds in the same way as the coming into being of beings and their stigmatization as beings rather than existentials. The "decision" passes from the ontic to the ontological precisely in the context of a philosophy of religious experience. This would be a proof, if such were necessary, that the kerygma—understood in Bultmann's terms as the preaching of a personal message—does not undermine philosophy but reinforces it and undergirds it through and through. Kierkegaard assumed this task as a pioneer in the genesis of an ontological deployment of existentiality. He established the *Either/Or* as the act, the place of a decision from which not only to think but also to live or position oneself: "What takes precedence in my Either/Or, is, then, the ethical. Therefore, the point is still not that of choosing something; the point is not the reality of that which is chosen but the reality of choosing."[19]

This clear statement orients the concept of decision in regard to its ontological dimension, outside of which it becomes no more than a simple matter of a Cartesian free will or Kantian responsibility. In the eyes of Kierkegaard, to decide is indeed not to choose this or that, as is the case with free will, or to assume that which has been chosen, as in the case of responsibility, *but to choose to choose or not to choose* and *to choose oneself in the choosing*. In other words, choosing is not separating beings, but, on the one hand, entering into the ontological act of choice upstream every choice (where non-choice is also a choice) and, on the other hand, discovering oneself in one's ipseity as a choosing being. According to the confessing philosopher, an absolute choice exists upon which every choice depends such that "for the greatness is not to be this or that but to be oneself, and every human being can be this if he so wills it."[20]

The decision appears primary not simply because it is deliberated or assumed. Rather than occurring in time, it disrupts the course of time and opens a new time: "then their eyes were opened and they recognized him," as the Gospel writer recounts about the disciples on the way to Emmaus (Lk 24:31). The connection of the decision to the kerygma is neither fortuitous nor exaggerated. The ethical stage of life in which the human chooses himself depends also and immediately on the religious stage where he repents. While Kierkegaard muses about his reader finding himself *coram Deo*, he writes "in the moment of choice; then he will choose himself, then he will also repent of whatever guilt may rest upon him from me."[21] We do not first choose only thereafter to repent, in a facile play of pardon, which gives license to every depravity. Rather, one chooses in choosing oneself, and in choosing oneself, one repents "of oneself," as it were, in the gap between the to-be and the should-be, which is less a result of the morality of a culpable conscience (as with Rousseau and Kant) than a consequence of a vis-à-vis with another existence capable of unveiling me—according to Kierkegaard, God. In an exemplary fashion in the Danish philosopher's thought, the decision for transformation accompanies the transformation of the concept of decision: being oneself—to choose oneself—is at the same time, a being for another or before another—to repent "of oneself." A significant distance separates culpability from repenting. Culpability is bound strictly to the interiority of the conscience; in repenting, the conscience is *coram Deo.* Morality gives way to religion. In this leap—now from morality to religion—resides the entire problematic of the decision, precisely in the context of a philosophy of religious experience, which is not satisfied with a philosophy of religion alone.

To Choose Oneself Choosing

In a first instance, reasoning from Kierkegaard to Heidegger is sound. Of course, Heidegger will progressively secularize, in his conception of philosophizing, what Kierkegaard carefully chose not to separate—that is, the experience of faith at the heart of the decision itself. Still, that every true choice consists not in choosing but in choosing to choose—what I will call here the choice of the King or the absolute choice—is precisely the lesson rediscovered by the philosopher of Marburg in his famous resolution about authentic Dasein. In *Being and Time*, he writes:

> When Da-sein thus brings itself back from the they, the they-self is modified in an existentiell manner so that it becomes *authentic* being-one's-self. This must be accompanied by *making up for not choosing.* But making up for not choosing signifies *choosing to make this choice*—deciding for a potentiality-of-being, and making this decision from one's own self. In choosing to make this choice, Dasein *makes possible*, first and foremost, its authentic potentiality-of-being.[22]

More clearly than Kierkegaard's absolute choice, Heidegger's choice of choice reveals the Dasein or the being-there of the human choosing oneself *as the origin of all choice* and thus, assuming itself as such.

The "turn" that Heidegger incessantly makes bears a significant cost. The consequence of a philosophy of religious experience, which over the course of time paradoxically turns into a philosophy of religion and then even into a plain philosophy, is that Dasein must be authentic (*eigentlich*). The aesthetic stage that stays within the indifference to choice certainly passes into the ethical stage where one chooses oneself. But by not passing through the religious and experiential stage where one chooses oneself at the same time as one repents results in forgetting the original situation of decision *coram Deo*, which marks the philosophy of religious experience. Such forgetfulness entails remaining uniquely before oneself or even before a God—but one all the more objectivized as he no longer plays the role of the One to whom one calls out (the God found in philosophies of religion). The Heideggerian "resolution" risks becoming nothing but a solipsism of the authentic Dasein, such that living would become a kind of struggle against a "free-floating ego" or an "I cast into the void," which implies that resolute Dasein alone can free himself for his world.[23] Irresolution is not indecision but the absence of determination: Dasein only exists as a decision that understands and projects itself.[24]

To Choose to Be Chosen

If the decision of transformation necessarily becomes, in a Christian or kerygmatic mode, a transformation of the concept of decision, this paradigm change barely takes place, if at all, with Heidegger and is even insufficiently radical with Kierkegaard. Indeed, for each of them, "choosing oneself" is the key problem, rather than "being chosen," at least insofar as the chooser remains in the ethical stage. Reasoning *from the absolute choice to the choice of choice* is sound, even though one only chooses oneself—before another for Kierkegaard or before oneself for Heidegger. Nevertheless, to push the kerygma and the decision (here in Chapter 4) to their limit, and not to stop at the "always believing" that designates the whole of humanity (see Chapter 3), entails accepting taking into account the dimension of *the [one] called* without confining *him* always to the anonymity of the call, which leads the philosopher to take refuge at every instance in his putative neutrality. In the framework of a philosophy of religious experience carried out to its logical conclusion, an appropriately identified notion of "election" becomes the proper name of the decision in Christianity as in Judaism. Satisfied neither with assuming an "I" in the footsteps of Kierkegaard nor with avoiding a neutral, impersonal "They" ["*On*"] à la Heidegger, the confessing believer constructs himself in a "We" (see §15). In this *We*, the kerygmatic decision of the believer is consecrated as an entry and incorporation into the Decision of God: "You did not choose me, but I chose you and appointed you so that you might go and bear fruit" (Jn 15:16).

In passing from the philosophical to the theological and then from the theological to the philosophical, we must agree now to descend, and no longer uniquely to ascend; that is, to begin with "God's decision in relation to the human" and not to dwell uniquely on the human decision before God. This descent would be the condition of a true transformation and incorporation of the concept of decision. As a sovereign decision, God's decision will not be content with the simple vis-à-vis with the human in his decision for or against himself, but will be aimed at the human himself in God's very decision such that our decision depends directly on God's. Indeed, Barth asserts in his *Church Dogmatics:*

> His command is the *sovereign, definite and good decision* concerning the character of our actions—*the decision from which we derive, under which stand and to which we continually move.*[25]

Another important step was taken in the transformation of the concept of decision as soon as the decision for transformation was made. Deciding is not choosing but responding. The person who decides is never first; he is always second. One does not decide a priori but only a posteriori. If this refrain is well-known, as it has been inflected and repeated many times in the many modes of the call described in phenomenology, Barth adds a couplet that shows the extent to which theology itself—in the two senses of the crossing of the Rubicon—becomes capable of modifying the philosophical perspective:

> For both the obedient and disobedient it means, when they are claimed, that they belong to it, that they are marked by it, that it qualifies them ineluctably. . . . It *not only demands* that he should make *a decision* in conformity with it, but as it does so, and as man decides in conformity or contradiction to it, it *presses a decision about man.*[26]

The ontic decision found in Descartes's free choice became ontological in Kierkegaard's absolute choice or in Heidegger's choice of choice. Now, with Barth, the decision becomes a question of the horizon of the One who decides, within which the believer finds himself decided or not. The priority and the precedence of the decision overshadow all, in a certain sense as when the thick cloud enveloped Moses upon his "hearing and understanding" God in order that the people "hear and understand" (Ex 19:19). The novelty consists not only in the opening or creation of a horizon by the decision but in the fact that this horizon of the decision is not first of all mine, but an Other's. I become then the respondent to him or the One who proclaimed himself first—before I did. In the kerygmatic and thus Christian decision, the human neither chooses to believe nor decides to commit himself to believing, but "falls" under the decision (de-*cadere* [to fall] and not simply de-*caedere* [to cut]), such that his decision to decide comes to pass according the decision of God—that is, in standing beneath God's wings as beneath his shadow. In other words, to refer this time to Bultmann, who consecrated the rupture of the asymmetrical and kerygmatic vis-à-vis as inaugurated in theology by Barth, *"Knowledge about God is in the first instance a knowledge which man has about himself and his finitude, and God is reckoned to be the power which breaks through this finitude of man and thereby raises him up to his real nature."*[27]

§15. Deciding Together

There Is No Choice

In passing the decision over to God, the human has in a sense freed himself of the aporias of the decision. He remains authentic (*eigentlich*) in his being capable of deciding. Yet now he gains, or rather receives, his authenticity in his inauthenticity. Most important, here, inauthenticity no longer indicates a regime of the neuter "they" but the recognition of mistake and incapacity in wanting to be always the first to decide, and to decide everything. What plays itself out here in the context of theology is replayed today in entire segments of phenomenology. The fields are indeed different along with the rules of play, but the game is one and the same. Whether gift, rupture of the epoché, manifestation as revelation, or exposition to the event or yet to saturation, the entire schema emerges largely from what was previously called the Protestant hermeneutic of the kerygma (see §13). In short, it emerges from the rupture of revelation and from the shared claim to an absolute novelty, the so-called "nonmetaphysical," which at times is not far from the act of total demythologization. In other words, the ideal of a pure faith is carried on in a pure phenomenology—intentional or counter-intentional, purely transparent and stripped of all obscurity—which Merleau-Ponty alone has attempted to counteract with the concept of perceptive faith or brute nature (see Chapter 3, §12). As shown above, the primacy of sense over nonsense (or the absence of sense) in phenomenology carries on and redoubles the phenomenological primacy of the flesh over the body as also of passivity over activity.[28]

As proof, the problem of "eventuality" is supposed to uncover a new conceptuality of the decided being. To decide for a transformation, as Romano underlines, "does not decide among possibilities, but decides in favor of the possible; it does not choose between adverse possibilities, but decides for the adversity of possibility."[29] In other words, Kierkegaard's and Heidegger's possibility is now replaced with *passibility*, as in Romano and Maldiney; deciding to decide becomes simply deciding to be open to the undecidable—"Understood eventually, the decision signifies instead the active dispossession from all original power over the possible. . . . It no longer signifies the exercise of a sovereign capability, but the summons to passibility."[30] Pindarus's dictum "become what you are," which Heidegger inherited from Kierkegaard and reiterated, is transformed here into "be what you are becoming." It marks, thus, the transformation of the "advenant" receiving, undergoing, and transforming himself at the contact and welcome of the "advenue."[31] As formulated in Marion's term of donation, "to decide on the gift" implies, at one and the same time, "to receive what was not expected," "renouncing autarchy" and even abandoning the will to give or to receive a gift. To choose the gift eliminates even the gift of the decision, at least insofar as it could be recognized and identified as a gift.[32]

Nevertheless, the question remains, whether in regard to Romano's exposition to the event or Marion's reception of the donation without cause or reciprocity: in such a possibility or passivity, is there not a form of "renouncement of the subject" or at least of its power of decision? What happens to Romano's *advenant* and Marion's *adonné* when he decisively chooses, indeed can *only* chose indecision, understood here as the opening to what cannot—maybe even never can be—decided? Is there not a surreptitious movement of the kerygmatic decision—the identified horizon of the divine over the human in theology—into a philosophical decision, described in phenomenology as an unidentified or neutral horizon of the event or the gift over the being-there?

The complexity of the question can but lead to a suggestive answer, requiring each and every one to decide the matter in relation to the nature of the established debate. Indeed, in Barth's theology, where the horizon is identified, as much as in French phenomenology, where the horizon is neutralized, the *advenant*'s exposition to the *advenue*, as well as the *adonné*'s to the donation, entails that I choose nothing that is given to me apart from the decision not to decide or to decide nothing. Simply put, "there's no choice"—apart from the choice to say, to decide, and to recognize that there is no choice. Of course it is not a question of Stoicism, determinism, or fatalism in a negation of freedom, but of apophaticism in a radicalization of existentiality. In a theological mode in the context of Protestantism as also in a philosophical mode according to the declension of phenomenology, theology and phenomenology have both become negative in the Dionysian sense of the term. As a result, the purification of the subject nearly leads to its elimination, except for its frame as pure receptacle or simple passivity.

Whether in Protestant theology or French phenomenology, the professed asymmetry leads thus, in my eyes, to such high praise of passivity that activity as a possible cooperation between humans and God is forgotten. Catholic theology, however, offers another teaching that could on its own account question a fair number of the commonplaces of phenomenology. Aquinas's treatise on "Providence" in *Contra Gentiles* argues and explains that *Deus causa est omnibus operantibus ut operentur*—God is the cause enabling all operating agents to operate—such that "the ultimate in goodness and perfection among the things to which the power of a *secondary agent* (*agens secundum*) extends is that which it can do *by the power of the primary agent* (*ex virtute agentis primi*), for the perfection of the power of the secondary agent is due to the primary agent."[33] This thesis must be clearly understood. While Aquinas's claim is well known and deserves to be remembered, its significance for this discussion of the concept of decision must be made explicit, especially insofar as one is attempting to elucidate it in relation to the kerygma and thus also within the framework of a philosophy of religious experience. For Aquinas, the dependence of the secondary cause on the first cause does not imply—and even excludes—all submission of a Barthian type to the pure decision of God as much as any Kierkegaardian absolute choice. On the contrary, inasmuch as "God works in us the willing and the doing of his good design" (Phil 2:13), God renders us not inoperative but capable of cooperating. God "operates in whatever is operating" (*Deum operari in quolibet operante*), in the words of a famous phrase from the *Summa theologia*.[34] Thus, we are first the seat of his operation precisely in order that we operate. Far from operating "in our place" or causing us to succumb to the horizon of his operation or Providence, God "co-operates," strictly speaking, with our operation. Translated into the problematic of the decision with a freedom of interpretation that is here appropriate, *Deus est causa decidendi omnibus decidentibus*—God is the cause of the decision of all that decides.

In Christianity, therefore, the decision is no longer a matter of "one" but "two," even "three," or yet "three in one." The incorporation of the human into God by his integration into the second person of the Trinity probably constitutes the unique character of the Christian concept of decision, according to the final schema (see §18) of the Trinitarian monadology inherited from St. Bonaventure and before him, drawn from St. Paul: "in him all things were created. . . . All things have been created through him and for him" (Col 1:16). We certainly cannot claim that *I* decide. At the same time, we will no longer be content to assert that *he* decides, whether it is a question of the power of God, the exposition to the event, or the evidence of donation. All power (*virtus*), understood as a first cause or a second cause, always entails, even necessitates and desires, a counter-power. The "force of the decision," known in the kerygma, waits now and as its ultimate consequence for the "decision of the force." The common, contemporary claim of the primacy of passivity over activity has forgotten the question of the force present in the capacity to decide by reducing egoity to a pure receptivity, incapable of determining itself. I am not suggesting a return to the unbridled Prometheism of a Nietzsche or to the all-encompassing apologetics of some Romanticism. Rather, if the force comes from an Other and will be shared, I am not reduced to exposing myself to it but to participating in it: as Christ promises on the day of his Ascension in the announcement of Pentecost, "you will receive *a Force* [*dunamin*] when the Holy Spirit comes on you" (Acts 1:8; my emphasis and translation).

Neither simply a gift offered to humans according to the linear Greek schema, nor uniquely the love of the Father and the Son as in the circular Latin model, the most appropriate name for the Holy Spirit today is the *dunamis* or Force (*Kraft*). Instead of "separating force from what it can accomplish" (which Nietzsche wrongly denounced as a paralogism), in the person of the Holy Spirit, Christianity fulfills all the Spirit's "force" as also God's. But this fulfillment in the Spirit is not uniquely given to us as a dispensation, but to give us the capacity to co-operate with it. Indeed, St. Paul proclaims to the Corinthians, "Each of you should give *what you have decided in your heart to give* (*kathôs proêrêtai tê kardia*) not reluctantly or under compulsion, for *God loves a cheerful giver*" (2 Cor 9:7).

The "In-Common" of Believing

From the "believing-in-common of the always believing" human (Chapter 3) then follows, evidently freely so, an "*in-common of believing* of the confessing believer," rooted this time in "the kerygma and the decision" (Chapter 4). In Nicolas of Cusa's magisterial treatise *De icona*, when he completes his demonstration that the all-seeing God of the painting hung on the north wall of the refectory "looks on all and each at the same time," he is waiting for "a brother in the community" (*socius*) to certify the veracity of this experience. In fact, everything takes place as if the communally shared *human saying*, as also the *ecclesial* gathering around the sacramentality, would confirm the individually decided *seeing of God*, without which one runs the risk of enclosing forever in a solipsism the act of believing that is intended to be communicated. Indeed, in the preface of *De icona*, one reads with astonishment, "So by his brother's [*socius*] showing he will come to know that the picture's face keepeth in sight all as they go on their way, although it be in contrary directions."[35]

In what Nicolas of Cusa paradoxically calls "the coincidence of opposites," the revealed newly crosses "the ford" that leads from God to the human. More accurately, it makes itself all the more divine as it passes through the human to whom it is to be delivered and entrusted. The witness or the reporter (*relatoris*)—my brother—reveals to me the effectivity of the Revealed. Phenomenological alterity follows the same pattern as monastic fraternity: "The other is an intentional transposition into others' lives, by which we seek to grasp what they themselves think"[36]—in short, *no alterity without community*. This is certainly true in phenomenology as well as for the being-in-common of humans per se. But it is all the more true in mysticism, as here in this case where the cardinal addresses himself intentionally to a community of monks constituted, or at least reinforced, by his "seeing in common." I will reach him, the Wholly Other as he is, not by first simply listening to him but in submitting myself to "him"— my brother—another as my "other self" or *alter ego*, and also as "other than myself" or *ego alter*. In this way, I will learn from him the effectivity of the All-seeing whose ever-impossible possibility I always and already believe on my own.

Paradoxically, thus, yet probably even more convincingly, the revelation of the word of *the other* or *the brother* attests to the goodness of the Wholly Other whom, on my own and wrongly so, I could also doubt [having already believed]. Following the example of the ecclesial and sacramental schema of baptism, marriage, or confirmation, a third person or a witness testifies and affirms *de visu* what I did not first believe or simply hear. It is because *he himself*—the other—also saw that he was seen by the all-seeing (God), while at the same time and in another place *I myself* also enjoyed such a seeing, so that *together*, the other and I, we could rejoice in this common vision of being seen and loved by him, the all-seeing God. Where one might have believed or at least thought that the posture of "kerygma and decision" in Chapter 4 was going to exclude the Christian from the status of the "always believing" human of Chapter 3, on the contrary, it leads him right back to it. Belief in God (*fides quod*) certainly does pass through God's belief in the human (*fides qua*), but this time united and reinforced by the unique trust of a human in another human, such that I have faith in another in order to also have faith in God (*fides cum*). The "in-common of believing" the kerygma joins up with—even as it returns to—the "believing-in-common" of the human per se, inasmuch as the Trinity establishes in an original and eternally decided way a *fellow-*

ship in faith, which is at the same time a *fellowship of the self*. Nicolas of Cusa pursues this further in *De icona* with prose reaching rarely attained heights:

> When I thus rest in the silence of contemplation, Thou, Lord, makest reply within my heart: "Be thou thine and I too will be thine. . . . If I be not mine own self, Thou art not mine. . . . Thou canst not be mine if I be not mine own. . . . Thou awaitest that I should choose to be mine own."[37]

Crossing

5

"Tiling" and Conversion

The pathway from hermeneutics in Part I to belief in Part II, or from interpreting to deciding, opened a space for a philosophy of religious experience that was not content with a philosophy of religion. The importance of the kerygma calls for the rediscovery or reestablishment of an act of philosophizing, as proved by Pascal and Kierkegaard in their day, for which the experience of believing is not dismissed as a matter of course. In this Part III, the time has come to formalize what this essay on the boundaries between philosophy and theology truly aims to express from the point of view of the disciplines themselves. Indeed, as indicated many times already, the effort to bring two disciplines such as philosophy and theology face-to-face cannot content itself with a forever frozen, even crystallized vis-à-vis. Rather, in making the effort and sharing the audacity of crossing the Rubicon, we cross the river and learn from the other bank what we never had known or perhaps had forgotten. The "pathways through the woods" (*Holzwege*) are not only "trails that need to be blazed" (per Heidegger) but also, most of all, adventures to be undertaken. I am before all else a philosopher and will not cease to insist upon this point. In attempting and daring to pass through, we cross the river certainly conscious of danger. But at the heart of the passage, we also suffer this alterity, from which we can never withdraw without at the very same time being modified by it. In remaining a philosopher, I accept a priori that theology may transform me—even though the point of departure, understood philosophically, is always anchored in a commonly shared humanity.

§16. The Horizon of Finitude

The Human's Experience and God's Experience

At first, we have no other experience of God than the human's. The departure point for all reflection, albeit theological reflection, is in this sense philosophical. Initially, we encounter the human per se, independently of all other belief or exposition to God. To recognize this is, on the one hand, to accept our state of creatureliness with its distance from the Creator, and on the other hand, to reject everything that, in one way or another, does not directly return to some kind of human experience as its source of meaning. Nothing is more to be feared, in fact, than the kinds of angelism that tend to confuse the human with the divine in an excess of divinization and any verbalism (a derivation of conceptualism) that is generally satisfied with abstract notions that never redirect us to some lived experience. From time to time in phenomenology as in theology, we find terms that say nothing *about* or *to* the human as long as they do not refer back to a mode of being of our experience. Along with Greisch, we must recognize that:

> Unless it effects a quite suspicious theological turn, phenomenology must forbid all speculation about the preexistence of the Word, the relation between kenosis and incarnation, the communication of the idioms, the hypostatic union and other such questions.[1]

But this is not the case in French phenomenology today—that is the very least one can say. Therefore, the famous and legitimate question about a "theological turn" was raised. In fact, theological objects, such as prayer, adoration, liturgy, the incarnate Word, have been directly engaged. These objects are studied phenomenologically (for example, via notions of listening, the gift, the world, the flesh) but without first passing through the human per se—that is, without falling under the properly human horizon of philosophy as such. Indeed, this movement is occurring as if the coincidence of phenomenology and theology has become so perfect that the revealed has gained on the given. It is as if we have discovered the infinite as the inevitable vanishing point of phenomenality, at most leaving to the finite the task of bearing its stamp in Descartes's image of the worker on his work. In my eyes, the philosopher is not simply the one who uses philosophical tools, including phenomenological ones, but he who respects and begins with the human per se—that is, from the horizon of the pure and simple existence of the human. Janicaud's question in the opening of *The Theological Turn in French Phenomenology* is therefore legitimate and must be heard, although the dogmatic tone of the book should be somewhat nuanced: "it is only a question of testing the coherence of an interpretive intuition concerning French phenomenology over the last thirty or so years. . . . And is this trait the rupture with immanent phenomenality?"[2]

Must we conclude that all theological modes of investigation should be prohibited to phenomenology? Not in the least. On the contrary, because philosophy and theology are not practiced together (see Chapter 6, §20), we do not know *where* and *when* we have been philosophers. The theological turn is not, in any case, to be either taken or left behind. In reality, everything depends on the point of departure and the endpoint. Paradoxically, it could well be the case that one is more of a philosopher by being at the same time a theologian, in the unity of the same person, than by always trying to pass as nothing but a philosopher while in fact also practicing theology. In my account, the condemnation of a theological turn accuses less "the turn itself" than the derived way of pretending not to have changed sides—although one has changed course but without intending to acknowledge it. Theology also has its institutional and ecclesial meaning and is practiced as an autonomous science. Theologians' suspicion of phenomenologists arises less from phenomenology itself, whose fecundity all see and recognize, than from their hegemonic pretension in desiring to resolve everything better than everyone else, including general theological questions and even exegetical ones.

Far too often in the current situation, everyone is sticking to his guns and entrenched positions, although the absence of advances, if not also the triviality of the postures, should be quite evident. Instead of joining one or another camp, I will call for another and new way of jointly practicing phenomenology and theology: more truly conformed to the specificity of the one—that is, the finitude of the human—and the other, the Incarnation of the Son. Merleau-Ponty reminds us quite correctly:

> it is a little too much to forget that Christianity is, among other things, the recognition of a mystery in the relations of man and God, which stems precisely from the fact that *the Christian God wants nothing to do with a vertical relation of subordination*. . . . Christ attests that God would both be fully God without becoming *fully man*. . . . Transcendence *no longer hangs over* man: he becomes, strangely, its *privileged bearer*.[3]

Indeed, philosophy and theology are distinguished, as will be shown, not so much by their respective contents (after all, the Eucharist, the Passion, or the Resurrection can also be approached philosophically) than by their different points of departure—from below or from above—and their modes of proceeding—heuristic or didactic. Finitude thus serves as the beginning of philosophy as well as theology insofar as no theologoumenon has any meaning outside of a lived experience or a philosophical "existential," which gives it meaning: for example, the body for the Incarnation, anguish for Gethsemane, eros for the Eucharist, birth for the Resurrection, wandering for sin, childhood for the Kingdom. In sum, it should be clear that a phenomenology from below precedes and grounds any theology from above.

Only in the overlaying (tiling) and transformation (conversion) of the below of philosophy by the above of theology can the one and the other respectively come to make sense.[4] This is not to say that philosophy cannot be conceived without theology, and vice versa. But each truly comes to makes sense only as philosophy offers theology what it possesses—the weight of humanity—and theology reveals itself capable of receiving and converting its meaning—by the Resurrection. The difference between the approaches of philosophy and theology, set forth at the beginning of this work, reveals Christology, the locus and source of their overlaying or "tiling," and the trinitarian perichoresis as the operator of their conversion. Perhaps, we will then decry once again the scandal of philosophy's annexation by theology unless philosophy's serving theology in this way is recognized as an honor and not slavery. Gilson rightfully reminds us that "To be of *service* a handmaid *must first exist*, and although it is true that the handmaid is not the mistress, *she belongs to the household.*"[5]

The Difference between the Ways

It is a mistake to seek to distinguish philosophy from theology on account of their objects rather than their methods. The wealth of philosophy lies in its ability to describe the mode of appearing of the theological. This claim no longer needs to be demonstrated, at least in the context of the latest developments of French phenomenology. Simply read Levinas's account of God and transcendence, Marion's notion of the gift and revelation, Henry's concepts of flesh and Incarnation, Chrétien's understanding of speech and the Word, Lacoste's notion of world and liturgy. The paradox consists in the fact that these theological objects have never been more clearly brought to light than now when they are described by means of philosophy—where philosophy in no way exhausts the content of theology and is required to undergo an unexpected and unhoped-for conversion. What was true for Augustine yesterday in relation to Platonism or for Aquinas with Aristotelianism is thus also true for us today with regard to phenomenology. Yesterday it was the return to oneself for Augustine or the status of reason for Aquinas; today, it is the horizon of finitude for Heidegger, which still waits to be investigated and transformed. Theology renews itself by means of philosophy, although theology is never content to use philosophy, but to transform it through and through.

Within the structure of these homologous aims—that is, the assumption and transformation of philosophy by theology—differences between the disciplines remain that constitute their specificity as much as their complementarity. Over-unifying confuses the methods; over-separating excludes the subject matters. Between philosophy and theology a *difference* must be maintained between (a) their ways, (b) their modes of proceeding, and (c) the status of the objects to be analyzed, while at the same time recognizing (d) the possible and paradoxical *community* of objects given to thought.

(a) First, from the point of view of their approaches or points of departure, it should be clear that philosophy does not proceed in the same way as theology. Even in the case of revelation or simply donation, philosophy never finds for itself another beginning point than the pure and simple humanity of the human—the human per se. Against every (contemporary?) temptation of angelism, Heidegger reminds us of the "problem of facticity—most radical phenomenology, which begins 'from below' in the genuine sense."[6] At first at least, philosophy must be content with its "from below," otherwise it runs the risk of falling into the void, imagining, like "the light dove," that it would fly better without the air's resistance.[7]

(b) Philosophy is distinguished from theology with regard to their modes of proceeding. In fact, at times in this respect, these two disciplines find themselves mutually incomprehensible. Theology appears to accept, usually without question, the didactic mode as the most adequate form of its discourse. What is said in opening must then also be repeated identically at the end, following upon a self-grounded, systematic ordering of the matter and by means of introductions to works, which, rather than wrestling with a question, generally consider the problem already solved or only needing to be presented. The dogmatic force of theology—rooted in the fact that the revealed is taken as given—is also the source of its problematic weakness, as soon as its inquiry seems to come first from God rather than from humans. In contrast, philosophy, at least since Descartes's *Metaphysical Meditations*, has made *heuristic development* its proper mode of reflection. Its beginning point—for example, hyperbolic doubt—is not the same as its findings offered at its endpoint—the status of the world on the basis of the cogito. The heuristic order of discovery in philosophy sets out a path to be followed, which the didactic order of teaching in theology often fails to make visible, in particular in its Germanic and systematic heritage (Barth, Bultmann, Moltmann, Kasper, Rahner, von Balthasar). At least on the basis of philosophy and the French practice of phenomenology, I should have the courage to ask: must we not accept in theology too an order of discovery beginning with the human—from below—that does not surrender immediately to the imperative of the order of teaching beginning with God—from above? In other words, is it necessary from the start to speak of creation when we experience first nothing but finitude, of trinitarian perichoresis when we first undergo the experience of the other human, or yet of Christic Incarnation when before all else we auto-affect ourselves in others, in our own flesh? Monica reminds her son Augustine that "The word spoken to me was not 'Where he is, there will you be also,' but 'Where you are, there will he be also.'"[8]

(c) Finally, the status of the object to be analyzed is different in philosophy and theology, not in terms of the object itself but according to the means of investigation. Heidegger's famous imperative in *Being and Time*, Chapter 2, §7, "higher than actuality stands possibility," serves well to distinguish these two disciplines—not to create a hierarchy (one might think rather the inverse) but to clearly specify each discipline.[9] Following Marion's vast and accurate investigation of the meaning of donation, the philosopher will consider merely *possible* what must be *actual* for the theologian. The philosopher does not actually believe in the Incarnation, the Eucharist, or the Resurrection—as they are revealed—apart from within the framework of theology itself. Theology opens itself, and paradoxically so, all the more to philosophy as it fears no damage to the actuality of the phenomenon due to the philosophical investigation: it allows its possibility to be analyzed by others. In this way, "catholicity" is understood in its strictest sense as "universality"—not in the sense of falling back on some identity, but in the opening to a mystery that is sometimes shared across significant differences.

(d) With respect to the object, paradoxically, philosophy and theology differ the least. Let me be clear. I am not claiming a false annexation of theology by philosophy; quite the contrary. But we can rejoice that phenomena such as prayer, listening, the Word, the Incarnation, the Eucharist, can also be described philosophically—without carrying out or replacing the work of theology. Where we might have believed that the greatest distance between philosophy and theology was found in the "matters at hand," we discover it to be in the "manners" of appearing and investigation. As object, the same phenomenon may well fall in distinct ways within the purview of multiple disciplines or, better, of different acts of consciousness. For example, the artist, the viewer, or the art critic may "see" a painting differently. Therefore, nothing impedes the existence of *a community of the object* despite or thanks to the diversity of intentional gazes, and even if the theological actuality of the message would prevail over its sole phenomenological possibility. The force of theology as a discourse beginning with God does not hinder philosophy as a discourse on the God-phenomenon appearing to the human. As a *descriptive phenomenology* and not a natural theology (!), the objects of theology do not cease to be within the purview of philosophy under the condition, nevertheless, to be restricted to "everything originarily (so to speak, in its 'personal' actuality) offered to us in intuition . . . , but also only within the limits in which it is presented there."[10]

On Contingency

To start with philosophy and to remain a philosopher means, therefore, first of all to uncover the philosopher's horizon: "the human per se" and "finitude as such," albeit encountered and transformed by God in the figure of the God-man. Nothing is more erroneous than the confusion of limit with limitation. Limit indicates simply the obstructed horizon of existence, following Heidegger, or yet the constitution of our created being, according to Aquinas. Limitation lays claim to the unlimited, as if our condition were not the one in which we find ourselves as incarnate beings—in Heidegger's terms, "In order to designate the finite in human beings it might suffice to cite any of our imperfections. In this way, we gain, at best, evidence for the fact that the human being is a finite creature."[11] One could certainly believe that the confession of such contingency is a responsibility of philosophy alone, as if theology had no other significance or goal than to surpass or forget it. The theologian Duns Scotus, however, opened the door to its possibility, although only in order to make all the more visible, on the other side, the absolute freedom of a God given unconditionally. The Franciscan doctor firmly and originally emphasizes, "I say that contingency is not merely privation or defect of Being like the deformity . . . which is sin. Rather, contingency is a positive mode of Being, just as necessity is another mode."[12] As the subtle Doctor opens a new horizon for modernity, the importance of his assertion lies not in the negation of infinity or even the possibility that God would assume and transform the mode of contingency given here. In reality, all that counts is the thickness of our being-here-below—the pilgrim human or the *homo viator*—who ceases finally attempting to escape into another world (as is the case with the Platonic leap) and recognizes pure and simple humanity as the starting point: "it cannot be shown by natural reason that something supernatural exists in the wayfarer, nor that it is required necessarily for his perfection."[13]

Of course, some will criticize this reading of Aquinas, condemning a certain univocity's deviation from analogy or the renunciation of the natural desire for God, despite the immediate evidence of our yearning for him. But that only indicates a failure to see that the heuristic point of departure—finitude—is not identical with the didactic endpoint—the transformation of finitude by the Resurrection. The radical limitation of *nature* to *my nature* does not deny the eventuality of the supernatural; quite the contrary. It requires only that the human as such be given, in order that the divine may graft itself on it. Yet Scotus takes a leap that we cannot accept or endorse (Chapter 6, §19), since he returns philosophically to contingency—that is, to the univocity of being, only in order to better detach himself from it theologically and assert the absoluteness of God. Nevertheless, far from marking an end, this *incipit* consecrates a beginning: the recognition of a mode of existence of the human per se, which God, in his Incarnation, comes to assume as much as transform.[14]

§17. On "Tiling" or Overlaying

On the Servant

Thus, we should not too quickly dispense with the preambles to faith (returning again to Aquinas). Even if not to prepare for theology, we should attend to preambles at least to recognize that philosophy still has a major role to play in the development (*manuductio*) of theology. To restrict philosophy to the simple rank of *preambula fidei* for theology is at once to trust it with too much and too little. Too much: because it risks then exceeding its proper limits. Too little: because it would be reduced to the simple status of auxiliary, appearing to be purely subject to theology rather than truly in a cooperative relation. After all is said and done, philosophy does not choose the theological approach. Rather, theology itself puts forward and honors philosophy in its midst. While too often misunderstood, Aquinas's formula preserves a certain meaning today, even if it cannot be directly received as such: *philosophia ancilla theologiae*.

In Aquinas's thought, theology never sought to subordinate philosophy to itself—in the sense of subjugating a rebel party—as argued according to a false conception, too often invoked, of a certain economy of natural theology in relation to revealed theology. Sacred Doctrine avails itself of the philosophical sciences, "as of the lesser and as handmaidens [*tamquam inferioribus et ancillis*]," not as serfs or slaves but as servants [*ancillas suas*] whom wisdom has called from the highest point of the city [*vocare ad arcem*] (Prv 9:3).[15] In short, the servant is honored to be elevated to serve and work in her master's house. In the same way, philosophy finds itself in a good position: after having first cared for its own goods—the human per se—it receives from theology the invitation to *dwell* there as well, just as Mary was the servant of the Lord (Lk 1:38) or as the human dwells in the Son and the Son in his Father (Jn 15:10).[16] Today philosophy seems to have forgotten *the honor of the theological*. By dint of claiming his autonomy, the philosopher became independent and then separated from the theological. Now long after the divorce has been completed, he returns to his old loves as to his first spouse. But is it sufficient to return to Aquinas to believe that the marriage is renewed? That may be to make too little of the fecundity of modern thought as well as the weightiness of the Incarnation itself.

The Natural and the Supernatural

The vagaries of philosophy's and theology's tumultuous past are not the only reason that they cannot remain today in a radical independence locked in a stony stare or frozen as a mask of Janus. The invitation comes from the very content of the Incarnation. If there is no other experience of God than that of the human (§16), it is because the disciple encounters the God-man precisely on human pathways. In other words, the theological encounters and transforms the philosophical through and through by walking along the philosophical way. Here we follow the possible double interpretation of the disciples' journey to Emmaus (Lk 24:31–32). The essence of the message could certainly reside in the extraordinary breaking of the bread where he disappears before their eyes—a phenomenology "from above" or the saturation of phenomena. One should not forget, however, as a complementary approach, to underline the fact that the evangelist mentions that, without having recognized him, their hearts were still burning within them, showing that in the ordinariness of this human is made known at the same time the extraordinary character of God—a phenomenology "from below" and of the ordinary character of the flesh.[17] In short, ever since God became man and showed himself as a man even in his Resurrection, we have access to Him *via humanity* and thus also through philosophy, albeit then to be transformed or "metamorphed" into God within the crucible of theology.

This "tiling"—namely, the *overlaying of philosophy by theology*—is thus always borne by the God-man himself, the Word made flesh, and results, in this way, from a decision by God rather than humanity. The model advanced by Bonaventure or Pascal of the relay of philosophy by theology—*theologia incipit ubi terminator cognitio philosophica* ("theology begins . . . [at] the very point at which philosophical knowledge ends")—no longer suffices without running the risk of leaving no place for the God-man to assume the human dimension.[18] At least at this stage of the meeting of the human and the divine, Aquinas's model of overlaying is preferable after it is somewhat transformed. Certainly, following Aquinas, Theology as Sacred Doctrine "is of another genus" (*differt secundum genus*) than the theology that is still a part of philosophy. There should be no confusion between the theological, whose origin is from above ("the light of supernatural reason or of divine revelation" [*lumen divinae revelationis*]) and the philosophical as such, which always comes from below ("the light of natural reason" [*lumen naturalis rationis*]). More clearly yet, the primacy of revelation over reason does not prevent (*nihil prohibet*) the objects investigated by the philosophical sciences (existence, unity, infinity) from being also and even first approached by the theological sciences ("I am who I am" [Ex 3:14]).[19]

God's Initiative

The contemporary consideration of finitude requires us now to account *positively* for the obstructed horizon of our existence as the starting point. Indeed, I pass first through the world and the cosmological ways because the way through God seems at first forbidden or impractical, as seen with the ontological arguments. Yet *the passage of the limit or the crossing through nature* [*meta-phusis*] and thus the passage through philosophy is not simply the best effort of a mind incapable of reaching God directly "on account of the weakness of our mind [*propter debilitatem intellectus nostri*]."[20] For Aquinas as well as for me, the *debilitas* is not only weakness: it is also the limit of our created being. It is less the degeneration of a state of infinitude than the recognition of our human condition. Christ's Incarnation itself, and God's taking charge of humanity, consecrate the limit as to what is intended, loved, and desired by the One who engendered us, transforming the span between the Creator and the creature into the place of the greatest proximity. The human is "a limited phenomenon" (§19) on two accounts: *philosophically* according to an observed, rather than desired, finitude, as with Heidegger; *theologically* according to the mode of a differentiated creation that calls for respect for the creaturely state, as in

Aquinas, rather than for its being always surpassed.[21] Without reducing God to a human being—the false accusation of an "anthropological reduction"—we should remember that God himself kenotically took "the form of a slave, being born in human likeness" (Phil 2:7), embracing our finitude all the more that he bore it himself to the point of fulfilling the mystery of the incarnate Word: "In order to be able to accept God without reducing him, as it were, in this acceptance to our finiteness, this acceptance must be borne by God himself."[22]

§18. Of Conversion or Transformation

Must we then conclude that "the subject is fundamentally and by its nature pure openness for absolutely everything, for being as such"—and therefore philosophy to God himself?[23] That would be to make too much of philosophy, which is incapable of exceeding the field of its immanence, the source of its greatness. Deleuze warns us to be wary of all thought that has an immediately religious connotation: "Religious authority wants immanence to be tolerated only *locally* or at an *intermediary level*, a little *like a terraced fountain* where water can briefly immanate on each level but on condition that it *comes from a higher source and falls lower down.*"[24] Philosophy must restrict itself to finitude understood not simply as the delimitation of the finite within the sphere of the infinite but as the ever-unsurpassable horizon of our existence as such. Such is the condition for adhering fully to our own humanity as also to our contemporaries' experience of life, at first "without" God.

Nevertheless, the God-man carries out the "tiling" or overlaying of the human and the divine. Thus, philosophy and theology come to "overlay" or "cover" each other in Christology. At the same time and in the same operation, the human being is converted into God in the Resurrection as humanity is incorporated into the divine, and thus philosophy into trinitarian theology. Indeed, the schema of the dovetailing of philosophy into theology is Thomistic: there is such "truth which faith professes and reason investigates" (God, Creation, Providence) but there is also "truth which surpasses reason" (the Trinity, the Incarnation, Redemption, the Resurrection).[25] Therefore, it is not simply a question of the assumption or integration of philosophy into theology but more importantly a matter of the "transformation" or "metamorphosis" of philosophy by theology. Christology discovered on the human way does not solely strike in a single flash, as it were, in order to repair Adam's sin—that is, through a leap of faith—but it arises also on the road to Emmaus with the disciples, upon Christ's sharing their sadness as also their very finitude, which would be the "tiling" or overlaying. While asserted didactically at the beginning of the *Summa theologia* (*Prima Pars*), the Trinity is nevertheless not brought to light heuristically until the end (*Tertia Pars*)—that is, in the mysteries of the life of Christ, the place of the incorporation and transformation of the human into God *in* the act of the Resurrection—thus with the transformation of philosophy into theology.[26]

The Monadological Principle

A single trinitarian axiom directs and settles philosophy's relationship to theology, even as all human reality is properly assumed and converted by God: "If this is said with a view to the creation, nevertheless it is true first of all in the inner life of God."[27] In the terms of the trinitarian monadology, which serves as our leitmotif, "nothing is produced in the human that is not first produced in God, apart from sin."[28] This is the theological weight—in the sense of the glory (*kavod*) as well as the burden (*pondus*)—of philosophy today, and all the more so, of the existentials. The weight of finitude will not be lightened as long as the Son who *suffers* it in his humanity will not have passed it himself on to the Father in his divinity.[29] The fleshly *eros* of the married couple will not receive its ultimate meaning as long as it will not also have been integrated and transformed in divine *agape*.[30] Philosophy is *transformed and converted* upon contact with theology: not in the sense of having its presumed capacities to deviate or its temptations toward autonomy restrained, but in the sense that it receives at once from the force of the Resurrection and the thickness of the Eucharist its ultimate, yet unexpected, meaning. The philosopher certainly has no other immediate desire for the absolute than to satisfy his pure and simple humanity by respecting the human per se, which is after all already a substantial commitment. The theologian, however, and him alone, introduces a surplus. He overtakes and draws the philosopher toward a conversion that is as unforeseen as radically new: the Resurrection itself.

Those who believe that they should still engage in the battle between philosophy and theology should now see that this clash would forever be sterile. According to the famous dialectic, the master of theology has come to fear his servant, philosophy, to the point of losing his supremacy and waiting for his chambermaid to assert her own truth: "there may be religion without philosophy, but there cannot be philosophy without religion, because philosophy includes religion within it."[31] Every single model of the interlocking of philosophy with theology, and vice versa, has been tested. With Aquinas, philosophy is included in theology according to the honor given by the wisdom of God to the wisdom of humanity. With

Hegel, theology is inverted and included in philosophy, since the conceptual truth of the latter arises from the sentimentalism of the former. The time for quarrels as well as for varieties of inclusion is over. The time has come for reciprocal fecundity in a radical transformation of the one by the other—particularly of philosophy *in* theology. Therefore, we will abandon the attempts (Chapter 6, §20) to "liberate philosophy by means of theology," as if "in the elevation of one who thinks (or philosophizes) is also found a liberation of his thought for philosophy."[32] Quite the opposite: today's task is to *liberate theology by means of philosophy* in order to give dogma its double consistence, human according to the existential dimension of philosophy and transformed by God according to the theological dimension of the Resurrection. Then we will perhaps find a *common grammar* with our contemporaries whose first language is the language of the human per se—finitude or humanity without God—yet accept receiving the metamorphosis of God—that is, the resurrection or humanity with God and the incorporation into him, or simply the Eucharist and the pilgrim's character. In this way, John Paul II challenged the bishops of Canada:

> we need a new apologetic, geared to the needs of today. . . . Such an apologetic will need to find a common "grammar" with those who see things differently and do not share our assumptions, lest we end up speaking different languages even though we may be using the same tongue.[33]

Of Meta-Physics

This treatment of philosophy is so tightly bound to theology that it is even converted into theology. I will thus investigate what place remains for metaphysics, denounced as it is by phenomenologists, yet highly sought after by theologians. Everything turns on what we mean by metaphysics as well as on the task, and even the idea, of philosophy itself.

As far as the term "metaphysics" is concerned, we are well aware of the repeatedly asserted amphibology of its meaning to the point where Heidegger made it the crucible of his critique:

> It is known that the initial, purely technical meaning of the expression μετὰ τὰ φυσικὰ (the collective term for those of Aristotle's treatises that were arranged [in sequence] after those belonging to the Physics) later became a philosophically interpreted characteristic of what is contained in these rearranged treatises. This change of meaning,

however, is not as harmless as people ordinarily think. . . . [Metaphysics] is a science that is, so to speak, outside of the field of physics, which lies on the other side of it.[34]

The "after" in its chronological meaning—a simple classification of the subject matters or themes under consideration—progressively comes to designate the "after" or the "beyond" in its ontological sense—the position of transcendence. In this way, all immanence of being (*qua* being) definitely pertains to the transcendence of God (as the Super Being). This is too well known to require further exposition.

Nevertheless, we should ask ourselves today, in light of the endless quest, if this putative metaphysics understood as ontotheology—namely, the act of leading being *qua* being [*ontos*] back to God as the super Being [*theos*]—is not another one of those paradises that is illusory and impossible to find. The recent history of philosophy in France provides sufficient evidence to answer in the affirmative. So-called ontotheology has been reduced to a discourse with ever-diminishing returns: students of philosophy take off on its trail but can never catch up with it or seek to prove themselves by demonstrating that in the author in question, of course, no ontotheology can be found. Plato, Aristotle, Augustine, Bonaventure, also Aquinas, Descartes, obviously, Pascal, Leibniz, even Hegel and Marx cannot be framed within the putative historical schema of ontotheology. After all, ontotheology is actually a concept derived from the work of Thomas Erfurt (the pseudo-Duns Scotus), which the young Heidegger himself studied; he then extended his project (inappropriately?) to the whole history of philosophy.[35]

Is this to say that ontotheology does not exist, and never could have existed, to the point of becoming a lure for all philosophers seeking novelty?—Certainly not. If the schema according to which all immanence leads immediately back to transcendence as its sufficient reason is no longer a given in philosophy, it remains present, however, in the depths of Christian consciousness. There it most often relates any event of the world immediately to Providence, albeit according to the order of a general theodicy rather than of true Christianity. In short, ontotheology might well have never existed *philosophically* or even *theologically*, even though believers alone would continue to adhere to it thoughtlessly.[36]

To Overtake the Overtaking

"Metaphysics," then, cannot and should not be radically eliminated in its end as well as in its content. This should be obvious if one accepts precisely no longer turning the question of ontotheology into an obsolete hobby-horse. To overplay its case gives it more importance than it can lay claim to. *The overtaking of metaphysics is overtaken.* At the same time, the sometimes ideological, or even political, forceful return of metaphysics within a certain strand of French spirituality or analytic philosophy can appear as violent as its past condemnation when phenomenology staked out certain trenchant positions. But boundaries are not crossed by erecting barriers. The struggles for influence and the recurrent changing of sides in the contemporary history of philosophy make the situation no less a kind of trench-warfare, of which all intelligence suggests that the fields are not as mined as they appear. "Crossing the Rubicon" is to accept the crossing as the possibility of being transformed by the other. Such is a condition of a philosophy of the passage (Chapter 6, §21), which the strategy of the leap renders null and void in seeking to separate everything (§19).

Meta ta phusica, metaphysics, is then no longer understood either as "after physics" in the chronological succession of themes or as its "beyond" in the ontological sense of its overtaking, but in the sense of its *crossing* or *traverse* in the experiential sense of its suffering [*pâtir*] as of its passage. To return to the pre-Socratics, *phusis* designates the "flux" of what "flows by and thus passes" without ever remaining. Metaphysics as the act of *traversing* across the physical or natural—*meta(trans)phusica*—entails agreeing to plunge into the Heraclitean river in which one can never bathe in the same way twice, and thus to suffer from the world and finitude—in philosophy—in order to pass it to another, the Father, the only One capable of bearing it with me—in theology. The suffering and the passage consecrate the *phusis* as the anchorage par excellence of thought, whether the philosophical horizon of the world or the theological metamorphosis of philosophy in the Resurrection. Horizontality marks the beginning and probably the only possible starting point (§16) for the atheist as also for the believer. Yet the opening word, "the human per se," is not the final word, "the human converted and transformed in God." This newly queried metaphysics, therefore, does not make us forget the world in which we are rooted, but requires us to cross it without ever being overtaken. In the words of von Balthasar, one must affirm that

> the Biblical perception of God cannot be spiritualized. . . . The distinctive Christian factor is that here we not only "start from" the corporeal and the sensory as from some religious material on which we can then perform the necessary abstractions; rather, we abide in the seeing, hearing, touching, the savoring and eating of this flesh and blood, which has borne and taken away the sin of the world.

From Valentinus to Bultmann this flesh and blood have been spiritualized and demythologized.[37]

Scotus's "horizon of finitude," Aquinas's "overlaying" such finitude in the figure of the God-man, and Bonaventure's notion of its "conversion" at the heart of a trinitarian monadology marks the three steps by which metaphysics indicates the crossing of the world (*meta-phusis*) carried out as much by the human as it is transformed by God. The audacity of the [crossing of the] Rubicon is this suffering and passage—without being overtaken, however. The crossing of the ford of this truly *small* river, yet with such *high* stakes, leaves no one indifferent—neither the one who leads his army, nor those who remain somewhat dumbfounded by such an act. Nevertheless, *alea iacta est*: "the die has been cast," as Caesar proclaimed before launching his conquest. The march is underway, and it must now be completed in Chapter 6, "Finally Theology." Then at last, the author as well as the reader will have the task of discovering a new opening with an "after" (or conclusion) that will not fail to newly orient them together.

6

Finally Theology

"Finally theology." A theologian should utter this phrase—not a philosopher. One could fear that the great crossing finally had no other goal than to push us across the ford, as if the crossing of the Rubicon signified only the time of an Iliad without an Odyssey. Yet my principal thesis is that the two-way journey, there and back again with a definite return, is necessary to give each riverbank its specificity. I am first of all a philosopher and want to remain one. I am all the more committed to remaining a philosopher after having engaged in a vis-à-vis without a mode of subsidiarity with another discipline. Barely a few years ago, at least in France, cries of treachery, renouncement, even defeat or blasphemy would probably have been heard. Will the philosopher capitulate—he who had acquired his rights to the highest struggle, convincing the theologian of his autonomy and ignoring all theological matters in his haughtiness? Today philosophy certainly is no longer kept separate, and the hour has perhaps struck for a so-called "return to theology." But should we so quickly proclaim, along with Gilson, a "rediscovered theology" in opposition and contradiction to a "lost theology"?[1] Is it sufficient to restore an ancient model, such as Aquinas's, as the satisfactory and unique paradigm, even if it traces the way for a distinction without confusion or separation, as we showed above (Chapter 5, §17)?

Certainly a *kairos* appears today to disrupt the *chronos*: a timely event in the course of time. Where one might have believed theology forgotten, even rejected, it returns in force at the heart of the French university in the discipline of philosophy, at least as much as in theology. This development could be praised or conversely deplored. But the fact remains evident and inescapable: ever since Levinas and Ricoeur, God has "come (again) to mind," such that today we are not ready to dispose [of this "idea"].

Nevertheless, the renewed interest in theology, or more precisely this philosophical treatment of theological matters, in no way signifies just any old return to or new rise of Christianity; quite the opposite. A great distance lies between interpretation of objects of faith and confession of faith. The posture of the not-explicitly-confessing philosopher who still makes use of theology is very common in France and sometimes is a most honorable one (Nancy, Badiou, Franck). Yet no move is more misguided than seeking to baptize everything and everyone—in particular the emboldened thinkers who seek to offer an alternative reading of revealed texts. On the contrary, *one enters the other's field in order to respect the boundaries.* It has long been forgotten, although I have not ceased here to drive the point home: only a well-conducted battle can lead sometimes to true peace. The crossing of the Rubicon follows the pattern of every intelligently led conquest. An adversary is not vanquished by crushing him. In seeking vengeance, he will not abandon his opposition. Instead, we study the adversary and, by dint of combat, come to know him. As with armies, exchanges (blows, words) take place. Our shared community is only observed *after the fact*; paradoxically, the battle becomes the place of a real alterity. In adventuring into others' camps, we also discover our own country and finally cease to believe and think that the grass is always greener on the other side of the fence.

Rather than forbidding the philosopher from "theologizing," we should, conversely, encourage him to practice everything. This declaration may appear so commonplace today that it must be all the more firmly highlighted. The universal scope of philosophy cannot end on the threshold of theology. Since the philosopher studies epistemology, aesthetics, ethics, anthropology, or sociology, it is difficult to understand why the theological sphere should be forbidden for the sole reason that theology itself is and sometimes, although not always, becomes confessional. More clearly yet and most astonishingly, we might ask whether the prohibition of theology for philosophers does not originate also with theologians themselves. Plainly, at least in Catholic theology, the theologian also practices philosophy. In fact, it is a requirement for his theological development. In fact, its necessity has meant that no one reproaches theologians for reading and drawing on philosophers—for example, Plato and Aristotle to Descartes, Kant, Hegel, Kierkegaard, and Nietzsche. But then it is certainly difficult to understand why the philosopher himself could not equally earn his keep in service to theology—for example, Augustine and Aquinas certainly, but also Luther, Barth, Rahner, Balthasar, Bultmann, Moltmann, Jüngel, and others. In short, the leitmotif of "finally theology," or of a "theological turn" all the more assumed as it is explicitly undertaken, does not signal a simple return to theology as with Gilson, as if it were lost today and in need of rediscovery. "Finally Theology" rings out only as the imperative driving the quest, which is here a conquest, at the very heart of a paradox that must now be deployed as also explained: "the more we theologize, the better we philosophize."[2]

§19. From the Threshold to the Leap

Philosophies of the Threshold

In our current context, the call for a "separated theology" is no longer heard. To continue making it a concern, albeit to oppose it, is to once again inscribe oneself in Gilson's battle, now passé. The *honor* of the servant welcomed in the master's house did not signify some subsidiarity of philosophy in relation to theology or even a return to Christian philosophy.[3] Arguments for theology are not needed now that it has become a given presence in the field of philosophy. Its proclamation—for some thinkers, even restoration or extension—is not at issue. Rather, its mode of articulation, or more accurately its "inter-dicts," precisely what has been non-said ["*non-dits*"], is in question, which now must be, if not crossed and overcome, at least passed and overtaken.

Everyone observes that the times have changed, *ad intra* and *ad extra*. *Ad intra*: in the way theologians do or should theologize, introducing a great part of their description into their theological discourses. *Ad extra*: in the way philosophers do or should philosophize, approaching theological objects as themselves sources of philosophical reflection—for example, the relation to the sacred text. A question endures, however: if we are not or are no longer under the conditions of "a separated philosophy," is what we are calling "philosophy of the threshold" truly passed and left in the past? In other words, can we rest forever with the quasi-dogma of the "starting-block" that Maurice Blondel in a certain sense inaugurated? To be sure, the supernatural is both necessary and inaccessible. To proclaim it, in 1893 at the time of the *Action*, was a radical novelty with a boldness of thought that must be rediscovered today. Far from closing doors to theology after the manner of Léon Brunschvicg or Émile Boutroux, the philosopher from Aix-en-Provence opened the field of philosophy to the horizon of theology, making a breakthrough and even opening a gaping hole in the wall separating philosophy from theology. In this way, Blondel created some open space that remained to be occupied and that de Lubac would eventually fill. If for Blondel the supernatural is "necessary but inaccessible," then revelation itself will dictate the conditions of its accessibility in "the mystery of the supernatural" of what has been revealed, according to de Lubac. The one *remains on the threshold* of the opening that he pierced; the other *invests the field* opened by the gaping hole.

Nevertheless, one must ask whether then as now the one ever truly meets up with the other. If philosophy and theology no longer stare stonily at each other, as in the case of a "separated philosophy," nor are only complementary in a "subaltern philosophy," are they not still, and always will remain, each in their separate field? Having become allies, have they actually met each other? After years of dividing up their tasks—the philosopher *opens* and the theologian *fills*—have not philosophy and theology progressively fallen into a division of labor where each shift's teams continue to be separated one from the other, even though the lines of production are interconnected? In other words, although theology can no longer be produced without philosophy and philosophy can indeed open onto theology without letting itself be annexed, have philosophers and theologians truly engaged in debates and deliberations? Have they at least communicated, but more importantly found that the work of the one could become the professional experience of the other? This is not to confuse the tasks, since each one has its proper approach to the material, but to introduce flexibility into the labor for a new and more fecund productivity. To further play out the metaphor: as "in a factory," in fashioning a discourse on God, both philosophers and theologians labor today and are better informed of the professional experience of the other insofar as they attend trainings in order to become familiar with and try out the other's job, not to usurp it, but to enrich it with their own experience and their original way of conceptualizing it.

What appears here as a request for a division of professions, rather than a division of tasks, is far from being realized. The threshold established by Blondel, which opened a space for de Lubac, remains the only model affirmed today, or rather, the only properly "legitimate" one. Ricoeur can thus be seen as its standard-bearer, repeating in his Protestant context what Blondel carried out in his Catholic one. The philosopher from Nanterre had many occasions to step across the threshold or brave the prohibition. Already in *Finitude and Culpability* (1960), where he discusses fallibility and sin, he could have addressed grace and even redemption, without which its meaning—even its philosophical meaning—is in a certain way obscured or at least amputated. Yet he did not do so. Theologians then entered the newly created space. This deliberate strategy also runs through the *Conflict of Interpretations* (1969). His textual hermeneutic clearly inherits the four senses of scripture from theology, but the status of the revealed is contemplated without ever being thematized or affirmed. The same attitude is found in *Time and Narrative* (1983), where the question of eternity is not examined, or at least not with regard to the theological conceptions of the final, general resurrection. This pattern continues even up until *Memory, History, Forgetting* (2000), where recognition and forgiveness are considered, but never in the sense of a divine action coming to transform everything. Like Blondel, Ricoeur is thus a man of the opening and breakthrough, but he never crosses the threshold or occupies a "rediscovered beyond" or at least "the beyond" in which we are to venture today.

Returning to the metaphorical thread of this essay, we might be led to believe that others might have crossed the Rubicon and braved the prohibition. After all, if Julius Caesar had not resolved to cross the Rubicon but had stopped there, returning now to Leibniz's phrase, nothing prevents us from thinking that other "monads" may have cast the die, albeit simply to carry out the divine plan, so harmoniously determined. Yet that is not the case. The armies may appear different today but the battle remains the same.

(a) First, to seek to "translate the Bible into Greek" is not enough to actually theologize, as Levinas makes clear. His aim is exclusively philosophical. The phenomenologist fears nothing more than to find himself labeled a Jewish theologian or exegete. The fact that everything comes from scripture or the sacred text as "a trace" does not require the showing of its trace—quite the contrary. (b) To deploy a textual hermeneutic on the basis of the revealed, but without ever saying a word about the figure of the one who revealed himself, as Ricoeur did, is thus again to split them apart in the very midst of a rapprochement. (c) Marion keeps his corpus as a whole as well as his books separated. That may well be a way to inhabit the two disciplines more fully and aptly. Yet at least in France, the gap remains. There is no actual joint practice of philosophy and theology. They remain separate fields, unless the material at times demands it, as in studying St. Augustine, for example.

(d) It is true that to oppose the liturgy of the human *coram Deo* to the obstructed horizon of human existence creates a passage from anguish to joy, or from the unease of being-there to the well-being of "being toward" as in Lacoste's work. The radicality of the rupture, however, consecrates again both the imperative of conversion and the logic of separation. If the chiaroscuro remains within the eschatological horizon, we might ask if the revealed does not once again overdetermine existentiality or the "being over-there" of our pure and simple "being there." (e) To work strictly with the scriptural texts as the basis for thought, in particular the Gospel of John as Henry promotes could lead one to believe in a new unity. But here also the encounter is distorted. Not knowing when we philosophize and when we theologize, as shown in §20, we cannot know who we are when we believe to be, at the same time, on both sides of the opening. (f) Finally, to claim, along with Chrétien, that the scriptural text itself is the place of philosophy's greatest literality is not to theologize anymore than philosophize. The one who stands on this side of the distinction between the disciplines certainly has the advantage of not needing to decide, but also forgets the significance of the prior debates about a separated philosophy. Clearly, no one crosses the Rubicon when he may have thought that he did so. No one practices philosophy and theology by appealing to the text as a literary given, authorizing oneself, at times wrongly, to dispose of what truly constitutes a tradition and is necessary for any real interpretation.

The Illusion of the Leap

From the threshold upon which philosophers stop at the doors of theology and leave to others the care for that task, should one then take the leap? I noted this question in passing, at least in reference to Scotus, but have yet to develop it. A common requirement for all contemporary phenomenologists who draw on theology is disjunction rather than conjunction, the gap rather than continuity, a rupture rather than an overlaying.

Pascal can serve as a figurehead and example in light of a rarely discussed interpretation of his text. The "God of Abraham, God of Isaac, God of Jacob, and not of the philosophers and scholars" found in his *Memorial*,[4] dating from 1654, serves as a prism for a philosophy that up until today takes its proper name not from being specifically philosophical, but from being nonphilosophical—that is, not "of the philosophers"— at least in the sense of rejecting any abrupt imposition of a discourse of God (*theo*-logia) that cancels out, at the same time, any discourse about God (theo-*logia*). In other words, the philosopher paradoxically negates his own discipline and renames it metaphysics or ontotheology in order to lay claim to a so-called "other" discipline that he newly calls philosophy. Yet this newly created philosopher remains well versed, and even dabbles, in theology without acknowledging or addressing it. In an exemplary fashion, the contemporary interpretation of Pascal's "three orders" displays this very problematic. "The infinite distance between bodies and minds is a figure of the infinitely more infinite distance between minds and charity, for charity is supernatural."[5] The ordering of the flesh, the spirit, and charity is telling. Each inferior order remains autonomous and foreign to the superior order, such that a radical rupture establishes itself between the spheres to the point of instituting a hierarchy of classes. The kings, the wealthy, and the captains (the people of the flesh) share nothing in common with the sages and the great geniuses (the people of the spirit) who look down on them or contemplate them from above. Having no need for fleshly or spiritual greatness, since God alone suffices, the saints (the people of love) alone are seen by God and the angels.[6] In sum, the superior level alone sees and supervises the inferior level, and not the opposite. As a result, the purity of the discourse about sanctity, whether philosophical or theological, is gained by denouncing any intermixing with a common humanity, who is not yet converted and "metamorphed." This angelic "swan dive," to say the least, produces, on the one hand, an overdetermination of Pascal's interpretation in the radical rupture between the human and the divine and, on the other hand, an apology for theological reason, which has nothing or barely anything in common with philosophical reason.

Turning first to Pascal's interpretation: neither the recourse to the God of Abraham, Isaac, and Jacob nor the presumed ruptures among the three orders of flesh, spirit, and charity are sufficient to consummate the separation to such a degree. An attentive reading of the *Memorial* and its interpretation leads us to the "figure" rather than the "rupture," to the God of Jesus Christ, cited immediately afterward, rather than to the denunciation of the previously rejected God of the philosophers: "God of Abraham, God of Isaac, God of Jacob, and not of the philosophers and scholars . . . God of Jesus Christ."[7] In fact, nothing requires or compels us to think of the God of Jesus Christ in a radical opposition to the God of the philosophers, even here in Pascal's work. After all, what gives itself *figuratively* as "the God of Abraham, Isaac, and Jacob" could just as well designate "the God of the philosophers and the scientists." The structure of Pascal's thought, inasmuch as it is biblical and not only philosophical, consists in *anticipation* rather than *opposition*, in *figuration* more than *separation*. Reread figuratively, the philosophers and the scientists, along with their God or their concept, are not so terribly heterogeneous to salvation that they cannot participate in it. They do not imply the condemnation of the whole of humanity for neither wanting nor succeeding to attain "love." The elitism of the third order, which is called "love" but generally excludes philosophers on account of their "thinking," forgets the essential character of the human per se, known in the prefiguration and continuity of genus's rather than in the opposition of classes. As proof, Pascal emphasized, as cited above, that the "infinite distance between bodies and minds is a figure of the infinitely more infinite distance between minds and charity." The *Memorial*'s notion of "the God of Abraham, Isaac, and Jacob" and of *also* the three orders of flesh, spirit, and love in the *Pensées* present relations of figuration rather than exclusion, differentiation more than disqualification.

The problem with the Jansenist concept of grace in theology can sometimes translate into an elitism of reason and philosophy, which a number of contemporary philosophers perpetuate without daring to openly acknowledge it. When read carefully and reread within a horizon of figuration, Pascal eludes that interpretation. Salvation is not a matter of separation but integration. All philosophy worthy of the name (and all theology, as well) would no longer look down on or contemplate from above the life lived *over-there* or *down-below*, without risking losing the double movement that goes from below to above and from above to below. We want to neither omit nor even denigrate each of the orders that constitute our common humanity. Theology from above, as indicated in Chapter 5, §16, can only be received from a philosophy from below. Failure to understand this problem leads at times to the more or less unacknowledged conversion of *theology from above* into *philosophy from above*, as if reason itself—even philosophy—could receive a supernatural or revealed status that cannot truly be directly attributed to it.

The philosophical apology for "the three orders" and the false opposition of the "God of Abraham, Isaac, and Jacob" to the "God of the philosophers and the scientists" produces a "pastorale" of the rupture rather than continuity, of the quest for purity more than the recognition of our own obscurity. Certainly that may be surprising. A similar attitude of "looking down on" or "surveying from the heights," as Merleau-Ponty also says, joins the phenomenological discourses on revealed reason and the evangelical practices of a pure and totally separated faith as the two ends of one same chain. Catholic theology took in the past a position against demythologization and de-hellenization, as shown in Chapter 4, §13. Today the philosophical quest for a pure rationality without admixture in the order of charity may have the same weakness as the argumentation previously denounced. In claiming to boldly separate what gives itself first as mixed by means of a "leap" into pure faith (or philosophy), we sometimes forget the obscurities and oscillations in all humans. When thinking any alterity "on the way"—on *his* way—upon a predetermined route, the Christian's "evidence" leads him often to forget the *Holzwege*, or the wild trails, upon which God can also reveal himself through humanity this time. It is a matter of finding a new equilibrium between the ways, or approaches, as well as between the *corpora*. Assuredly this entails accounting for the rupture in Bonaventure's work, for the continuity in Aquinas, and for St. Damien's immediate conversion before Christ in Saint Francis's account, but also the slow and laborious discussion with the Cathar innkeeper in Toulouse in St. Dominic's writings.

The Limited Phenomenon

The appeal to the double interpretation of the Lukan passage describing the experience of the disciples on the road to Emmaus (§17) introduced Marion's approach determined by his concepts of excess or the saturated phenomenon. But in counterpoint, it indicates also a way via poverty or the limited phenomenon, which I am here advancing. In reality, these two approaches are not opposed: they signal two different, even complementary, ways to consider the rupture and the opening; that is, the absoluteness of revelation but also the possibility of transformation. Surely the "Rubicon" could flow between the two "banks" of philosophy and theology, provided that, from the human point of view, one accepts crossing from the one to the other. No one will pick a fight when and where the armies are advancing into battle, each one according to its own marching orders and according to its proper strategy. No one engages in battle by mistake if clearly aware of fighting a different war.

Nevertheless, even if the pathway of transformation begins with the human per se and takes precedence over the absoluteness of the revelation of God or reason, no argument for humanism could constitute alone the meaning of Christianity. The well-known saying by Irenaeus in *Adversus Haereses* that "God was made a man among men so that man may become God" is precisely why divinization serves as the horizon for humanization, or the condition of the divine as the desire of the human.[8] Yet in insisting too much on the brilliance of the Greek tradition, from Irenaeus to Denis the Aeropagite after the timely rediscovery of the church fathers during Vatican II, we have forgotten the greatest strengths of the Latin tradition from Tertullian to Aquinas. This forgetfulness is compounded by an ancient misinterpretation of the thought of St. Augustine, which believes and mistakenly judges that the weight of sin constitutes the whole of the Latin tradition. As a consequence, we have turned today to the primacy of glory as the unique mode of Christianity.

Aquinas, however, at the very heart of the Catholic tradition, never ceased to emphasize that *Deus non est primum quid a nobis cognoscitur*—that is, "God is not the first object of *our* knowledge."[9] Of course, there is the unlimited. Certainly we would always prefer the evidence of illumination to fumbling around in darkness. And clearly, we want to believe to have already arrived when we have barely set out on our way. Yet, as Aquinas says, "our soul, as long as we live in this life, has its being in corporeal matter; hence naturally it knows only what has a form in matter. . . . Hence it is impossible for the soul of man in this life to see the essence of God."[10] Everything has been said. We would like to see God in his essence, but we only discover his existence. We desire the saturated, but we see only the limited. We would like to be clothed in the garments of angels, but we find ourselves only in human skin.

We could regret not having arrived. We could increase the pace only to be weakened in other ways. This is neither God's plan nor the human's, however, as soon as we realize that we pass through the God-man. The *status viae* or the horizon of finitude—that is, the properly philosophical discourse of the human—is not simply the consolation prize of the being-there *in patria* or of the life in beatitude—namely, the theological reasoning of God. Even in the new life after the final resurrection, Aquinas surprisingly declares as he speaks of beatification, "the created light of glory received into any created intellect cannot be infinite."[11] Precisely, "perpetually, then, the soul will not be without the body."[12] In other words, and this is the full force of Aquinas's thought and his teaching for us today, the limit or finitude is not the only fact about the human being-there that would need to be overcome or should be opposed by the verticality of a God who comes abruptly to change everything. It belongs through and through to our humanity, because "nothing can be received from beyond one's own measure."[13] Since the human is created *within the limit*, precisely on account of his status of *creature*, he does not expect to escape into the unlimitedness of the uncreated. He will wait only for the splendor of the One who desires to dwell at the heart of his finite condition, to shine within him. To forget this limit *qua* creature is to seek wrongly to leave behind our God-given human position. After all, God offers it to us as our vocation: to let us then be converted and "metamorphed" within his divine Trinity.

Humanity's temptation—perhaps also the key temptation of a certain form of contemporary and Christian philosophy—is to seek to escape into the unlimited, when, in fact, the human being is desired and considered within the limit, or yet to invest in the secret hope of our being-over-there or being-up-above, when we are first called to remain and love our *being-there* in its *here-below*. Where finitude is only observed in philosophy, it is, on the contrary, *sought* and *desired in theology*. Perhaps this is the greatest gap between philosophy and theology, now understood in terms of the difference between the concepts of world and creation. While we are "purely nature" from Cajetan to Heidegger, we discover ourselves "creatures" from Aquinas to von Balthasar. The reality is the same: finitude or the human per se. Nevertheless, the interpretation is different: cornered in our being-there for Heidegger, on the one side, and awaited in our being-here-below for Aquinas, on the other. Far from breaking away from the whole of humanity or making his own path into the unique modality, the Christian offers another reading of what is first given to every human. The attitude is not exclusionary or a demand for conversion, but the meeting of a diversity of interpretations and relationships. Knowing where to dwell, that is, in his humanity, the philosopher will not or no longer need to regret not being a theologian or need to play the theological game without knowing his specific philosophical task. On the contrary, he receives from theology itself the right and the duty, or, better the vocation, to be and remain always a philosopher—in the same way that Christ as the figure of the God-man enjoins us paradoxically to attend also to the human and go through humanity in order to find God there. Therefore, a principle of proportionality will govern the exercise of philosophy in relation to the joint practice of theology: after the opposition or the simple complementarity of the disciplines, the relay takes place finally here in their connection as much as cross-fertilization.[14]

§20. The Principle of Proportionality

The More We Theologize, the Better We Philosophize

The thesis of a passage toward theology, following the image of a two-way crossing of the Rubicon—"there and back again"—could offer the impression that I am ready to confuse everything or usurp the garments of the other and appear, as it were, in disguise. Such assertions are based on mistaken principles and are at variance with history. They must be denounced. In fact, the exact opposite is the case: we forget what constitutes our own attire at times because we do not know how to wear the other's clothing.

Philosophia ancilla theologiae—philosophy is a servant of theology—returning to Aquinas's formula (§17) no longer means being content to recognize only that the servant is surely not the mistress of the house and must not be destroyed in order to continue serving the master.[15] Even if she is present in the house and even resides in the home itself, still sometimes, she must be invited into the master's apartments and not restrict herself to the simple role of serving. In refusing to share his intimacy, even his bed, the master stands guard over his sphere of influence, which the servant will always seek to usurp. Yet to accuse the disciplines of adultery, or even indict a possible illegitimate child, is to fail to understand that the lovers have been married at all times and are bound for eternity. Aquinas is not a philosopher or a theologian but philosopher *and* theologian. Moreover, what Aquinas accomplished in his position—that is, maintaining *in the unity of a same being*, both philosophy and theology—theologically explaining for example the question of the Trinity (*Prima Pars* of the *Summa theologiae*) or of the Incarnation (*Tertia Pars*), as well as philosophically how the human being in his action is taken up in this act of return to God without losing anything of his humanity (*Secunda Pars*)— was not accomplished by Gilson any more than by all the other protagonists of contemporary phenomenology. Of course, the solution is not simply to return to Aquinas. It consists in showing the extent to which his gesture, which founds Catholicism, at the same time, forbids us to be satisfied today with the simple strategy of "threshold" and "complementarity." The prohibition of the passage of philosophy to theology is not a matter of forbidden fruit or even an error in which not to fall. Only the history of philosophy and theology erected that wall. The twentieth century created the breach in it; the twenty-first century will have to find a passage through it.

The principle of proportionality according to which "the more we theologize, the better we philosophize" will serve as the leitmotiv for this liberated theology.[16] The ambiguity faced today is not, as mistakenly believed, that philosophy opens onto theology or takes over its field, but that it no longer knows when the discourse of the self-proclaimed philosopher falls under the jurisdiction of philosophy or belongs to theology. In reality, we must theologize if we want to truly philosophize, at least when philosophy claims to reach theology's threshold. Neither the scriptures nor the exegete alone can remain philosophers' sole partners, as is the case in the gestures of hermeneutics or phenomenology today (for example, the exegetes are Ricoeur's partners and the Gospel of John, Henry's). Tradition imposes the passage through theology and its study as such, even in an ecclesial and institutional mode. The proportionality of this saying— the more we theologize, the better we philosophize—appears with great clarity only in the practice of both disciplines. Knowing precisely when and where we pass into theology, we know exactly when and where we were in philosophy, and vice versa. Finitude, or the human per se, returning to dearly held formulas, are indeed starting points for philosophy and under the jurisdiction of the philosopher (§16). But only as this finitude is then rejoined (§17) and transformed (Chapter 5, §18) in the recited and assumed act of the Resurrection, is it made known that we were actually within the realm of true humanity and thus of philosophy—not of divinity concealed under the cover of humanity—that is, theology. The starting points are all the more *philosophical* when the endpoints are *theological*. This position can be summarized as the principle of "the philosopher before all else," which should be adopted today not against theology but, on the contrary, for it, in order to dwell otherwise and better situated within it.[17]

The Counterblow

The movement from the conquest to the crossing of the Rubicon—in opposition to the philosophies of the threshold and the leap (§19)—and from the recognition of the meaning of the limit to the proportional relation of philosophy and theology (§20) ultimately generates a counterblow upon philosophy itself, or at least upon phenomenology. Indeed, ever since the dawn of the theological turn, if one is to believe Janicaud, beginning with the publication of Levinas's *Totality and Infinity* in 1961, we have not ceased making theological inquiries on the basis of phenomenology, recognizing that a notion of "the God who comes to mind" could also be developed phenomenologically. One question must still be answered. If phenomenology can utterly renew the approach to the divine on its own account with a fecundity that must be honored today, would not theology itself also have the means, in a "rebound" or a "backlash," to question phenomenology as such, even to make it see its incapacities or at least its insufficiencies?

As denounced earlier, contemporary phenomenology exhibits a triple excess that must be restated, not to leave it behind but to consider them otherwise: first, the hypertrophy of the flesh over against the body; second, the surplus of sense over nonsense; third, the over-determination of passivity with respect to activity. The deviations of the flesh led to its stigmatization, which was so completely and adeptly typified that nothing remained of the body or the organic—the *Korper*—by dint of drawing it into a simple lived interiority. Between the extended body and the lived body, it was thus necessary to find and define *the spread body*—that is, the body on this side of any signification, all the way into the depths of its interior chaos. Christ indwells this very body in his Eucharist.[18]

The questioning of phenomenology itself, and its very capacity to attend to non-sense or the organic body, arises from the counterblow of theology on phenomenology—not the opposite. Everything changes here: it is no longer the flesh or *Leib* that explains Christ's Incarnation as with Henry, but Christ's Incarnation that questions *Leib* or the meaning of its consistence *qua* body, according to my own perspective. This means retracing one's steps, since the approach is now taken in reverse direction: the move is now from the theological to the phenomenological, and no longer from the phenomenological to the theological. Only without reading Tertullian or in reading him poorly, is it possible to think that the flesh of Christ is no more than an illustration of the lived body in its interiority or auto-affection. Rather, it is a body "spread out" in its organic character, as inaccessible to conceptuality as it is determinative for my affectivity. The wonders that astonished the church fathers as they argued against the Gnostics, in particular against Valentinus, were precisely that Christ himself had, like us,

> the muscles as turf, the bones as rocks, even a sort of pebbles round the nipples. Look upon the clinging bands of the sinews as the fibres of roots, the branching meanderings of the veins as the twistings of rivers, the down as moss, the hair as grass, even the very treasures of the marrow in its secret place as the goldmines of the flesh.[19]

Here, it is not a question of the appearance of a body or the reduction of the body to a lived experience, but a matter of the corporeal and biological human reality of this God-man, which establishes his kinship with "our race" (Acts 17:26). Certainly he is not portrayed here as the Christos Angelos, evanescent within a glorious cloud, which, however desirable it would be, is evidently false. In losing the thickness of the body, the heart of the divine's—but also the very human's—incarnation is lost.

The time has thus come to question phenomenology on the basis of theology and not always and again to develop theology phenomenologically. Criticisms may arise mistakenly asserting that I am engaging in a radical theologization of phenomenology or a phenomenological turn of French theology. In this case, the error is to believe that it is appropriate first of all and exclusively to theologize. I am not following or want to follow that approach. Rather than writing theology, I desire to write philosophy, but I will philosophize that much better if I agree also to do theology. The paradox is that precisely where and how philosophy and theology have been separated is now where and how they should properly be united. Only in uniting philosophy and theology can we see that we are consciously crossing the ford at the same time from philosopher to theologian and reciprocally from theologian to philosopher. The whole movement is held and maintained in the unity of the same being and according to a mutually fecund investigation.

The Liberation of Theology by Philosophy

A few years ago, in an ongoing Hegelian gesture, claims of a liberation of philosophy by theology were still resounding in that "in the elevation of one who thinks (or philosophizes) is also found a liberation of his thought for philosophy."[20] In direct contrast, I propose here a liberation of theology by philosophy (as already indicated in §18) by which philosophy discovers its marks of nobility and one of its principal raison d'êtres. A philosophy of religion *is not identical* to a philosophy of religious experience (§13). An account of the experience of faith as such, albeit rooted in a form of belief originally shared by all humanity (see Chapter 3, "Always Believing"), must itself be undertaken in order to account for a distinct conceptuality. Augustine, Pascal, Kierkegaard, even Nietzsche himself cannot be studied independently of this mode of faith (or nonfaith), which produces a discourse anchored in a truth that is not content with simply being objectivized. The significant question and line of demarcation is not whether one is or is not a "confessing believer." At the very least, we should recognize that a confession, or a refusal to confess, energizes this type of discourse, whose subjective heart must be engaged—otherwise we run the risk of missing the authentic and unsurpassable realities that are the sources of inspiration for what is simply stated or conceptualized.

To liberate theology by means of philosophy and not the opposite is neither to renounce philosophy nor even to reduce it to an ancillary role (§17). On the contrary, philosophy will be all the stronger as it will have proved its power of deliverance precisely at the point where the theologian would probably have remained in a purely didactic exposition if he had not also found the philosopher's heuristic capacity to question and enroot thought in the figure of the human per se. As the philosopher and the theologian cross the Rubicon, they will have no choice in passing each other but to let themselves be transformed—each one by the other. The first will teach the second about the human journey. The second will make the first see that he cannot refuse to open himself—upon a decision, of course (Chapter 4, §14)—to the transcendence of the One who comes to "metamorphose" everything, to the extent to which he has first assumed it in its entirety. Philosophy liberates theology not only insofar as it "prepares it" (*preambula fidei*) but also as it makes it its own object according to a heuristic, descriptive—but not actualizing—mode (§16). Theology receives itself from philosophy at the same time as it opens onto it and offers it the actuality of an act of faith that only the revealed and its "in-common" can at once provoke and accompany (Chapter 4, §15). Working neither in pure opposition nor in simple complementarity—and even less in competition, the two disciplines present themselves and articulate a discourse according to a common *ascesis* or spiritual exercise—its source of movement, as it were—whether it is the *askesis* of ancient philosophy or the examination of the conscience in the Christian tradition.[21]

§21. A Sigh of Relief

Finally Theology

The phrase "finally theology" sounds first like an avowal, but also a program. The battle against the previously much-heralded declaration of a "separated philosophy" no longer needs to be carried out. We have learned this from Gilson's past work in his endeavor to set forth a rediscovered theology. But more is to be found in the release, liberation, or even relief that is drawn from the act of "crossing the Rubicon." In fact, to brave the prohibition and pass from philosophy to theology (and vice-versa) makes it possible to follow the path without hesitation, step into the breach, and pass through the opening. The stranger's country becomes my own land, without confining me to the status of an expatriate. Of course, no one will forget his country of origin. But we will also remember that only our country of origin makes the opportunity to travel possible, and that we must finally oppose patriotism's code of silence and disciplinary boundaries and divisions, the transformation of ourselves by that which is foreign.

Finally Theology

"Finally" or in-the-end ultimately indicates theology "at the end"—not that the theologian always has the last word, as if the philosopher had no other destiny than to be the subaltern in a battle that was wrongly engaged. "Finally theology" indicates a finale that was already present at the beginning. Yet the ending does not impose itself; from the start, it was a matter of the design and proper character of the incarnate God. Since God became man, and that was his choice, it is first through the human that we reach God, only seeing after the fact and with a heart still burning that he was already walking at our side when he was speaking to us along the way (Lk 24:32). The relationship between philosophy and theology is similar to the intimate connection between the Incarnation and the Resurrection. Only a prolepsis, according to Pannenberg, causes the end to shed light on the beginning, or upon the discovery that one is all the more a philosopher if one has also braved the fields of one's theological partners and friends.

Alea iacta est

As Julius Caesar, through his interpreter Suetonius, exclaimed "*alea iacta est*," so must we: "the die has been cast." As in all battles, it matters little whether or not other infantrymen have been enlisted. Quality and quantity are not cut of the same cloth. Moreover, the rightfulness of the crossing alone was sufficient to justify it. Finally, "*entente*" [in French] has two meanings: *listening* but also *agreement*. In this double sense, we should listen for and agree on what such a crossing of the ford might have demanded, or yet led us to believe or think. Indeed, one is never walking alone there where one has enlisted and committed oneself:

> A being of splendid size and beauty suddenly appeared, sitting close by, and playing music on a reed. . . . From one of [the soldiers], the apparition seized a trumpet, leapt down to the river, and with a huge blast sounded the call to arms and crossed over to the other bank [*pertendit ad alteram ripam*]. Then said Caesar: "*Let us go where the gods have shown us the way and the injustice of our enemy calls. The die is cast* [*alea iacta est*]."[22]

Epilogue: And Then . . . ?

§22. First to Live

Primum vivere deinde philosophari—"first live and then philosophize." This famous saying of the ancients reminds us what is at stake in the act of writing and thinking. We do not first write and then live afterward or "on the side," as it were. Rather, *we live and then we write.* The first imperative is not to know how to write but to learn to live; otherwise we run the risk of having nothing to say. The particularity of the philosopher is that he participates in the incarnate. No error is greater than his confusing himself for an abstraction, whereby he would become a cut (*ab-stracto*) being. Moreover, *thought and writing are themselves acts of life.* We should not seek first to see, then to judge, and then to act—nor yet first to reflect, then to live, and then to reread—as if judgment or rereading themselves did not emerge from the modality of living. *The circle of life and thought* belongs to life or better yet *constitutes* life. Forgetting this reality leads the most determined actors as well as thinkers into the deadliest separation of the practical from the theoretical. There is no life without thought or thought without life—in the complementarity of intuition and concept most definitely, but also in the unity of the experience of thought as the thought of experience. Phenomenology's teaching that the life of thought is a mode of the thought of life is a heritage that none should forget.

Thus, nothing is more concrete than the act of philosophizing that the decision to cross the Rubicon calls forth, insofar as it determines a posture that, even if not necessarily shared by all, cannot not generate inquiry. There is no benefit, however, in knowing who lost or won, or in engaging in polemics, and even less in believing that one has finally arrived. An essay on "the borderlands," as indicated in the subtitle of this work, is not a battle to determine and definitively trace new or old boundaries. I have made no claim to some orthodoxy or presumed loyalty to a so-called origin of phenomenology, following Janicaud's model in *The Theological Turn in French Phenomenology*. To cross the Rubicon is not to seek combat but to advance or orient thought otherwise. We must avoid crossing and passing too rapidly along our way, as if the first battle had just been won. On the contrary, we must come to rest at, camp, and navigate the river whose two banks cannot be separated. The image of Caesar crossing the Rubicon implies for this thinker leaving neither Cisalpine Gaul nor Emilie-Romagna, regardless of which bank is designated as philosophy or theology. This essay on the borderlands remains "within" the boundary zone, even if it were to delimit "a neutral zone" where it is certainly not easy to live but where the risk of meeting the stranger is high.

§23. The Afterward of the Afterward

"The *afterward* of metaphysics" is no longer in question inasmuch as it delimited a "river bank" or "a defensive wall" beyond which reside those who do not know how to pass it and remain therefore in an outdated mode of philosophy. No one could deny that even its very overcoming has today been overcome without once again playing out all the "essays," which have already, and quite rightly so, been transformed. There is no question, however, of simply returning to the past in a deplorable reactionary mode, as if the trumpet call resounded this time for metaphysics' revenge upon phenomenology, according to the definitely antiquated standards of the rearguard. The virulence with which certain so-called "metaphysicians" lay claim to metaphysics over against phenomenology is comparable to the ardor with which certain phenomenologists, in their time, claimed to have overcome metaphysics (Chapter 5, §18)—no one can deny it. The phenomenological practice of philosophy clearly has the great merit of having analyzed and questioned metaphysics, which it claims to have surpassed (in its full sweep from Aristotle to Hegel), profoundly renewing the interpretation of a corpus that others would also like to rediscover today.

Leaving thus the first "afterward" (in a sense, the "before") to those who still seek controversy, all that counts from my standpoint and for today is "the afterward of the afterward"—which is the relief of a philosophy that may or may not have claimed to have surpassed metaphysics. "And then?" [*Et après?*]—this French expression certainly acknowledges "what" comes after, but also the possibility of pursuing it "oneself," no longer bound to who [what] engendered one. Indeed, what is at stake is not to either stick with or escape from a mode of thinking to which one is attached—for example, phenomenology. We remain forever marked by who [what] gave birth to us: probably in phenomenology, this mark is a "descriptivity" that no other mode of thinking could surpass. Yet description itself can evolve. Remaining a phenomenologist today does not require securing the boundaries—whether for or against metaphysics— but rather accepting the need to cross the barricades. The crossing of the Rubicon not only joins the two banks (philosophy and theology) by a single thread but also "casts the end of the rope" (in the nautical sense of the phrase) to metaphysics itself. Phenomenology and metaphysics can thus discover, if not a place for *conciliation*, at least terms for the *discussion*.

§24. With an Exposed Face

In contrast, then, to Descartes's "comedian stepping onto the theater of the world" and turning instead to Péguy's "stranger who will quickly bring them to agreement," the philosopher advances undisguised—*larvatus prodeo*—in order not to risk making himself and his work pass strictly for philosophy when it has also a theological impetus.[1] The mask only masks whoever believes himself to be masked. In the carnival of philosophy, it is better to advance without shame than to disguise what, in any case, is meant to be brought out into the open: "No one after lighting a lamp puts it under the bushel basket, but on the lampstand, and it gives light to all in the house" (Mt 5:15). Even though we do not advance masked before humans (*larvatus prodeo*), we definitely advance masked before God (*larvatus pro Deo*), at least in the sense that the assumption of the "humus" of the human (finitude) cannot immediately lay claim to the glory of God— that is, the Resurrection.[2] Strangely enough, Ovid carries the day over Descartes by advancing no longer veiled but undisguised, not masked but nearly in the nude: *non larvatus* (as Descartes), *sed detecta fronte* (as Ovid), *prodeo*.[3]

"Crossing the Rubicon" is therefore not a reaction in relation to an assigned problem in some set of subject matters—namely, philosophy and theology—and to the mode of being of their approaches, as described by phenomenology, both of which we can only praise and expand. By this, I mean the following. First, negatively: the times have changed and we can no longer demand, according to a nearly unanimous posture, "the sort of controlled schizophrenia that has always been my rule of thought."[4] Rather than dividing philosophy and theology up into two utterly separate worlds, we will practice the one as well as the other, seeking in ourselves a new mode of unity. Second, positively: we build now upon this radical contemporary modification in the way of philosophizing. Indeed, the whole of French phenomenology, whether or not understood in terms of a theological turn, has this particularity: it was and still is able to deploy *philosophema* that are at the same time *theologoumena*, such as Levinas's face, Chrétien's speech, Henry's flesh, Marion's gift, Lacoste's liturgy. All that remains to be done, then, is to "transform the essay" or "push to the limit" what has given itself up until now strictly in a veiled mode, or with such prudence that the professions of philosophizing sometimes prevent the crossing of the ford. As a result, philosophy has restricted itself to the threshold of the theological discipline, which could actually be practiced at the very same time. This step had to be taken. Elsewhere I have already undertaken part of the crossing. All that was missing was its justification according to the new given, which today and in the days to come must be considered. To conclude with a quasi-prophetic vision of the philosopher Stanislas Breton:

> At this stage where the *boldness of the question* and the *responsibility of the response* are all that count, what does it matter that one calls oneself a *theologian* or *philosopher*: the *spirit*, which blows where it will, will know to *recognize its own*.[5]

Acknowledgments

Thanks to Yves Roullière and Paul Gilbert, who needled me into beginning this book, and to Jérôme Alexander and Jérôme de Gramont, for their ever most helpful editorial attentiveness.

Notes

Introduction

1. The *Blackwell Encyclopedia of Modern Christian Thought* says, "There is no concept of an immortal soul in the Old Testament, nor does the New Testament ever call the human soul immortal" (Cambridge: Blackwell, 1995), 101.

2. Henri de Lubac, *The Drama of Atheist Humanism* (San Francisco: Ignatius Press, 1995).

3. Emmanuel Falque, *The Metamorphosis of Finitude*, trans. George Hughes (New York: Fordham University Press, 2012), 73.

4. Given that English-speaking philosophers of religion such as Kevin Hart, Anthony Steinbock, Bruce Ellis Benson, and J. Aaron Simmons are currently doing their own proper work in phenomenology, we could remove the qualifier "French" from Janicaud's statement and speak more broadly of a "theological turn in phenomenology"; see Brad Onishi, "Emmanuel Falque and the New Theological Turn in Phenomenology," paper prepared for Autour Emmanuel Falque, Orsay, July 2014.

5. Dietrich Bonhoeffer got the phrase from Grotius; see his letter to Eberhard Bethge, 16 July 16 1944, in Bonhoeffer, *Letters and Papers from Prison* (New York: Touchstone, 1997), 360.

6. See Alain Saudan, *Penser Dieu autrement* (Paris: Éditions Germina, 2013), 12.

7. Quoted in ibid., 11.

8. Friedrich Nietzsche, *Thus Spoke Zarathustra* (Blacksburg: Thrifty Books, 2009), 41.

9. Christina Gschwandtner, *Postmodern Apologetics? Arguments for God in Contemporary Philosophy* (New York: Fordham University Press, 2012), 5ff.

10. Onishi, "Emmanuel Falque," 4.

11. Falque, "Phénoménologie de l'extraordinaire," in *Éditions de Minuit*, no. 78 (June 2003): 52–76.

12. Falque, *Le combat amoureux* (Paris: Hermann, 2014), 137–93. Chapter 4, in fact, presents a revised and expanded version of his 2003 "Phénoménologie de l'extraordinaire."

13. Ibid., 10. Falque borrows this phraseology from Jean-Louis Chrétien.

14. Ibid., 11.

15. Falque, *Metamorphosis of Finitude.*

16. Falque, "*Larvatus pro Deo*: Jean-Luc Marion's Phenomenology and Theology," in *Counter Experiences: Reading Jean-Luc Marion,* ed. Kevin Hart (Notre Dame: University of Notre Dame Press, 2007), 181–200.

17. Falque, *God, the Flesh, and the Other,* trans. William Christian Hackett (Evanston: Northwestern University Press, 2014).

18. Kevin Hart, introduction to Hart, *Counter Experiences,* 1.

19. Falque, "*Larvatus Pro Deo,*" 195.

20. Quoted in Falque, "*Larvatus Pro Deo,*" 185.

21. See Jean-Luc Marion, *La Rigueur des Choses: Entretiens avec Dan Arbib* (Paris: Éditions Flammarion, 2012).

22. Karl Barth, *Church Dogmatics* (Alexandria, Va.: Alexander Street Press, 2010), §38.

23. Rudolf Bultmann, "The Problem of Natural Revelation," in *Faith and Understanding* (Paris: Seuil, 1970), 466.

24. Falque, "*Larvatus Pro Deo,*" 195.

25. Marion, *Being Given,* trans. Jeffrey Kosky (Stanford: Stanford University Press, 2002), 235.

26. Ibid., 264.

27. Joeri Schrijvers, "On Doing Theology 'After' Ontotheology: Notes on a French Debate," *New Blackfriars* 87, no. 1009 (May 2006): 309.

28. Gschwandtner, "Corporeality, Animality, Beastiality: Emmanuel Falque on Incarnate Flesh," *Analecta Hermeneutica* 4 (2012): 1–16; see also her essay in *Postmodern Apologetics.*

29. Edmund Husserl, *Zur Phänomenologie der Intersubjektivität I,* Husserliana XIII (The Hague: Martinus Nijhoff, 1973), 57ff.

30. Jean-Louis Chrétien, *L' Appel et la réponse* (Paris: Minuit, 1992) 102ff. Incidentally, Jacques Derrida noticed in *Le Toucher* that Chrétien fails to mention his debt to Jean-Luc Nancy; see Derrida, *On Touching: Jean-Luc Nancy* (Stanford: Stanford University Press, 2005), 261.

31. Aristotle, *De anima* II.11.423b14.

32. Husserl, *Ideas Pertaining to a Pure Phenomenology and a Phenomenological Philosophy* (*Ideas I*), trans. F. Kersten (The Hague: Martinus Nijhoff, 1982), 57.

33. Husserl, *Zur Phänomenologie der Intersubjektivität II*, Husserliana XIII (The Hague: Martinus Nijhoff, 1973), 261.

34. Marion, *In Excess* (New York: Fordham University Press, 2002), 98.

35. Ibid., 99.

36. Kathryn Tanner, "Theology at the Limits of Phenomenology," in *Counter Experiences*, 205.

37. Marion, *Being Given*, 243.

38. In sum, Shane Mackinlay argues that Marion has achieved something much more modest than he supposes—he has argued not for phenomena excluded from Kantian relation but simply for additional kinds of relations not denominated by Kant; see Mackinlay, *Interpreting Excess* (New York: Fordham University Press, 2010), 130ff.

39. Falque's affinities with Marion become apparent especially in *Le Passeur de Gesthemani* (Paris: Éditions du Cerf, 2004).

40. Translation mine; Falque, *Les noces de l'agneau* (Paris: Cerf, 2011), 24. Falque charges Heidegger with a similar mis-emphasis. By failing to hold on to his own *existentiell* analytic in the progress of *Being and Time*, Heidegger misses the personal and affective character of suffering, intellectualizes moods, and generally disincarnates Dasein.

41. Translation mine; Falque, *Les noces de l'agneau*, 23.

42. Falque is not alone in this judgment. Gilles Deleuze, Jacques Derrida, John Caputo, and Roberto Walton all worry that phenomenologists tend to discorporate the flesh.

43. Edgar Allen Poe, "Descent into the Maelström," in *The Fall of the House of Usher and Other Writings*, ed. David Galloway (London: Penguin Classics, 2003).

44. See Frederick Copplestone, *A History of Philosophy*, vol. 1, *Greece and Rome* (New York: Doubleday, 1993), 469.

45. Falque, *Dieu, la chair, et l'autre* (Paris: Presses Universitaires France, 2008).

46. Here my worry is different from Falque's. Given that the subspecies *homo sapiens sapiens* exhibited modern anatomy and phenotypes at least 200,000 years ago, it is hard to see how evolutionary time destabilizes the concept of human animality. What Falque should be more concerned about, as is Thomas Carlson, are technological contractions of evolutionary time and unparalleled incursions into the human biotic; see Carlson, *The Indiscrete Image* (Chicago: University of Chicago Press, 2008).

47. Gschwandtner doubts that Falque really improves on Augustine's anthropocentricism much by denying animals consciousness rather than voice; see "Emmanuel Falque: A God of Suffering and Resurrection," in her *Postmodern Apologetics*, 201.

48. Ibid., 163.

49. Falque, "Phénoménologie de l'extraordinaire," 52.

50. Falque, *Les noces de l'agneau*, 293.

51. Thomas Aquinas, *Summa theologica*, I. 1.8 ad. 2.

52. Falque, *Les noces de l'agneau*, 188. Falque traces Marion's dim view of the perfectibility of the intellect to a misreading of Aquinas that is over-determined by a Pascalian subordination of the order of knowledge to love, which is then mapped on to Aquinas's distinction between *theologia rationalis* and *sacra doctrina*, respectively.

53. Aquinas, *Summa theologica*, Ia.105.5.

54. Eberhard Jüngel, *God as the Mystery of the World* (Grand Rapids: Eerdmans, 1983) 1:2.

55. See Saudan, *Penser Dieu autrement*, 167.

56. Falque, *Metamorphosis of Finitude*, 82ff.

57. Marion, *Being Given*, 238ff.

58. Falque, "*Larvatus Pro Deo*," 192ff.

59. Ibid., 193. To these objections, I would add that Marion in §24, at least, does not draw his focal examples of Christ's saturation from resurrection appearances at all. It is not clear on Marion's account, therefore, what the Resurrection *adds* to Christ's saturated phenomenality, which is already par excellence before the Resurrection. Moreover, one cannot help but wonder whether or not Marion avoids Resurrection appearances precisely because they are frequently marked by an anonymous thinness—not by a bedazzling excess—of intuition, as in the unrecognized appearance along the road to Emmaus.

60. See Chapter 2.

61. Ibid., 161.

62. Ibid., 89.

63. Ibid., 8.

64. Bonhoeffer, *Résistance et soumission* (Geneva: Labor et Fides, 2006), 438.

65. See Chapter 3.

66. Ibid.

67. Ibid., 126.

68. See Saudan, *Penser Dieu autrement*.

Opening

1. G.-W. Leibniz, "Discourse on Metaphysics," in *Philosophical Essays*, trans. Roger Ariew and Daniel Garber (Indianapolis: Hackett, 1989), 44–45.

2. Suetonius, *Lives of the Caesars*, trans. Catharine Edwards, Oxford World's Classics (Oxford: Oxford University Press, 2000). He writes, "at dawn, he located a guide [*duce reperto*] and found the route on foot, following narrow paths. He caught up with his cohorts at the *River [flumen]* Rubicon, which was *the boundary of his province*, where he paused for a while, thinking over the magnitude of what he was planning, then turning to his closest companions, he said: '*Even now we can still turn back. But once we have crossed that little bridge [ponticulum], everything must be decided by arms*.' As he paused [*cunctanti*], the following portent occurred. A being of splendid size and beauty suddenly appeared, sitting close by, and playing music on a reed. . . . From one of [the soldiers], the

apparition seized a trumpet, leapt down to the river, and with a huge blast sounded the call to arms and crossed over to the other bank [*pertendit ad alteram ripam*]. Then said Caesar: '*Let us go where the gods have shown us the way and the injustice of our enemy calls. The die is cast* [*iacta alea est*—most often transcribed as *alea jacta est*]'" (16–17; my emphasis).

3. For the relationship between medieval philosophy and phenomenology, see Emmanuel Falque, *God, the Flesh, and the Other: From Irenaeus to Duns Scotus*, trans. William Christian Hackett (Evanston: Northwestern University Press, 2014), 13–42; especially the "Introduction": "*Fons signatus*: La source scellée." As for the relation between phenomenology and theology, a series of works about contemporary phenomenologists lay out the terrain (see for example, the forthcoming *Disputes phénoménologiques: Entre phénoménologie et théologie*). In another step, this present work now addresses the relation between philosophy and theology, inclusive of hermeneutical questions.

4. See John Chrysostom, "Homily IX: 1 Cor. 3:12–15, [5] v. 12," in *Homilies of St. John Chrysostom: Commentaries on the First Epistle of St. Paul the Apostle to the Corinthians*, Rev. Oxford Translation, ed. Philip Schaff (London: Oxford, 1889); my emphasis and bracketed additions. [Note that the author cites a translation of Chrysostom's "The Homily on the Cannanite" (PG 51, col. 458ff.), by Willibrord Witters, found in "La prière," in *Cahiers de la Pierre qui vire* (Paris: DDB, 1954), 176–77.]

5. ["La grande traversée"; The French title, *Passer le Rubicon*, is translated according to the English idiom "*crossing* the Rubicon." Falque will deploy the full set of French terms within this semantic field, "passer, le passage, la traversée, la traverse, traverser, franchir. . . ." All of these can be translated as *crossing* in English, although passer and passage are more temporal notions connoting the duration of an event and of movement *through*, including distinct stages or moments, thus also passing *by* or *beyond*; *traverser* and *la traverse* are more spatial in their connotations—crossing as going or traveling *across* some extended, determinate space; *franchir* is crossing *over* something definite and determinate in a single moment, such as an obstacle. Keeping these distinctions in mind, as a general rule, this translator still rendered all three—*passer, traverser,* and *franchir*—as crossing, noting in brackets the specific French term when pertinent.]

6. St. Bonaventure, "Prologue," §6, no. 5, in *Works of St. Bonaventure: Breviloquium*, Bonaventure Texts in Translation Series, ed. Robert J. Karris, trans. Dominic V. Monti (St. Bonaventure, N.Y.: Franciscan Institute Publications, 2005), 9:22; my emphasis. See also my commentary in Falque, *Saint Bonaventure et l'entrée de Dieu en théologie: La somme théologique du Breviloquium* (Paris: Vrin, 2000); especially the Introduction, "L'hypothèse phénoménologique et le breviloquium," 19–27.

7. See the Acknowledgments.

8. See Alain Saudan, *Penser Dieu autrement: L'oeuvre d'Emmanuel Falque* (Paris: Germina, 2013). Saudan's recent publication perfectly complements this

present work and offers an excellent introduction to my thought as also to the positions taken here.

9. ["Evidence" is here used in a Husserlian phenomenological sense. Falque is highlighting how an investigation into the spiritual senses can be understood as emphasizing the role of *subjective* intuition in fulfilling the intention, such that the phenomena are known in full "*Evidenz*".]

10. ["The Word" of John 1 (the greek, Logos) is commonly translated in French as *le Verbe*. Here in the context of "(specifically written) linguistic voices" and elsewhere throughout the text, Falque builds on this dynamic verbal and vocal character of the Logos. The fact that Falque will alternately use *la Parole*, that is, the Speech, only reinforces the point. —Trans.]

11. [See Baruch Spinoza, *Ethics*, trans. Samuel Shirley, ed. Seymour Feldman (Indianapolis: Hackett, 1992), 105 (*Etica* III.ii, Scholium).]

12. [See Emmanuel Levinas, *Otherwise than Being, or, Beyond Essence*, trans. Alphonso Lingis (Pittsburg: Duquesne University Press, 1998).]

13. See my "triptych": Falque, *Le passeur de Gethsémani: Angoisse, souffrance, et mort* (Paris: Les Editions du Cerf, 1999); *Métamorphose de la finitude: Essai philosophique sur la naissance et la résurrection* (Paris: Les Editions du Cerf, 2004), trans. *Metamorphosis of Finitude: An Essay on Birth and Resurrection* (New York: Fordham University Press, 2012); *Les noces de l'agneau: Essai philosophique sur le corps et l'eucharistie* (Paris: Les Editions du Cerf, 2011).

14. [Falque's use of "*tuilage et conversion*" in this theological context appears unique; cf. Ricoeur's notion of "*tuilage et recouvrement*," where *recouvrement* is the French translation of Husserl's concept of *Deckung* denoting the structure of the pre-predicative synthesis of moments of incomplete intuition that result in a indeterminate unity: the varied moments of intentional relation in sensibility "cover" each other or "overlay" each other in forming a temporally extended conscious act (without becoming a determinate object in relation to cognition). Here, *recouvrement* will be translated as *overlaying* (more than simply overlapping, with a sense of a unity generated by an activity of *covering over and recovering*), and *tuilage*, with its connotations drawn from the literal sense of roof tiles overlaying each other, will simply remain *tiling*, to preserve the uniqueness of the term. —Trans.]

15. See my commentary "L'hypothèse monadologique," in Falque, *Saint Bonaventure et l'entrée de Dieu en théologie*, Collections "Études de philosophie médiévales" (Paris: Vrin, 2000), 75–78.

16. See Thomas Aquinas, *Scriptum Super Sententiis*, Lib. III, D. 49, q.2, a.1.

17. Ignatius of Loyola, *Spiritual Exercises and Selected Works*, ed. George E. Ganss, SJ (Mahwah, N.J.: Paulist Press, 1991), 121: "For just as taking a walk, traveling on foot, and running are *physical exercises*, so is the name of *spiritual exercises* given to any means of preparing and disposing our soul to rid itself of all its disordered affection" (my emphasis); Pierre Hadot, *What Is Ancient Philosophy?*, trans. Michael Chase (Cambridge, Mass.: Belknap Press, 2002), 179–80: "Throughout our investigation, we have encountered 'exercises' (*askêsis, meletê*)

in every school, even among the Skeptics; that is to say, we have found voluntary, personal practices intended to cause a transformation of the self."

18. Cf. Hans-Georg Gadamer, "The Concept of Experience (Erfahrung) and the Essence of the Hermeneutic Experience," in *Truth and Method*, 3rd ed. (New York: Continuum, 2006), 340–55. In particular: "'learning through suffering' (*pathei mathos*). This phrase does not mean only that we become wise through suffering. . . . What man has to learn through suffering is not this or that particular thing but insight into the *limitations of humanity*, into the absoluteness of the *barrier* [*limite*; —Trans.] that separates man from the divine. . . . Thus experience is experience of *human finitude*. . . . Real experience is that whereby man becomes *aware of his finiteness*" (350–51; my emphasis).

19. This expression was first formulated and put to work in the context of medieval philosophy, in my work *God, the Flesh, and the Other: From Irenaeus to Duns Scotus*, trans. William Christian Hackett (Evanston: Northwestern University Press, 2014); see especially the subsection entitled "Philosophy and Theology."

20. Joachim Du Bellay, "Sonnet 31," in *Les regrets* [1558] (Paris: Livre de Poche, 2002), 72 [English—Trans.].

1. Is Hermeneutics Fundamental?

1. Emmanuel Levinas, "Is Ontology Fundamental?," in *Entre Nous: Thinking-of-the-Other*, trans. Michael B. Smith (London: Continuum, 2006), 1–10.

2. Gregory the Great, "Homily VII," in Book I of *The Homilies of St. Gregory the Great on the Book of the Prophet Ezekiel*, trans. Theodosia Tomkinson and Juliana Cownie (Etna, Calif.: Center for Traditionalist Orthodox Studies, 1990). [Cf. the Latin text, *Liber Primus*, Homilia 19, pt. 8, in *Sancti Gregorii PP: I Magni Romani Pontificis Homiliarum in Ezechielem Prophetam Libri*: "quia divina eloquia cum legente crescent"]. See the commentary on this formula by Jean Greisch, Chap. 2, "Lire pour grandir," in *Entendre d'une autre oreille: Les enjeux philosophiques d'une herméneutique biblique* (Paris: Bayard, 2006), 48–52; and by Jean-Louis Chrétien, "Allowing Oneself to Be Read Authoritatively by the Holy Scripture," in *Under the Gaze of the Bible*, trans. John Marson Dunaway (New York: Fordham University Press, 2015), 6–22, esp. 20.

3. Paul Claudel, *The Essence of the Bible*, trans. Wade Baskin (New York: Philosophical Library, 1957), 33.

4. Henri de Lubac, *History and Spirit: The Understanding of Scripture according to Origen*, trans. Anne Englund Nash (San Francisco: Ignatius Press, 2007), 386; cited in Chrétien, *Under the Gaze of the Bible*, 19.

5. Cf. my contribution to the work of Jean Greisch, "Le tournant de la facticity," in *Le souci du passage: Mélanges offerts à Jean Greisch* (Paris: Cerf, 2004), 209, 223; esp. 215.

6. [Transversality denotes a concept of places of passage between different levels of the real and domains of discourse. The notion was introduced in French thought by Felix Guattari. See, for example, his first use of the term in a work,

first published in 1972, most recently as Guattari, *Psychanalyse et transversalité: Essai d'analyse institutionnelle* (Paris: Éditions La Découverte, 2003).]

7. [The French *relève* means *relief* as in taking over the position, picking up the task, or changing of the guard or arrival of the new shift.]

8. This is a formula of Augustine of Dacia as translated and cited by Paul Beauchamp, "Sens de l'écriture," in *Dictionnaire Critique de Théologie*, by Jean-Yves Lacoste (Paris: Presses Universitaires de France, 1998), 1087 [English–Trans.]. For a commentary on Augustine of Dacia, see also Greisch, "L'autre quadriparti: Le quadruple sens de l'écriture," in *Entendre d'une autre oreille*, 144–52.

9. Paul Ricoeur, "Philosophical Hermeneutics and Biblical Hermeneutics," in *From Text to Action: Essays in Hermeneutics*, trans. Kathleen Blamey and John B. Thompson (Evanston: Northwestern University Press, 1991), 2:89–102.

10. Ricoeur, "The Hermeneutical Function of Distanciation" in *From Text to Action*, 85.

11. Ibid., 84; see esp. "The Relation of Speaking and Writing," 83–84.

12. Ibid., 85–86; see also the entire section "The World of the Text," 84–86.

13. Ibid., 87–88 (my emphasis); see the entire section "Self-Understanding in Front of the Work," 87–88.

14. Ibid., 88.

15. Ibid., 87.

16. See Ricoeur, *Oneself as Another*, trans. Kathleen Blamey (Chicago: University of Chicago Press, 1992). [Note that "constitute" is here used in the phenomenological sense of some meaning constituted in and by consciousness.]

17. Ricoeur, "Philosophical Hermeneutics and Biblical Hermeneutics," 92.

18. [Falque is working off the French text: Edmund Husserl, *Méditations cartésiennes*, trans. Gabrielle Peiffer and Emmanuel Levinas (Paris: Vrin, 1980), 33 [English—Trans.]. Cf. the English translation based on a variant manuscript: Edmund Husserl, *Cartesian Meditations: An Introduction to Phenomenology*, trans. Dorien Cairns (Norwell: Kluwer, 1999), 38–39.]

19. Claude Romano, *Au coeur de la raison: La phénoménology* (Paris: Gallimard, 2010), 12.

20. Ibid., 874.

21. Ricoeur, "Existence and Hermeneutics," in *The Conflict of Interpretations: Essays in Hermeneutics*, ed. Don Ihde (Evanston: Northwestern University Press, 1974), 3. In addition to that opening essay originally published in French in 1969, see also his 1975 article published as "For a Hermeneutical Phenomenology," Chap. 1 in *From Text to Action*, 23–52.

22. Ricoeur, "Existence and Hermeneutics," 6.

23. Ibid., 10.

24. Ricoeur, *From Text to Action*, 32.

25. Ibid., 84.

26. Ibid., 69.

27. Ricoeur, "Explanation and Understanding," in *From Text to Action*, 130.

28. Ricoeur, "The Task of Hermeneutics," in *From Text to Action*, 69.

29. Levinas, "Is Ontology Fundamental?" in *Entre Nous*, 1–10.

30. Ibid., 5 (my emphasis).

31. Ricoeur, "The Task of Hermeneutics," 71 (my emphasis).

32. Ibid. Ricoeur adds, "The very title of the work confronts the Heideggerian concept of truth with the Diltheyan concept of method. The question is to what extent the work deserves to be called *Truth and Method*, and whether it ought not to be entitled instead *Truth or Method*. For if Heidegger was able to elude the debate with the human sciences by a sovereign movement of transcendence, Gadamer can only plunge himself into an ever more bitter debate, precisely because he takes Dilthey's question seriously."

33. See Dominique Janicaud, *Phenomenology and the "Theological Turn": The French Debate*, trans. Bernard G. Prusak (New York: Fordham University Press, 2000); Jean Grondin, *Le tournant herméneutique de la théologie* (Paris: Presses Universitaires de France, 2003)—for the "double turn," see 99. For an explicitly "phenomenological theology" attempted by two doctors in theology, see Franco Manzi and Giovanni Cesare Pagazzi, *Le regard du fils: Christologie phénoménologique*, trans. Paul Gilbert (Brussels: Lessius, 2006).

34. Dominique Janicaud, *Phenomenology "Wide Open,"* trans. Charles N. Cabral (New York: Fordham University Press, 2005), 48, 57.

35. See Martin Heidegger, *Being and Time*, trans. Joan Stambaugh (Albany: State University of New York Press, 2010), §7, and Ricoeur, Part 1, "For a Hermeneutical Phenomenology," in *From Text to Action*.

36. John Paul II, "The Relationship between Faith and Reason," in *"Fides et ratio": On the Relationship between Faith and Reason: Encyclical Letter of John Paul II* (Boston: Pauline Books and Media, 1998).

37. Benedict XVI, *The Word of the Lord: Verbum Domini* (Boston: Pauline Books and Media, 2010), §16.

38. Ricoeur, "Phenomenology and Hermeneutics," 31–32.

39. Ricoeur, "The Hermeneutical Function of Distanciation," 83.

40. Ibid., 87–88, and Ricoeur, "Philosophical Hermeneutics and Biblical Hermeneutics," in *From Text to Action*, 92.

41. Ricoeur, "Philosophical Hermeneutics and Biblical Hermeneutics," 93.

42. Romano, *Au coeur de la raison*, 883–84 [English—Trans.].

43. René Descartes, *Discourse on Method, Optics, Geometry, and Metereology*, trans. Paul J. Olscamp (Indianapolis: Hackett, 2001), 12.

44. St. Bonaventure, *Collations on the Six Days*, trans. Jose de Vinck, Works of Bonaventure 5 (Quincy, Mass.: Franciscan Press, 1995), bk. XIII, §12, v. 390.

45. See my commentary "Reading the Book," in Falque, *God, the Flesh, and the Other: From Irenaeus to Duns Scotus*, trans. William Christian Hackett (Evanston: Northwestern University Press, 2014), 314–17.

46. Hugh of Saint-Victor, *De diebus tribus* (Did. VI, PL. 176, 814B), as cited in St. Bonaventure, *Works of St. Bonaventure: Breviloquium*, ed. Robert J. Karris, trans. Dominic V. Monti, Bonaventure Texts in Translation 9 (St. Bonaventure, N.Y.: Franciscan Institute Publications, 2005), 63.

47. Levinas, *Alterity and Transcendence*, trans. Michael B. Smith (New York: Columbia University Press, 1999), 173 (my emphasis).

48. See Levinas, *Of God Who Comes to Mind*, trans. Bettina Bergo (Stanford: Stanford University Press, 1998).

49. Rodolphe Calin, *Levinas et l'exception du soi* (Paris: Presses Universitaires de France, 2005), 334, 343.

50. Levinas, *Beyond the Verse: Talmudic Readings and Lectures*, trans. Gary D. Mole (London: Athlone Press, 1994), x, 121.

51. Levinas, *In the Time of the Nations*, trans. Michael B. Smith (London: Athlone Press, 1994), 114.

52. Calin, *Levinas et l'exception du soi*, 336–37.

53. Levinas, *In the Time of the Nations*, 41.

54. Claudel, "Second Ode: The Spirit and the Water," in *Five Great Odes*, trans. E. Lucie-Smith (London: Rapp and Carroll, 1967), 29 (my emphasis).

55. Heidegger, *On the Way to Language*, trans. Joan Stambaugh (New York: Harper and Row, 1971), 12.

56. Ibid., 9–10.

57. Chrétien, *The Ark of Speech*, trans. Andrew Brown (New York: Routledge, 2004), 2.

58. See my chapter on Irenaeus, "The Ark of the Flesh," in Falque, *God, the Flesh, and the Other*.

59. Maurice Merleau-Ponty, "Faith and Good Faith" [1945], in *Sense and Non-Sense*, trans. H. L. Dreyfus and P. A. Dreyfus (Evanston: Northwestern University Press, 1992), 174. See also the commentary in the substantive article by Emmanuel de Saint-Aubert, "L'incarnation change tout," *Transversalités* 112 (October–December 2009): 147–86.

60. Marcel Jousse, *L'anthropologie du geste*, vol. 2, *La manducation de la parole* (Paris: Gallimard, 1975), 31–60. For the image of the two tables of the word and the Eucharist, see the Second Vatican Council, *Dei Verbum*, §21.

61. Benedict XVI, *Verbum Domini*, §55.

62. See the chapter "Incorporation," §30, in Falque, *Les noces de l'agneau: Essai philosophique sur le corps et l'eucharistie* (Paris: Cerf, 2011), 348–54.

63. Pope Paul VI, *Decree on the Ministry and Life of Priests: Presbyterorum Ordinis* (Second Vatican Council: December 7, 1965), no. 18. A complement to this text is found in the *Constitution on the Sacred Liturgy: Sacrosanctum Concilium* (also promulgated by Pope Paul VI, December 4, 1963), no. 56: "The two parts which, in a certain sense, go to make up the Mass, namely, the liturgy of the word and the eucharistic liturgy, are so closely connected with each other that they form but one single act of worship."

64. St. Jerome, "Homily 57 on Psalm 147," in *The Homilies of St. Jerome*, trans. Marie Liguori Ewald, Fathers of the Church (Washington D.C.: The Catholic University of America Press, 1964), 1:410; Origen, *On First Principles*, with a new foreword by John C. Cavadini, trans. G. W. Butterworth (Notre

Dame: Ave Maria Press, 2013), IV.2.8; as cited in Benedict XVI, *Post-Synodal Apostolic Exhortation Verbum Domini*, §56.

65. Edmund Husserl, *Ideas: General Introduction to Pure Phenomenology* (New York: Routledge, 2012), 180: "On [transcendental phenomenology's] own ground it must come to the point, not of treating experiences as so much dead material . . . but rather . . . as *intentional*, and that *purely through its eidetic essence as 'consciousness-of.'*"

66. This return to Heidegger's important notion of "factical life" will be advanced further in the context of a "hermeneutic of the decision"; see Chap. 4, "Kerygma and Decision," especially §13b: "Philosophy of religion and philosophy of religious experience."

67. This is the justification of the approach developed in my first work, *Le passeur de Gethsémani*, in particular in Part 2, "Le Christ devant l'angoisse de la mort" (65–121). This position, in reality, was firmly taken already very early on: "Contre toute prétention par trop hégémonique de la théologie herméneutique aujourd'hui—et sans que l'horizon d'une *phénoménologie descriptive* n'occulte néanmoins le necessaire processus de parole par lequel elle ne peut accéder à la description—le Christ "entrant en agonie" (*agonia*) verbalise moins, selon nous, de facon langagière l'épreuve métaphysique de son angoisse qu'il ne l'exhibe au contraire par le seul *vécu charnel* de sa "sueur devenue comme des caillots de sang tombant à terre"; 138 (Lk 22: 44).

68. Ricoeur, "Philosophical Hermeneutics and Biblical Hermeneutics," 90 (my emphasis).

69. Heidegger, "The Concept of Logos," §7, in *Being and Time*, 28; cf. Aristotle, *De interpretatione* I.4.17a3–7, in *The Complete Works of Aristotle: Rev. Oxford Translation*, ed. Jonathan Barnes (Princeton: Princeton University Press, 1984), 26. Especially: "Every sentence is significant (not as a tool but, as we said, by convention), but not every sentence is a statement-making sentence, but only those in which there is truth or falsity. There is not truth or falsity in every sentence: a prayer is a sentence but is neither true nor false" (26). John Scot Erigenus provides a particularly pertinent illustration of this claim when he makes the apophantic (manifestation in discourse) a condition for the apophatic (God beyond language)—see Chap. 2, "Dieu phénomène [Jean Scot Erigène]," in Falque, *God, the Flesh, and the Other*; see especially "L'apophantique ou l'écrin du logos" (107–23).

70. Ricoeur, "Hermeneutical Function of Distanciation," in *From Text to Action*, 86.

71. Chrétien, "Allowing Oneself to Be Read Authoritatively by the Holy Scripture," in *Under the Gaze of the Bible*, 6–22.

72. Ibid., 10 and 11 (my emphasis).

73. Claudel, *Essence of the Bible*, 34.

74. Ibid., 10.

75. Joseph Conrad, "Preface," in *The Nigger of the Narcissus: A Tale of the Forecastle* (New York: Doubleday, Page, 1916), x–xi.

76. Hugh of Saint-Victor, "La parole de Dieu," in *Six Opuscules Spirituels*, Sources chrétiennes, no. 155, trans. Roger Baron (Paris: Les Éditions du Cerf, 1969), 63. Also see my forthcoming commentary on medieval philosophy in "Hughes de Saint-Victoire: Lire le Monde au Moyen-Âge," *Actes du colloque de la Société internationale de philosophie médiévale* (Paris: Centre Sèvres, 2007).

2. For a Hermeneutic of the Body and the Voice

1. Hugh of Saint-Victor, "La parole de Dieu," in *Six opuscules spirituels*, Sources chrétiennes, no. 155, trans. Roger Baron (Paris: Les Éditions du Cerf, 1969), 63.

2. See Falque, *Les noces de l'agneau: Essai philosophique sur le corps et l'eucharistie* (Paris: Les Éditions du Cerf, 2011)—especially the Introduction, "L'embardée de la chair" (21–38) and Chap. 1, "La philosophie à la limite" (39–72).

3. A formula from Servius, as cited in Giorgio Agamben, *Language and Death: The Place of Negativity*, trans. Karen Pinkus and Michael Hardt (Minneapolis: University of Minnesota Press, 2006), 32. This work and seminar are especially exemplary and suggestive for reflection on this monumental "forgetfulness of the voice," even in philosophy itself.

4. Denis Vasse, "Preface" to Jean-Louis Chrétien's *L'arbre de la voix* (Paris: Bayard, 2010), 11 (my emphasis) [English—trans.].

5. Jacques Derrida, *Voice and Phenomenon: Introduction to the Problem of the Sign in Husserl's Phenomenology*, trans. Leonard Lawlor (Evanston: Northwestern University Press, 2011). The first French edition was *La voix et le phénomène* (Paris: Presses Universitaires de France, 1967); also, see Chrétien, *La voix nue: Phénoménologie de la promesse* (Paris: Éditions de Minuit, 1990).

6. Derrida, *Voice and Phenomenon*, 67–68.

7. Ibid., 60–66.

8. Aristotle, *De interpretatione* 1.16a.3–4, in *The Complete Works of Aristotle: The Revised Oxford Translation*, ed. Jonathan Barnes, Bollingen Series (Princeton: Princeton University Press, 1984), 1:25.

9. Derrida, *Of Grammatology*, trans. Gayatri Chakravorty Spivak (Baltimore: Johns Hopkins University Press, 1997), 3.

10. Derrida, "Plato's Pharmacy," in *Dissemination*, trans. Barbara Johnson (Chicago: University of Chicago Press, 1983), 67–129. Note especially: "But before, as it were, his adequacy of replacement and usurpation, Thoth is essentially the god of writing" (143) and "Thus it is that the god of writing can become the god of the creative speech" (173n29).

11. Agamben, *Language and Death*, 39 (my emphasis); see also a critique of Derrida by way of his opposition to Merleau-Ponty as relayed by Françoise Dastur, "La grammatologie," in Chap. 1, "Chair et langage," in *Chair et langage: Essais sur Merleau-Ponty* (Versanne: Encre-Marine, 2001), 21–25.

12. Martin Heidegger, *Being and Time*, trans. Joan Stambaugh (Albany: State University of New York Press, 2010), 284 (my emphasis).

13. Ibid., 255 (my emphasis).

14. Ibid., 258 (author's emphasis).

15. Agamben, *Language and Death*, 37.

16. Chrétien, *La voix nue*, 7.

17. Maurice Merleau-Ponty, *Signs*, trans. Richard McCleary (Evanston: Northwestern University Press, 1964), 42–43 (emphasis in text). This thought was already germinating in Chap.6, "The Body as Expression and Speech," in Merleau-Ponty, *Phenomenology of Perception*, trans. Donald Landes (New York: Routledge, 2012), 179–244 and developed later in "The Specter of a Pure Language," in his *The Prose of the World*, trans. John O'Neill (Evanston: Northwestern University Press, 1973), 3–8.

18. Although not developed in its many facets, the syntagm of the "raw voice" was proposed by Jean-Max Dussert in his "La voix crue" (master's thesis, Institut catholique de Paris, 2002).

19. Merleau-Ponty, *Signs*, 43.

20. Charles Péguy, "Dialogue de l'histoire et de l'âme charnelle," in *Oeuvres en prose completes* (Paris: Gallimard, 1992), 3:727–28 [English—Trans.].

21. See Dussert, "La voix crue," for an account of the true covering over of the voice by the why; also, cf. Ps. 22:2: "My God, my God, why have you forsaken me? Why are you so far from saving me, so far from my cries of anguish?"

22. I will not further develop this theological perspective here, since it is not the primary goal of the present essay. Others can carry on the task. For a full treatment of the cry of the passion, see Falque, "L'excès du corps souffrant," in *Le passeur de Gethsémani: Angoisse, souffrance, et mort* (Paris: Les Éditions du Cerf, 1999), 157–60.

23. Hugh of Saint-Victor, "La parole de Dieu," 63. See formula cited above, concluding Chap. 1, fn 76 [English—Trans.].

24. Cf. Blaise Pascal, "Letter to Mademoiselle De Roanez," in *Letters and Other Minor Works*, trans. M. L. Booth and O. W. Wright (New York: Digireads. com, 2011), 22: "[God] remained concealed under the veil of nature that covers him till the Incarnation, and when it was necessary that he should appear, he concealed himself still the more in covering himself with humanity. . . . And finally, when he wished to fulfill the promise that he made to his apostles to remain with men until his final coming, he chose to remain in the strangest and most obscure secret of all, which are the species of the Eucharist."

25. As translated by Eginhard Peter Meijering, in his *Hilary of Poitiers, On the Trinity: De trinitate* 1.1–19, 2, 3 (Leiden: E. J. Brill, 1982), 96; my Latin emphasis in brackets.

26. St. Irenaeus, "Against Heresies," book V, chap. XV, §4, in *Anti-Nicene Fathers*, ed. Alexander Roberts and James Donaldson (Peabody: Hendrickson, 1996), 1:544 [revisions on basis of French—Trans.].

27. Derrida, *Voice and Phenomenon: Introduction to the Problem of the Sign in Husserl's Phenomenology*, trans. Leonard Lawlor (Evanston: Northwestern University Press, 2011), 68.

28. Agamben, "Language and History," in *Collected Essays in Philosophy*, ed. and trans. Daniel Heller-Roazen (Stanford: Stanford University Press, 1999), 107.

29. Ibid.

30. Aristotle, *De interpretatione* 1.16a.3–4.

31. Agamben, *Infancy and History: Essays on the Destruction of Experience*, trans. Liz Heron (London: Verso, 1993), 9.

32. As translated by Agamben in *Language and Death*, 38.

33. Aristotle, *Politics* (2.1253a.9–11), in *The Complete Works of Aristotle*, Rev. Oxford Translation, ed. Jonathan Barnes, Bollingen Series (Princeton: Princeton University Press, 1984), 2:1988.

34. Ibid., 2.1253a.15.

35. Falque, *Les noces de l'agneau*, §15, 158, especially 157–61 as source of premises for this present work.

36. Agamben, *Infancy and History*, 8–9.

37. Agamben, *Language and Death*, 108 (author's italics).

38. See Falque, Chap. 5, "The Resurrection Changes Everything," in *The Metamorphosis of Finitude*, trans. George Hughes (New York: Fordham University Press, 2012), 62–80, for further discussion of this movement of abandon and transformation as ends of the Resurrection.

39. Franz Kafka, *The Metamorphosis*, trans. Willa Muir and Edwin Muir (New York: Schocken, 1946), 13.

40. Gilles Deleuze and Félix Guattari, *Kafka: Toward a Minor Literature*, trans. Dana Polan (Minneapolis: University of Minneapolis Press, 1986), 21.

41. [*La voix corporante.*]

42. Aristotle, *On the Soul* (8.420b.29–34), in *Complete Works of Aristotle*, 670.

43. Descartes, *Discourse on Method, Optics, Geometry, and Metereology*, trans. Paul J. Olscamp (Indianapolis: Hackett, 2001), 46: "For it is a very remarkable thing that no men are so dull and stupid—not excepting even the insane—that they are not capable of *arranging various words together*, and making *discourse* from them through which they *make their thoughts understood*; and on the contrary, there is *no other animal*, no matter how perfect and happily born, which can do the same thing" (my emphasis).

44. Agamben, *Infancy and History*, 8.

45. See Falque, "La vie corporante," in *Les noces de l'agneau*, §4, 63–72: *Leiben* is used here more in the Nietzschean sense than the Husserlian.

46. Ibid.

47. Merleau-Ponty, *The Prose of the World*, ed. Claude Lefort, trans. John O'Neill (Evanston: Northwestern University Press, 1973), 140–41.

48. St. Augustine, "Psalm CXL," in *On the Psalms*, trans. J. E. Tweed, in *Nicene and Post-Nicene Fathers*, ed. Philip Schaff, First Series (Buffalo, N.Y.: Christian Literature, 1888), 8:641.

49. "Eucharistic Prayer II," in *The Roman Missal*, trans. International Commission on English in the Liturgy, 3rd typical ed. (Washington D.C.: United States Catholic Conference of Bishops, 2011), 646.

50. *Cathéchisme de l'Église catholique* (Paris: Mame, 1992), no. 1353, 291 [English—Trans.].

51. Augustine, "Psalm LXXXVI," in *On the Psalms*, 410. Note that the English translation of the Latin first names it Psalm 86 and second offers the following translation of the Latin: "Let us therefore recognize *in Him our words, and His words in us.*"

52. Jean-Pierre Sonnet, *Le corps voisé* (Châtelineau: Le Taillis Pré, 2002), 17 [English—Trans.].

3. Always Believing

1. Blaise Pascal, *Pensées*, ed. and trans. Roger Ariew (Indianapolis: Hackett, 2004), 212 (B233/S680/L418).

2. Karl Barth, *Evangelical Theology: An Introduction*, trans. Grover Foley (Grand Rapids: Eerdmans, 1979), 76. In context: "When a man becomes involved in theological science, its object does not allow him to set himself apart from it or to claim independence and autarchic self-sufficiency. . . . This object disturbs him—and not merely from afar, the way a lightning flash on the horizon might disturb one. This object seeks him out and finds him precisely where he stands, and it is just *there* that this object has already sought and found him. It *met, encountered, and challenged him.* It invaded, surprised, and captured him. It assumed control over him. As to himself, the light 'dawned' on him, and he was ushered up from the audience to the stage" (75–76). [Note that the French translation (Geneva: Labor et Fides, 1962) reads, "De son côté, le théologien a été en quelque sorte 'inséré dans le tableau,' tire de la sale de spectacle et jeté sur la scène" (62).]

3. Edmund Husserl, §7, "The World as the Universal Ground of Belief Pregiven for Every Experience of Individual Objects," in *Experience and Judgment*, trans. James Spencer Churchill and Karl Ameriks (Evanston: Northwestern University Press, 1973), 30; also Husserl, §104, "The Doxic Modalities as Modifications," in *Ideas Pertaining to a Pure Phenomenology and a Phenomenological Philosophy (Ideas I)*, trans. F. Kersten (The Hague: Martinus Nijhoff, 1982): "A proper expression is needed which takes account of this special place and blots out every memory of the conventional placing of certainty and other belief-modes on par. We introduce the term *primal belief* or *protodoxa*, by which the intentional retrorelatedness, elaborated by us, of all belief-modalities is suitably expressed" (252). Note that Falque's French translation (Paris: Seuil, 1950) reads the last sentence as: "il permet de marquer de façon adequate la référence intentionelle que nous avons soulignée de toutes les 'modalités de croyance' à la croyance-mère" (358).

4. Maurice Merleau-Ponty, *The Visible and the Invisible*, trans. Alphonso Lingis (Evanston: Northwestern University Press, 1969), 35.

5. Ibid., 3, editor note 1: "Opposite the title of the section, the author notes: 'Notion of faith to be specified. It is not faith in the sense of decision but in the sense of what is before any position, animal and [?] faith.'"

6. While they are not clearly articulated in relation to each other or at least in the same way that we are doing so here, a significant exposition of the set of modalities of "believing" (from the "believe that" to the "believe in") appears in Paul Ricoeur, "Croyance," in *Encyclopaedia universalis* (Paris: 1978), 5:171–76. For a yet more complete account with excellent phenomenological analyses, see Philippe Fontaine, *La croyance* (Paris: Ellipses, 2003).

7. Charles Péguy, "Note conjointe sur M. Descartes," in *Oeuvres en prose complètes* (Paris: Gallimard, 1992), 1280 [English—Trans.].

8. Husserl, §32, "The phenomenological ἐποχή," in *Ideas I*, 61. As for the difference between Husserl's and Descartes's approaches, see the old but excellent contribution by Alexandre Löwit, "L'épochê de Husserl et le doute de Descartes," *Revue de Métaphysique et de Morale* (October 1957): 399–415.

9. Ibid. (author's italics)—Husserl's critique of the passage from the *cogito* to the *res cogitans* is found in §10, "Digression: Descartes' Failure to Make the Transcendental Turn," in *Cartesian Meditations*, trans. Dorion Cairns (The Hague: Martinus Nijhoff, 1950), 23–24.

10. Husserl, Chap. 2, "Universal Structures of Pure Consciousness," in *Ideas I*, 171.

11. Alfred Schütz, *Le chercheur et le quotidien: Phénoménologie des sciences sociales* (Paris: Klincksiek, 1987), 1:229, as cited and commented by Bruce Bégout, in "Alfred Schütz et l'épochê de l'attitude naturelle," *Revue Alter* 11 (2003): 165–92. Bégout writes, "Phenomenology taught us the concept of the phenomenological epoché or the suspension of our belief in the reality of the world, as the means to *surpass* the natural attitude by radicalizing the Cartesian method of philosophical doubt. We suggest that in the natural attitude, a human being also use a *specific kind of epoché*, altogether other than the phenomenologist's. *He does not suspend his belief in the external world and its objects, but on the contrary, suspends all doubt about their existence.* He puts in parentheses the doubt that the world and its objects may be other than the way they appear to him. We propose to call that epoché, the *epoché of the natural attitude*" (179; my emphasis).

12. Husserl, *The Crisis of European Sciences and Transcendental Phenomenology*, trans. David Carr (Evanston: Northwestern University Press, 1970), 241.

13. Husserl, *Experience and Judgment*, 30 (author's italics).

14. Martin Heidegger, *The Phenomenology of Religious Life*, trans. Matthias Fritsch and Jennifer Anna Gosetti-Ferencei (Bloomington: Indiana University Press, 2010), 248. See also the commentary by Sylvain Camilleri, "Foi," in *Phénoménologie de la religion et herméneutique théologique dans la pensée du jeune Heidegger* (Dordrecht: Springer, 2007), 447–68.

15. See the Credo of the Council of Nicea. With regard to the interpretation of St. Paul's notion of "believing," see Giorgio Agamben, "Belief In," in *The Time That Remains: A Commentary on the Letter to the Romans*, trans. Patricia Dailey (Stanford: Stanford University Press, 2005), 126–29. (Agamben builds on Bultmann's *Theology of the New Testament* [New York: Scribner, 1951].)

16. Heidegger, §31, "Da-sein as Understanding," in *Being and Time*, trans. Joan Stambaugh (Albany: State University of New York Press, 2010), 135.

17. Ibid., 140.

18. Ibid., §32, "Understanding and Interpretation," 140–41. See also Jean Greisch's commentary, *Ontologie et temporalité* (Paris: Presses Universitaires de France, 1994), 188.

19. The status of the me in the dative—"to me"—is clearly defined by Jean-Luc Marion in book V, "The Gifted," in *Being Given*, trans. Jeffrey L. Kosky (Stanford: Stanford University Press, 2002), 248–319; see especially §25, "The Aporias of the 'Subject': From the Subject to the Receiver," 248–61.

20. Hans-Georg Gadamer, "The Hermeneutical Circle and the Problem of Prejudices," in *Truth and Method*, trans., rev. Joel Weinsheimer and Donald G. Marshall (New York: Continuum, 1989, 2004), 268.

21. See Emmanuel Falque, §5, "The Preemption of the Infinite," in *The Metamorphosis of Finitude*, trans. George Hughes (New York: Fordham University Press, 2012), 16–18.

22. Gadamer, "Hermeneutical Circle," 272 (my italics). See also Jean Grondin's excellent commentary in *Introduction à Hans-Georg Gadamer* (Paris: Cerf, 1999), 128: "Gadamer gives up so little of the ideal of a critical elucidation of prejudices that he himself will critique a Cartesian prejudice: the prejudice against prejudices!" (my italics [English—Trans.]).

23. Merleau-Ponty, *Signs*, trans. Richard McCleary (Evanston: Northwestern University Press, 1964), 41–42.

24. Gadamer, "Hermeneutical Circle," 273.

25. Gadamer, "Prejudices as Conditions of Understanding," in *Truth and Method*, 277–304; Heidegger, §35, "Idle Talk"; §36, "Curiosity"; and §37, "Ambiguity," in *Being and Time*, 157–63.

26. Ludwig Wittgenstein, *On Certainty*, ed. G. E. M. Anscombe and Georg Henrik von Wright, trans. Denis Paul and G. E. M. Anscombe (New York: Harper and Row, 1972), 60. See the commentary on indubitable basic beliefs by Roger Pouivet, *Qu'est-ce que croire?* (Paris: Vrin, 2003), 77.

27. Wittgenstein, *On Certainty*, 60, 62.

28. Husserl, Appendice XVIII (to §34, "Exposition of the Problem of a Science of the Life-World"), in *La crise des sciences européennes et la phénoménologie transcendentale (Krisis)* (Paris: Gallimard, 1962), 515. [This Appendix is not included in the English volume: English—Trans.]

29. See a twofold illustration in Bégout's commentary on Husserl's *Krisis*, in *Découverte du quotidien* (Paris: Allia, 2005), 510–14; see also Tzvetan Todorov, *Éloge du quotidien: Essai sur la peinture hollandaise du XVIIIe siècle* (Paris: Seuil, 1997), in particular Chap. 1, "Le genre du quotidien," 9–26.

30. Merleau-Ponty, *Signs*, 146.

31. Merleau-Ponty, *Visible and the Invisible*, 30.

32. Merleau-Ponty, *Signs*, 146.

33. Jean-Yves Lacoste, *Experience and the Absolute: Disputed Questions on the Humanity of Man* (New York: Fordham University Press, 1994), 105.

34. Husserl, §58, "The Transcendency, God, Excluded," in *Ideas I*, 134. See also Lacoste's formula "Atheism of Life," in *Experience and the Absolute*, 105.

35. Heidegger, *Intérprétations phénoménologiques d'Aristote*, trans. J. Fr. Courtine (Mauvezin: T.E.R, 1992), 27.14 and 53.15; cited in Jean Greisch's commentary "Facticité et atheism," in *L'arbre de vie et l'arbre du savoir* (Paris: Cerf, 2000), 216–19. [Trans. note: the English translation lacks these appendices' notes; cf. Heidegger, *Phenomenological Interpretations of Aristotle: Initiation into Phenomenological research*, trans. Richard Rojcewicz (Bloomington: Indiana University Press, 2001), 148–49.]

36. Greisch, *L'arbre de vie et l'arbre du savoir*, 217.

37. Françoise Dastur, "Heidegger et la théologie," in *Revue Philosophique de Louvain* 92, nos. 2–3 (1994): 245 (my emphasis) [English—Trans.]. This suspicion of "crypto-theology" (accusing Heidegger of concealing his theological roots) maintains him within the theological sphere; cf. Karl Löwith, *My Life in Germany before and after 1933: A Report*, trans. Elizabeth King (Champaign: University of Illinois Press, 1994), 31. This is a clear statement of Heidegger's theological sources that has common currency today with the "Christianizing" interpretation of his works, which is certainly based in this texts (see, for example, Heidegger, *On the Way to Language*, trans. Peter D. Hertz (New York: HarperCollins, 1971) but which I do not think can establish or legitimize some compatibility or non-incompatibility between "existential atheism" and "philosophy of religion."

38. Emmanuel Levinas, *Totality and Infinity: An Essay on Exteriority*, trans. Alphonso Lingis (Pittsburgh: Duquesne University Press, 1969), 148.

39. Ibid., 58.

40. Aquinas, *Summa theologica*, I.a., q.2, a.1, resp.

41. Ibid., I.a., q.2 a.2 ad.1.

42. I am here synthesizing elements from Falque, "Limite théologique et finitude phénoménologique chez saint Thomas d'Aquin," *Revue des Sciences Philosophiques et Théologiques* 92 (July–September 2008): 527–56.

43. Karl Rahner, *Foundations of Christian Faith*, trans. William V. Dych (New York: Seabury Press, 1978), 21.

44. Ibid.

45. Ibid., 24 and 25.

46. See Falque, Chapter 1, "La philosophie à la limite," in *Les noces de l'agneau* (Paris: Cerf, 2011), 39–72.

47. Husserl, *Philosophie première*, vol. 2, *Théorie de la réduction phénoménologique*, trans. Arion L. Kelkel (Paris: Presses Universitaires de France, 1972), 67 [English—Trans.].

48. Husserl, *Idées directrices pour une phénoménologie et philosophie phénoménologique*, trans. Paul Ricoeur (Paris: Gallimard, 1950), 162n1 [footnote absent in English; English here by translator]. Thank you to my friend and colleague Jérôme de Gramont for pointing it out.

49. Husserl, §49, "Absolute Consciousness as the Residuum after the Annihilation of the World," in *Ideas I*, 109–12.

50. Levinas, "Insomnia," in *Existence and Existents*, trans. Alphonso Lingis (Pittsburgh: Duquesne University Press, 1978), 61; see also its counterpart in Levinas, "Existence without Existents," in *Time and the Other*, trans. Richard A. Cohen (Pittsburgh: Duquesne University Press, 1987), 48–49.

51. Levinas, "Insomnia," 51.

52. Ibid., 52.

53. Merleau-Ponty, "La nature ou le monde du silence," in *Maurice Merleau-Ponty: La nature ou le monde du silence*, ed. Emmanuel de Saint-Aubert (Paris: Hermann, 2008), 53.

54. Merleau-Ponty, *Visible and the Invisible*, 140 and 147.

55. Thanks to Jérôme de Gramont for indicating this rapprochement between Merleau-Ponty and Maurice Blanchot's notion of the "neuter"; see de Gramont, "Blanchot et Merleau-Ponty," in *Blanchot et la phénoménologie* (Paris: Corlevour, 2011), 88 [English—Trans.].

56. Merleau-Ponty, *Phenomenology of Perception*, trans. Donald A. Landes (New York: Routledge, 2013), lxxii; and Merleau-Ponty, *The Eye and the Spirit* in *the Primacy of Perception*, trans. William Cobb, ed. James Edie (Evanston: Northwestern University Press, 1964), 160.

57. Husserl, *Cartesian Meditations* [§16, 33] as reformulated by Merleau-Ponty in *Visible and the Invisible*, 4: "It is the things themselves, from the depths of their silence, that [philosophy] wishes to bring to expression." [Trans. note: Falque cites Merleau-Ponty's "elle veut conduire à l'expression," *Le visible et l'invisible* (Paris: Gallimard, 1964), 18, as "*la parole* veut conduire," although the immediate antecedent is "la philosophie."]

58. This perspective was fully developed in Falque, "Descente dans l'abîme," in *Les noces de l'agneau*, 39–124. With regard to the world of silence, see the accurate (but unfortunately forgotten) contribution of Max Picard, *The World of Silence*, trans. Stanley Godwin, with a Preface by Gabriel Marcel (Chicago: H. Regnery, 1952). Picard was a Jew who converted to Catholicism in the 1930s and followed in the footsteps of Husserl and Max Scheler.

59. Merleau-Ponty, *Visible and the Invisible*, 148.

60. Levinas, *Existence and Existents*, 55 and 56 (my emphasis).

61. Chrétien, *Promesses Furtives* (Paris: Minuit, 2004), 35 [English.—Trans.].

4. Kerygma and Decision

1. Cf. Emmanuel Falque, Chap. 5, "Resurrection Changes Everything," in *The Metamorphosis of Finitude*, trans. George Hughes (New York: Fordham University Press, 2012), 111–30.

2. Claude Romano, *Event and Time*, trans. Stephen E. Lewis (New York: Fordham University Press, 2014), 188.

3. Paul Ricoeur, "Philosophical Hermeneutics and Biblical Hermeneutics," in *From Text to Action: Essays in Hermeneutics*, trans. Kathleen Blamey

and John B. Thompson (Evanston: Northwestern University Press, 1991), 2:92 and 97.

4. Karl Barth, *Evangelical Theology: An Introduction*, trans. Grover Foley (Grand Rapids: Eerdmans, 1979), 104.

5. René Marlé, "Y a-t-il un problem catholique de la demythization?" in "Problema della Demittizzazione," by Enrico Castelli, *Archivio di Filosofia* 1–2 (1961): 158–59 (my emphasis).

6. Ricoeur, "Preface to Bultmann," in *The Conflict of Interpretations: Essays in Hermeneutics*, ed. Don Ihde (Evanston: Northwestern University Press, 1974), 382.

7. Rudolf Bultmann, *Interpreting Faith for the Modern Era*, ed. Roger A. Johnson (Minneapolis: Fortress Press, 1991), 300 (my emphasis).

8. Bultmann, "The Historicity of Man and Faith," in *Existence and Faith: Shorter Writings of Rudolf Bultmann*, trans. Schubert M. Ogden (New York: Meridian, 1960), 107–8.

9. Contra this ever repeated, unfounded, and even often thoughtless privileging of passivity, see Falque, Chap. 1, "La philosophie à la limite," in *Les noces de l'agneau* (Paris: Cerf, 2011), 39–72.

10. Henry Duméry, *Critique et religion: Problèmes de method en philosophie de la religion* (Paris: Société d'Édition d'Énseignment Supérieur, 1957), 18 [English—Trans.].

11. See Jean Greisch (building on Duméry), "Philosophie de la religion et philosophie religieuse," in *Le Buisson ardent et les lumières de la raison* (Paris: Cerf, 2002), 1:34–36. Despite the belated decision, I prefer the syntagm "philosophy of religious experience" to "religious philosophy"—the second having always been rightly the object of many doubts, including by those who chose to use it; see Jean Hering, *Phénoménologie et philosophie religieuse: Érude sur la thérie de la connaissance religieuse* (Paris: Felix Alcan, 1925), 7: "We could not bring ourselves to use indiscriminately the designations 'religious philosophy' and 'philosophy of religion' as many authors have done" (see Chap. 2, "Comment la philosophie religieuse est tombée dans le psychologisme," 8–15). Indeed, "philosophy" cannot be said to be "religious," without running the risk of psychologizing, but only "experience," which it examines, whether or not it is shared by the reader of an author who could not himself deny it (for example, Pascal, Kierkegaard).

12. Martin Heidegger, *The Phenomenology of Religious Life*, trans. Matthias Fritsch and Jennifer Anna Gosetti-Ferencei (Bloomington: Indiana University Press, 2010), 14.

13. See also the commentary by Sylvain Camilleri, *Phénoménologie de la religion et l'herméneutique théologique dans la pensée due jeune Heidegger: Commentaire analytique des fondements philosophiques de la mystique médiévale (1916–1919)* (Dordrecht: Springer Science and Business Media, 2007), 85; Google ebook, https://books.google.com/books?id=qrY_vPwJKMMC&printsec =frontcover&source=gbs_ge_summary_r&cad=0#v=onepage&q=dames &f=false. Further, the title change of vol. 60 of the *Gesamtausgabe* from "Phenom-

enology of Religious Consciousness" to "The Phenomenology of Religious Life" is explained by the editor, indicating Heidegger's notebooks: "Later the word 'consciousness' is crossed out by Heidegger and replaced with the word 'life'" ("Afterword of the Editor of the Lecture Course Summer Semester 1921 and of the Outlines and Sketches 1918–19," in *The Phenomenology of Religious Life*, 259).

14. See that true discourse on the method of "the phenomenological investigation of religious consciousness" found in Heidegger's lectures of 1918–19 (not held), on "The Philosophical Foundations of Medieval Mysticism" in *Phenomenology of Religious Life*, 231–33. He sets forth negative and positive definitions of a phenomenology of religious consciousness, justifications for the philosophical foundations of medieval mysticism, and the determination of the mystical by lived experiences and a theory of life. Perhaps, we would find in the early Heidegger (1915–21) more than elsewhere, or at least *otherwise* than elsewhere, the roots of what has already been underway in my own works for many years, and that Heidegger himself abandoned (with his break with Catholicism in 1921 as accounted in his "Letter to Krebs").

15. Heidegger, *Phenomenology of Religious Life*, 237. [Translator's note: Heidegger outlines the following questions for his lecture: "The question of whether non-religious persons understand the analysis as well is [to be distinguished] from the question of whether only religious persons can have a genuine 'absolute' givenness, and further, whether that somehow limits the 'essential validity' of the analysis, which, after all, is entirely independent of the number of those who recognize and understand."]

16. Ibid., 232.

17. Heidegger, §3, "Factical Life Experience as the Point of Departure," in ibid., 7.

18. Bernard of Clairvaux, "Letter 107: To Henry Murdac," in *The Letters of St. Bernard of Clairvaux*, trans. Bruno Scott James (Kalamazoo: Cistercian Publications, 1998), 156.

19. Søren Kierkegaard, *Kierkegaard's Writings: Either/Or*, Part II, trans. Howard V. Hong and Edna H. Hong (Princeton: Princeton University Press, 1987), 4:176.

20. Ibid., 177.

21. Ibid., 217.

22. Heidegger, §54, "The Problem of the Attestation of an Authentic Existentiell Possibility," in *Being and Time*, trans. Joan Stambaugh (Albany: State University of New York Press, 2010), 248.

23. Ibid., §60, "The Existential Structure of the Authentic Potentiality-of-Being Attested in Conscience," in *Being and Time*, 274. Martineau translates "ein freischwebendes Ich" as "un moi flottant en l'air" (see Heidegger, *Etre et Temps*, trans. Emmanuel Martineau [Paris: Authentica, 1985]) and Vezin as "un je lâché dans le vide" (see Heidegger, Etre et Temps, trans. François Vezin [Paris: Gallimard, 1986]). [Stambaugh's English is "a free-floating ego"—Trans.]

24. Ibid., 272–77, especially 275.

25. Karl Barth, §38, "The Command as the Decision of God," in *Church Dogmatics* II, ed. G. W. Bromley and T. F. Torrance, trans. G. T. Thompson and Harold Knight (Edinburgh: T. and T. Clark, 1957), 2:632 (my emphasis).

26. Ibid. (my emphasis).

27. Bultmann, "The Question of Natural Revelation," in *Essays: Philosophical and Theological*, trans. J. C. G. Greig (New York: Macmillan, 1955), 98 (author's italics).

28. See Falque, "Introduction: L'embardée de la chair," in *Les noces de l'agneau*, 23–38.

29. Romano, *Event and Time*, 188.

30. Ibid.

31. Ibid.; see all of §15, "The Present and Transformation," 185–92.

32. See Jean-Luc Marion, "To Decide on the Gift," in *Being Given: Toward a Phenomenology of Givenness*, trans. Jeffrey L. Kosky (Stanford: Stanford University Press, 2002), 111–13. The ignorance of the gift here is rightly traced to its initial theological context in Marion's work that follows up on *Being Given*; see Marion, *Le croire pour le voir* (Paris: Communio, 2012), 179–93: "Recognition of the Gift"; and in particular, 182–84: "Knowing God's gift" (an interpretation of the Christ's word to the Samaritan woman, "'If you knew the gift of God' (Jn 4:10) . . . , then it would no longer be such precisely if you *knew* it."

33. Aquinas, *Summa contra Gentiles: On the Truth of the Catholic Faith*, book 3, *Providence*, Part I, trans. Vernon J. Bourke (Garden City, N.Y.: Doubleday, 1956), 220 (Chap. 67:1) and 219 (Chap. 66:5).

34. Aquinas, *Summa theologiae, Divine Government*, trans. T. C. O'Brien (New York: Blackfriars, McGraw-Hill, 1975), 14:74–75 (*Ia*. q.105 a.5: "Whether God is active in every agent cause").

35. Nicolas of Cusa, *The Vision of God*, introduction by Evelyn Underhill, trans. Emma Gurney Salter (New York: Frederick Ungar, 1928), 5.

36. Robert Toulemont, *L'essence de la société selon Husserl* (Paris: PUF, 1962), 77 [English—Trans.]; cf. Edmund Husserl, *Cartesian Meditations: An Introduction to Phenomenology*, trans. Dorien Cairns (Norwell: Kluwer, 1999), §53.

37. Nicolas of Cusa, *Vision of God*, 32. Regarding this *transversality of believing* in Nicolas of Cusa as it founds a new mode of horizontality, see Michel de Certeau, "Nicolas de Cues: Le secret d'un regard," *Traverses* 30–31 (March 1984): 70–85: "In this Preface, the model is no longer (or no longer uniquely) biblical. . . . The threshold of *sociality* appears with the help of a *partner* . . . , at first in a coordination of *acting*, then in an agreement with respect to the *saying*" (82, my emphasis) [English—Trans.].

5. "Tiling" and Conversion

1. Jean Greisch, "Les limites de la chair," in *Incarnation: Actes di colloque Enrico Castelli* (Rome: 1988), ed. Marco M. Olivetti (Milan: Biblioteca dell'Archivio di Filosofia, 1999), 61 [English —Trans.].

2. Dominique Janicaud, *Phenomenology and the "Theological Turn": The French Debate*, trans. Bernard G. Prusak (New York: Fordham University Press, 2000), 17.

3. Maurice Merleau-Ponty, *Signs*, trans. Richard McCleary (Evanston: Northwestern University Press, 1964), 70–71 (my emphasis).

4. [In the French, this chapter's title is "*Tuilage et Conversion*." For more on the translation of "tuilage," see the "Opening," footnote 14, for an explanation of the translation of "*tuilage et recouvrement*."—Trans.]

5. Étienne Gilson, *The Philosopher and Theology*, trans. Cécile Gilson (New York: Random House, 1962), 101 (my emphasis). For Gilson—but not for me—this implies necessarily a "Christian philosophy," as if "an apostolic use of philosophy, conceived as an auxiliary to the work of redemption," could be immediately reiterated today, without any other end than "this use made of reason within faith and for it" (186 and 193). Certainly, I agree that one can "philosophize in a Christian way" (198), but it could be neither paradigmatic nor exclusive of all other ways of thinking. More accurately, in philosophizing with and via those who do not philosophize directly in a Christian mode, Christianity will reach the depths of its own humanity as such and see the "power" of the One whom it believes capable of bringing about its transformation.

6. Martin Heidegger, *Phenomenological Interpretations of Aristotle*, trans. Richard Rojcewicz (Bloomington: Indiana University Press, 2001), 146 (as cited by Jean Greisch in "Les limites de la chair," 61).

7. See Emmanuel Kant, *Critique of Pure Reason*, trans. and ed. Paul Guyer and Allen Wood (Cambridge: Cambridge University Press, 1998), 129: "The light dove, in free flight cutting through the air the resistance of which it feels, could get the idea that it could do even better in airless space."

8. Augustine, *Confessions*, trans. Henry Chadwick, Oxford World's Classics (Oxford: Oxford University Press, 2009), 50.

9. Heidegger, *Being and Time*, trans. Joan Stambaugh (Albany: State University of New York Press, 2010), 34. [Note that Falque's French translation reads "plus haut que *l'effectivité* se tient la possibilité" —translator's italics.]

10. Edmund Husserl, §24, "The Principle of Principles," in *Ideas Pertaining to a Pure Phenomenology and a Phenomenological Philosophy (Ideas I)*, trans. F. Kersten (The Hague: Martinus Nijhoff, 1982), 44.

11. Heidegger, §39, "The Problem of a Possible Determination of Finitude in Human Beings," in *Kant and the Problem of Metaphysics*, trans. Richard Taft (Bloomington: Indiana University Press, 1990, 1997), 154.

12. John Duns Scotus, cited and commented by Hannah Arendt, in "Two: Thinking," in *The Life of the Mind*, vol. 1, *Thinking*; vol. 2, *Willing*, ed. Mary McCarthy (New York: Harcourt, Inc., 1977, 1978), 134–35.

13. Scotus, "Prologue of the Ordinatio," trans. Peter L. P. Simpson (unpublished manuscript, December 2012), 9, Adobe PDF file accessed 22 February 2015, http://www.aristotelophile.com/Books/Translations/Scotus%20Prologue.pdf.

14. For a fuller treatment of this interpretation of Scotus, see Chapter 9, "L'autre singulier (Jean Duns Scotus)," in Emmanuel Falque, *Dieu, la chair, et l'autre* (Paris: Presses Universitaires France, 2008), 429–70, and especially "Le cadre de la finitude," 433–45.

15. Thomas Aquinas, "Whether Sacred Doctrine is Nobler than Other Sciences?" *Summa theologica* Ia. q.1 a.5 ad.2 and sed contra (Christian Classics Ethereal Library), Adobe PDF file, 10–11.

16. See Gilson, *Philosopher and Theology*, 101.

17. See Jean-Luc Marion, "Luke: Blessing" in *Prolegomena to Charity*, trans. Stephen E. Lewis (New York: Fordham University Press, 2002), 127–36; also Falque, §6, "Christian Specificity and the Ordinariness of the Flesh," in *The Metamorphosis of Finitude*, trans. George Hughes (New York: Fordham University Press, 2012), 19–20.

18. See St. Bonaventure, *Works of St. Bonaventure: Breviloquium*, Bonaventure Texts in Translation Series, ed. Robert J. Karris, trans. Dominic V. Monti (St. Bonaventure, N.Y.: Franciscan Institute Publications, 2005), 28.

19. Aquinas, *Summa theologica*, Ia. q.1 a.1 ad.2, 5–6.

20. Ibid., Ia. q.1 a.5 ad.2, 11. With regard to the passage through the world (the cosmological ways or arguments) as second-best to the direct way through God (the ontological argument), see Ia. q.2 a.1 resp.: "Therefore I say that this proposition, 'God exists' (*Deus est*) of itself is self-evident (*per se nota est*), for the predicate is the same as the subject. . . . Now because we do not know the essence of God, the proposition is not self-evident to us (*non est nobis per se nota*); but needs to be demonstrated by things that are more known to us (*per ea quae sunt magis nota quoad nos*), though less known in their nature—namely, by effects (*scilicet per effectus*)" (23–24).

21. For a more complete analysis of the human subject determined as a "limited phenomenon," see Falque, "Limite théologique et finitude phénoménologique chez Thomas d'Aquin," in *Revue des Sciences Philosophiques et Théologiques* 92 (July–September 2008): 527–58.

22. Karl Rahner, *Foundations of Christian Faith*, trans. William V. Dych (New York: Seabury Press, 1978), 128 (my emphasis). See also the accurate commentary by Vincent Holzer on how the different understandings of the "anthropological reduction" created the opposition between Rahner and Hans Urs von Balthasar, as explained in Holzer, *Le Dieu Trinité dans l'histoire: Le différend théologique Balthasar-Rahner* (Paris: Cerf, 1995), 333: "If Rahner asserts a measure of divinity for humans, he does not consider it a measure of divinity grasped and understood by humans, but as a measure of the self by God offered to humans."

23. Rahner, *Foundations*, 20.

24. Gilles Deleuze and Felix Guattari, *What Is Philosophy?* trans. Graham Burchell and Hugh Tomlinson (New York: Columbia University Press, 1994), 45 (my emphasis).

25. Aquinas, *Summa contra Gentiles*, book I, *God*, 9:3 and 3:2, trans. Anton C. Pegis (New York: Hanover House, 1955).

26. This argument is powerfully developed and demonstrated by Étienne Vetö, in *Du Christ à la Trinité: Penser les mystères du Christ après Thomas D'Aquin et Balthasar* (Paris: Cerf, 2012), 357: "In a sense, it is a question of reconstructing a model of the movement by which *the primitive faith in the Trinity would have developed out of the mysteries of Christ*" (my emphasis). Vetö finds this very model in Aquinas in the *Summa theologica* II-IIae. q.2, a.8 ad.2: "Before Christ's coming, faith in the Trinity lay hidden in the faith of the learned, but through Christ and the apostles it was shown to the world" (with Vetö's commentary on the "Return to the Question of Revelation of the Trinity" [205–11]) [English of Vetö's text by Trans.].

27. Hans Urs von Balthasar, *The Glory of the Lord: A Theological Aesthetics; Studies in Theological Style: Clerical Styles*, ed. John Riches, trans. Andrew Louth, Francis McDonagh, and Brian McNeil (San Francisco: Ignatius Press, 1984), 2:290.

28. See Falque, "L'hypothèse monadologique," in *Saint Bonaventure et l'entrée de Dieu en théologie: La somme théologique du Breviloquium* (Paris: Vrin, 2000), 75–78.

29. See Falque, *Le passeur de Gethsémani: Angoisse, souffrance, et mort* (Paris: Les Editions du Cerf, 1999), and *Metamorphosis of Finitude*.

30. See Falque, *Les noces de l'agneau*.

31. Georg Wilhelm Friedrich Hegel, "Preface," *The Encyclopedia of the Philosophical Sciences with the Zusätze*, Part I, *The Encyclopedia Logic*, trans. T. F. Geraets, W. A. Suchting, and H. S. Harris, 2nd ed. (Indianapolis: Hackett, 1991), 12.

32. Von Balthasar, "Regagner une philosophie à partir de la théologie," in *Pour une philosophie chrétienne: Philosophie et théologie* (Brussels: Lethielleux, 1984), 175–87 (citation 182–83) [English—Trans.].

33. John-Paul II, "Address of His Holiness John Paul II to the Bishops of Western Canada on their 'Ad Limina' Visit," Sunday, 30 October 1999 (Rome: Libreria Editrice Vaticana, 1999).

34. Heidegger, *Kant and the Problem of Metaphysics*, 4.

35. See Heidegger, "The Theory of Categories and Meaning in Duns Scotus" (Postdoctoral diss., University of Freiburg, 1915). For a contemporary discussion of the status of metaphysics, see my account in Falque, "Après la métaphysique? Le poids de la vie selon saint Augustin," inaugural colloquium of the Institut d'études médiévales (IEM), at the Institut catholique de Paris, June 2010 (Paris: Vrin, forthcoming).

36. See Falque, "Dieu nous éprouve-t-il ou faut-il sauver la providence?" *La Vie spirituelle* 734 (March 2000): 71–91.

37. Von Balthasar, *The Glory of the Lord: A Theological Aesthetics*, vol. 1, *Seeing the Forms*, ed. Joseph Fessia and John Riches, trans. Erasmo Leiva-Merikakis (San Francisco: Ignatius Press, 1982), 313–14.

6. Finally Theology

1. See Étienne Gilson, *The Philosopher and Theology* (New York: Random House, 1962), especially Chapter 5, "Theology Regained" (86–105) and Chapter 6, "Theology Lost" (62–85).

2. See the opening of Emmanuel Falque, *Dieu, la chair, et l'autre* (Paris: Presses Universitaires France, 2008), 35, for the first statement of this leitmotif.

3. See Chapter 5, footnote 5.

4. Blaise Pascal, "The Memorial" (S742/L913), in *Pensées*, ed. and trans. Roger Ariew (Indianapolis: Hackett, 2004), 266.

5. Ibid. (L308/S339), 92.

6. Ibid., 92–93.

7. Ibid., "The Memorial," 266.

8. [Cf. Irenaeus of Lyon, *Against the Heresies*, book 4, XX.4: "Now this is His Word, our Lord Jesus Christ, who in the last times was made a man among men, that he might join the end to the beginning, that is, man to God," and book 4, XX.7: "revealing God indeed to men, but presenting man to God."]

9. Aquinas, *Summa theologica* Ia q.88 a.3 resp.

10. Ibid., Ia q.12 a.11. resp.

11. Ibid., Ia q.12 a.7 resp.

12. Aquinas, Chapter 79, "That through Christ the Resurrection of the Bodies is to Come," in *Summa contra Gentiles*, book IV, no. 10.

13. Aquinas, *Supra sententiorum* I. d.8 q.1 a.2 s.c.2: "Anything that comes to participate in something is in it according to the mode of that with which it is participating [*in eo per modum participantis*] because nothing can be received from beyond one's own measure [*quia nihil potest recipere ultra mensuram suam*]. Thus, since the mode of every created thing is finite, all created things receive a finite being" [English—Trans.]; see the remarkable commentary by Jean-Pierre Torell in his *Saint Thomas maître spiritual* (Paris: Cerf, 1996), 335 (and its possible actualization in André Gravil, *Philosophie et finitude* (Paris: Cerf, 2007), 109).

14. See Falque, "Limite théologique et finitude phénoménologique chez Thomas d'Aquin," *Revue des Sciences Philosophiques et Théologiques*, colloque du Centenaire (July–September 2008), 527–56.

15. See Gilson as cited above in Chapter 5, footnote 5; cf. Aquinas, *Summa theologica* Ia q.1 a.5 ad.2: The sacred sciences "makes use of them as of the lesser, and as handmaidens."

16. See Falque, *Dieu, la chair et l'autre*, 35.

17. See my first contribution to this question, which probably provided the impetus for this present reflection: Falque, "Philosophie et théologie: Nouvelles frontiers," *Études* (February 2006): 201–10, and especially "Philosophe avant tout," 205–9.

18. See Falque, "L'embardée de la chair," especially §1, "Le résidu du corps" (for the "spread body"), in *Les noces de l'agneau*, 23–38.

19. See Tertullian, *Treatise on the Incarnation (or On the Flesh of Christ [De carne Christi])*, ed. and trans. Ernest Evans (New York: S.P.C.K., 1956), IX.3,

137. See also my complementary commentary, Chap. 5, "La consistence de la chair [Tertullien]," in Falque, *Dieu, la chair et l'autre*.

20. Hans Urs von Balthasar, "Regagner une philosophie à partir de la théologie," in *Pour une philosophie chrétienne: Philosophie et théologie* (Brussels: Lethielleux, 1984), 182–83 (my emphasis) [English—Trans.].

21. You will have recognized here two sides, which could be of the same coin: "ancient philosophy" (Pierre Hadot, *Philosophy as a Way of Life: Spiritual Exercises from Socrates to Foucault*, ed. Arnold Davidson, trans. Michael Chase [Malden: Blackwell, 1995]), and "the Christian tradition" (Ignatius of Loyola, *Spiritual Exercises and Selected Works*, ed. George E. Ganss [Mahwah: Paulist Press, 1991]).

22. Suetonius, *Lives of the Caesars*, trans. Catharine Edwards, Oxford World's Classics (Oxford: Oxford University Press, 2000), 16–17. Note that *alea iacta est* is the customary reversal of Suetonius's own *iacta alea est*.

Epilogue: And Then . . . ?

1. See Charles Péguy, *Note conjointe sur M. Descartes*, in *Oeuvres en prose complètes* (Paris: Gallimard and Pléiade, 1992), 1458 [English—Trans.]; and René Descartes, *Philosophical Writings*, trans. Elizabeth Anscombe and Peter Thomas Geach (Indianapolis: Bobbs-Merrill, 1971), 3: "Just as comedians are counseled not to let shame appear on their foreheads, and so put on a mask (*personam induunt*): so likewise, now that I am to mount the stage of the world, where I have been a spectator, I come forward in a mask (*larvatus prodeo*)."

2. For the wordplay (*larvatus prodeo / larvatus pro Deo*), see Léon Brunschvicg, "Mathématique et métaphysique chez Descartes," in *Revue de Métaphysique et de Morale* 34, no. 3 (1927): 323. He writes, "Descartes will thus confide to his public that he resolved to conceal everything in shadows according to the saying whose ingenious turn of phrase was so quickly turned against him, but with a little charity, whose true intention can readily be reestablished: *larvatus pro Deo*" [English—Trans.].

3. Ovid, "Tristia," in *The Poems of Exile: Tristia and the Black Sea*, trans. Peter Green (Berkeley: University of California Press, 1994), 6: "when you are admitted to my inner sanctum, and reach your own house, the curved bookcase, you will see your brothers there ranged in order, all, whom the same careful study crafted. The rest of the crowd will *show* their titles *openly* [*ostendet apertos*], carrying their names on their *exposed faces* (*et sua detecta nomina fronte geret*)."

4. Paul Ricoeur, *Critique and Conviction*, trans. Kathleen Blamey (New York: Columbia University Press, 1998), 2. See also the accurate observation by Isabelle Bochet, precisely on account of such a division, in *Augustin dans la pensée de Paul Ricoeur* (Paris: Facultés Jésuites de Paris, 2004), 100: "Ricoeur notably inflects Augustine's conceptions with his constant concern to maintain the distinction between faith and philosophy" [English—Trans.].

5. Stanislas Breton, "La querelle des denominations," in *Heidegger et la question de Dieu*, ed. Richard Kearney and Joseph O'Leary (Paris: Grasset, 1980), 268 (my emphasis) [English—Trans.].

Index

162nn16,21,25, 163nn34,37–39,
164nn52,57,59, 177n19, 182n32,
184n17
Marlé, René 180n5
Merleau-Ponty, Maurice 6, 19, 48,
61–62, 71, 79–81, 86–87, 89–91,
93, 95–97, 112, 123, 144, 170n59,
172n11, 173nn17,19, 174n47, 175n4,
177nn23,30–32, 179nn53–57,59,
183n3

Nicolas of Cusa 115–17, 182nn35,37

O'Leary, Joseph 187n5
Olivetti, Marco M. 182n1
Origen 30, 50, 167n4, 170n64
Ovid 157, 187n3

Pagazzi, Giovanni Cesare 169n33
Pannenberg, Wolfhart 152
Pascal, Blaise 3, 78, 80, 92, 104, 106, 121,
130, 134, 142–44, 151, 164n52,
173n24, 175n1, 180n11, 186n4
Péguy, Charles xi, 4, 63, 80, 157, 173n20,
176n7, 187n1
Picard, Max 179n58
Pouivet, Roger 177n26

Rahner, Karl 2, 11, 78, 93–94, 97, 126,
139, 178n43, 184n22
Ricoeur, Paul 11–12, 18, 20, 29–52,
54–56, 58, 73, 86, 100–2, 138,

140–41, 148, 166n14, 168nn9–
17,21–28, 169nn31–32,35,38–41,
171nn68,70, 176n6, 178n48, 179n3,
180n6, 187n4
Romano, Claude 8, 20, 35, 42, 103,
112–13, 168n19, 169n42, 179n2,
182n29

Saint-Aubert, Emmanuel de 170n59,
179n53
Saudan, Alain 161n6, 164nn55,68,
165n8
Schütz, Alfred 82, 176n11
Servius 57, 172n3
Sonnet, Jean-Pierre 175n52
Suetonius 15, 53, 164n2, 187n22

Tertullian 18, 19, 145, 150, 186n19
Thomas Aquinas 3, 9–10, 19, 23, 32, 84,
92, 114, 125, 127–32, 134, 136–37,
139, 145–48, 164nn51–53, 166n16,
178n40, 182nn33–34, 184nn15,19,
185nn25–26, 186nn9–15
Todorov, Tzvetan 177n29
Torell, Jean-Pierre 186n13
Toulemont, Robert 182n36

Vasse, Denis 172n4
Vatican II 145
Veto, Étienne 185n26

Wittgenstein, Ludwig 87–88, 177nn26–27

This page represents a continuation of the copyright page.

Library of Congress Cataloging-in-Publication Data

Names: Falque, Emmanuel, 1963– author.
Title: Crossing the Rubicon : the borderlands of philosophy and theology /
    Emmanuel Falque ; translated by Reuben Shank ; introduction by Matthew
    Farley.
Other titles: Passer le Rubicon. English
Description: First edition. | New York, NY : Fordham University Press, 2016.
    | Series: Perspectives in Continental philosophy | Includes
    bibliographical references and index.
Identifiers: LCCN 2015035227| ISBN 9780823269877 (cloth : alk. paper) | ISBN
    9780823269884 (pbk. : alk. paper)
Subjects: LCSH: Philosophical theology.
Classification: LCC BT40 .F2713 2016 | DDC 261.5/1—dc23
LC record available at https://lccn.loc.gov/2015035227

Perspectives in Continental Philosophy

John D. Caputo, series editor

Jean-Luc Marion, *The Idol and Distance: Five Studies.* Translated with an introduction by Thomas A. Carlson.

Jeffrey Dudiak, *The Intrigue of Ethics: A Reading of the Idea of Discourse in the Thought of Emmanuel Levinas.*

Robyn Horner, *Rethinking God as Gift: Marion, Derrida, and the Limits of Phenomenology.*

Mark Dooley, *The Politics of Exodus: Søren Kierkegaard's Ethics of Responsibility.*

Merold Westphal, *Overcoming Onto-Theology: Toward a Postmodern Christian Faith.*

Edith Wyschogrod, Jean-Joseph Goux, and Eric Boynton, eds., *The Enigma of Gift and Sacrifice.*

Stanislas Breton, *The Word and the Cross.* Translated with an introduction by Jacquelyn Porter.

Jean-Luc Marion, *Prolegomena to Charity.* Translated by Stephen E. Lewis.

Peter H. Spader, *Scheler's Ethical Personalism: Its Logic, Development, and Promise.*

Jean-Louis Chrétien, *The Unforgettable and the Unhoped For.* Translated by Jeffrey Bloechl.

Don Cupitt, *Is Nothing Sacred? The Non-Realist Philosophy of Religion: Selected Essays.*

Jean-Luc Marion, *In Excess: Studies of Saturated Phenomena.* Translated by Robyn Horner and Vincent Berraud.

Phillip Goodchild, *Rethinking Philosophy of Religion: Approaches from Continental Philosophy.*

William J. Richardson, S.J., *Heidegger: Through Phenomenology to Thought.*

Jeffrey Andrew Barash, *Martin Heidegger and the Problem of Historical Meaning.*

Jean-Louis Chrétien, *Hand to Hand: Listening to the Work of Art.* Translated by Stephen E. Lewis.

Jean-Louis Chrétien, *The Call and the Response.* Translated with an introduction by Anne Davenport.

D. C. Schindler, *Han Urs von Balthasar and the Dramatic Structure of Truth: A Philosophical Investigation.*

Julian Wolfreys, ed., *Thinking Difference: Critics in Conversation.*

Allen Scult, *Being Jewish/Reading Heidegger: An Ontological Encounter.*

Richard Kearney, *Debates in Continental Philosophy: Conversations with Contemporary Thinkers.*

Jennifer Anna Gosetti-Ferencei, *Heidegger, Hölderlin, and the Subject of Poetic Language: Toward a New Poetics of Dasein.*

Jolita Pons, *Stealing a Gift: Kierkegaard's Pseudonyms and the Bible.*

Jean-Yves Lacoste, *Experience and the Absolute: Disputed Questions on the Humanity of Man.* Translated by Mark Raftery-Skehan.

Charles P. Bigger, *Between* Chora *and the Good: Metaphor's Metaphysical Neighborhood.*

Dominique Janicaud, *Phenomenology "Wide Open": After the French Debate.* Translated by Charles N. Cabral.

Ian Leask and Eoin Cassidy, eds., *Givenness and God: Questions of Jean-Luc Marion.*

Jacques Derrida, *Sovereignties in Question: The Poetics of Paul Celan.* Edited by Thomas Dutoit and Outi Pasanen.

William Desmond, *Is There a Sabbath for Thought? Between Religion and Philosophy.*

Bruce Ellis Benson and Norman Wirzba, eds., *The Phenomenology of Prayer.*

S. Clark Buckner and Matthew Statler, eds., *Styles of Piety: Practicing Philosophy after the Death of God.*

Kevin Hart and Barbara Wall, eds., *The Experience of God: A Postmodern Response.*

John Panteleimon Manoussakis, *After God: Richard Kearney and the Religious Turn in Continental Philosophy.*

John Martis, *Philippe Lacoue-Labarthe: Representation and the Loss of the Subject.*

Jean-Luc Nancy, *The Ground of the Image.*

Edith Wyschogrod, *Crossover Queries: Dwelling with Negatives, Embodying Philosophy's Others.*

Gerald Bruns, *On the Anarchy of Poetry and Philosophy: A Guide for the Unruly.*

Brian Treanor, *Aspects of Alterity: Levinas, Marcel, and the Contemporary Debate.*

Simon Morgan Wortham, *Counter-Institutions: Jacques Derrida and the Question of the University.*

Leonard Lawlor, *The Implications of Immanence: Toward a New Concept of Life.*

Clayton Crockett, *Interstices of the Sublime: Theology and Psychoanalytic Theory.*

Bettina Bergo, Joseph Cohen, and Raphael Zagury-Orly, eds., *Judeities: Questions for Jacques Derrida.* Translated by Bettina Bergo and Michael B. Smith.

Jean-Luc Marion, *On the Ego and on God: Further Cartesian Questions.* Translated by Christina M. Gschwandtner.

Jean-Luc Nancy, *Philosophical Chronicles.* Translated by Franson Manjali.

Jean-Luc Nancy, *Dis-Enclosure: The Deconstruction of Christianity.* Translated by Bettina Bergo, Gabriel Malenfant, and Michael B. Smith.

Andrea Hurst, *Derrida Vis-à-vis Lacan: Interweaving Deconstruction and Psychoanalysis.*

Jean-Luc Nancy, *Noli me tangere: On the Raising of the Body.* Translated by Sarah Clift, Pascale-Anne Brault, and Michael Naas.

Jacques Derrida, *The Animal That Therefore I Am.* Edited by Marie-Louise Mallet, translated by David Wills.

Jean-Luc Marion, *The Visible and the Revealed.* Translated by Christina M. Gschwandtner and others.

Michel Henry, *Material Phenomenology.* Translated by Scott Davidson.

Jean-Luc Nancy, *Corpus.* Translated by Richard A. Rand.

Joshua Kates, *Fielding Derrida.*

Michael Naas, *Derrida From Now On.*

Shannon Sullivan and Dennis J. Schmidt, eds., *Difficulties of Ethical Life.*

Catherine Malabou, *What Should We Do with Our Brain?* Translated by Sebastian Rand, Introduction by Marc Jeannerod.

Claude Romano, *Event and World*. Translated by Shane Mackinlay.

Vanessa Lemm, *Nietzsche's Animal Philosophy: Culture, Politics, and the Animality of the Human Being*.

B. Keith Putt, ed., *Gazing Through a Prism Darkly: Reflections on Merold Westphal's Hermeneutical Epistemology*.

Eric Boynton and Martin Kavka, eds., *Saintly Influence: Edith Wyschogrod and the Possibilities of Philosophy of Religion*.

Shane Mackinlay, *Interpreting Excess: Jean-Luc Marion, Saturated Phenomena, and Hermeneutics*.

Kevin Hart and Michael A. Signer, eds., *The Exorbitant: Emmanuel Levinas Between Jews and Christians*.

Bruce Ellis Benson and Norman Wirzba, eds., *Words of Life: New Theological Turns in French Phenomenology*.

William Robert, *Trials: Of Antigone and Jesus*.

Brian Treanor and Henry Isaac Venema, eds., *A Passion for the Possible: Thinking with Paul Ricoeur*.

Kas Saghafi, *Apparitions—Of Derrida's Other*.

Nick Mansfield, *The God Who Deconstructs Himself: Sovereignty and Subjectivity Between Freud, Bataille, and Derrida*.

Don Ihde, *Heidegger's Technologies: Postphenomenological Perspectives*.

Suzi Adams, *Castoriadis's Ontology: Being and Creation*.

Richard Kearney and Kascha Semonovitch, eds., *Phenomenologies of the Stranger: Between Hostility and Hospitality*.

Michael Naas, *Miracle and Machine: Jacques Derrida and the Two Sources of Religion, Science, and the Media*.

Alena Alexandrova, Ignaas Devisch, Laurens ten Kate, and Aukje van Rooden, *Re-treating Religion: Deconstructing Christianity with Jean-Luc Nancy*. Preamble by Jean-Luc Nancy.

Emmanuel Falque, *The Metamorphosis of Finitude: An Essay on Birth and Resurrection*. Translated by George Hughes.

Scott M. Campbell, *The Early Heidegger's Philosophy of Life: Facticity, Being, and Language*.

Françoise Dastur, *How Are We to Confront Death? An Introduction to Philosophy*. Translated by Robert Vallier. Foreword by David Farrell Krell.

Christina M. Gschwandtner, *Postmodern Apologetics? Arguments for God in Contemporary Philosophy*.

Ben Morgan, *On Becoming God: Late Medieval Mysticism and the Modern Western Self*.

Neal DeRoo, *Futurity in Phenomenology: Promise and Method in Husserl, Levinas, and Derrida*.

Sarah LaChance Adams and Caroline R. Lundquist, eds., *Coming to Life: Philosophies of Pregnancy, Childbirth, and Mothering*.

Thomas Claviez, ed., *The Conditions of Hospitality: Ethics, Politics, and Aesthetics on the Threshold of the Possible.*

Roland Faber and Jeremy Fackenthal, eds., *Theopoetic Folds: Philosophizing Multifariousness.*

Jean-Luc Marion, *The Essential Writings.* Edited by Kevin Hart.

Adam S. Miller, *Speculative Grace: Bruno Latour and Object-Oriented Theology.* Foreword by Levi R. Bryant.

Jean-Luc Nancy, *Corpus II: Writings on Sexuality.*

David Nowell Smith, *Sounding/Silence: Martin Heidegger at the Limits of Poetics.*

Gregory C. Stallings, Manuel Asensi, and Carl Good, eds., *Material Spirit: Religion and Literature Intranscendent.*

Claude Romano, *Event and Time.* Translated by Stephen E. Lewis.

Frank Chouraqui, *Ambiguity and the Absolute: Nietzsche and Merleau-Ponty on the Question of Truth.*

Noëlle Vahanian, *The Rebellious No: Variations on a Secular Theology of Language.*

Michael Naas, *The End of the World and Other Teachable Moments: Jacques Derrida's Final Seminar.*

Jean-Louis Chrétien, *Under the Gaze of the Bible.* Translated by John Marson Dunaway.

Edward Baring and Peter E. Gordon, eds., *The Trace of God: Derrida and Religion.*

Vanessa Lemm, ed., *Nietzsche and the Becoming of Life.*

Aaron T. Looney, *Vladimir Jankélévitch: The Time of Forgiveness.*

Richard Kearney and Brian Treanor, eds., *Carnal Hermeneutics.*

Tarek R. Dika and W. Chris Hackett, *Quiet Powers of the Possible: Interviews in Contemporary French Phenomenology.* Foreword by Richard Kearney.

Jeremy Biles and Kent L. Brintnall, eds., *Georges Bataille and the Study of Religion.*

William S. Allen, *Aesthetics of Negativity: Blanchot, Adorno, and Autonomy.*

Don Ihde, *Husserl's Missing Technologies.*

Colby Dickinson and Stéphane Symons (eds.), *Walter Benjamin and Theology.*

Emmanuel Falque, *Crossing the Rubicon: The Borderlands of Philosophy and Theology.* Translated by Reuben Shank. Introduction by Matthew Farley.